Lecture Notes in Computer Science   **12395**

Founding Editors

Gerhard Goos
  Karlsruhe Institute of Technology, Karlsruhe, Germany
Juris Hartmanis
  Cornell University, Ithaca, NY, USA

Editorial Board Members

Elisa Bertino
  Purdue University, West Lafayette, IN, USA
Wen Gao
  Peking University, Beijing, China
Bernhard Steffen ⓘ
  TU Dortmund University, Dortmund, Germany
Gerhard Woeginger ⓘ
  RWTH Aachen, Aachen, Germany
Moti Yung
  Columbia University, New York, NY, USA

More information about this series at http://www.springer.com/series/7410

Stefanos Gritzalis · Edgar R. Weippl ·
Gabriele Kotsis · A Min Tjoa ·
Ismail Khalil (Eds.)

Trust, Privacy and Security in Digital Business

17th International Conference, TrustBus 2020
Bratislava, Slovakia, September 14–17, 2020
Proceedings

Springer

Editors
Stefanos Gritzalis
School of Engineering
University of the Aegean
Karlovassi, Samos, Greece

Gabriele Kotsis
Johannes Kepler University of Linz
Linz, Oberösterreich, Austria

Ismail Khalil
Johannes Kepler University of Linz
Linz, Oberösterreich, Austria

Edgar R. Weippl
SBA Research
Vienna, Wien, Austria

A Min Tjoa
Vienna University of Technology
Vienna, Wien, Austria

ISSN 0302-9743   ISSN 1611-3349   (electronic)
Lecture Notes in Computer Science
ISBN 978-3-030-58985-1   ISBN 978-3-030-58986-8   (eBook)
https://doi.org/10.1007/978-3-030-58986-8

LNCS Sublibrary: SL4 – Security and Cryptology

This Springer imprint is published by the registered company Springer Nature Switzerland AG
The registered company address is: Gewerbestrasse 11, 6330 Cham, Switzerland

Preface

This volume presents the proceedings of the 17th International Conference on Trust, Privacy and Security in Digital Business (TrustBus 2020), held as a virtual conference during September 14–17, 2020. This year's conference continued the tradition of being a forum for disseminating original research results and practical experiences.

TrustBus 2020 brought together academic researchers and industry partners to discuss the state of the art in technology for establishing trust, privacy, and security in digital business. The conference program included four technical paper sessions covering a broad range of topics, from permission models and cloud, privacy, proactive security measures, to cyber-physical systems. The papers were selected by the Program Committee via a rigorous reviewing process (each paper was assigned to four referees for review) and 11 papers were finally selected for presentation as full papers and 3 as short papers. The main topics of the accepted papers are related to privacy; this reflects the importance of this topic, in particular in Europe. A strong focus on this topic established Europe as the leader in this domain of research.

The success of this conference was a result of the effort of many people. We would like to express our appreciation to the Program Committee members and external reviewers for their hard work, and to the members of the Organizing Committee.

We would also like to thank Ismail Khalil for his help, for promoting the conference, and for his continued support of the TrustBus conference series. Special thanks go to the Editorial Director of Springer for including these conference proceedings in the *Lecture Notes in Computer Science* series.

Last but not least, our thanks go to all the authors who submitted their papers, and to all the participants. We hope you find the proceedings stimulating and beneficial for your future research.

September 2020

Stefanos Gritzalis
Edgar R. Weippl

Organization

General Chair

Sokratis K. Katsikas   Norwegian University of Science and Technology, Norway, and Open University of Cyprus, Cyprus

Program Committee Chairs

Stefanos Gritzalis   University of Piraeus, Greece
Edgar R. Weippl   University of Vienna, SBA Research, Austria

Steering Committee

Gabriele Kotsis   Johannes Kepler University Linz, Austria
A Min Tjoa   Vienna University of Technology, Austria
Ismail Khalil   Johannes Kepler University Linz, Austria

Program Committee and Reviewers

Cheng-Kang Chu	Institute for Infocomm Research, Singapore
Nathan Clarke	University of Plymouth, UK
Frédéric Cuppens	Télécom Bretagne, France
Sabrina De Capitani di Vimercati	Università degli Studi di Milano, Italy
Vasiliki Diamantopoulou	University of the Aegean, Greece
Prokopios Drogkaris	ENISA, Greece
Eduardo B. Fernandez	Florida Atlantic University, USA
Jose-Luis Ferrer-Gomila	University of the Balearic Islands, Spain
Simone Fischer-Hübner	Karlstad University, Sweden
Sara Foresti	DI, Università degli Studi di Milano, Italy
Steven Furnell	University of Plymouth, UK
Jürgen Fuß	University of Applied Sciences Upper Austria, Austria
Dimitris Gritzalis	Athens University of Economics and Business, Greece
Christos Kalloniatis	University of the Aegean, Greece
Georgios Kambourakis	University of the Aegean, Greece
Maria Karyda	University of the Aegean, Greece
Spyros Kokolakis	University of the Aegean, Greece
Stephan Krenn	AIT Austrian Institute of Technology GmbH, Austria
Costas Lambrinoudakis	University of Piraeus, Greece
Antonio Lioy	Politecnico di Torino, Italy
Olivier Markowitch	Université Libre de Bruxelles (ULB), Belgium
Fabio Martinelli	IIT-CNR, Italy

David Megias	Open University of Catalonia, Spain
Chris Mitchell	Royal Holloway, University of London, UK
Haralambos Mouratidis	University of Brighton, UK
Rolf Oppliger	eSECURITY Technologies, Switzerland
Andreas Pashalidis	BSI, Germany
Günther Pernul	Universität Regensburg, Germany
Nikolaos Pitropakis	Edinburgh Napier University, UK
Ruben Rios	University of Malaga, Spain
Panagiotis Rizomiliotis	Harokopio University of Athens, Greece
Pierangela Samarati	Università degli Studi di Milano, Italy
Miguel Soriano	Universitat Politècnica de Catalunya, Spain
Stephanie Teufel	University of Fribourg, iimt, Switzerland
A Min Tjoa	Vienna University of Technology, Austria
Christos Xenakis	University of Piraeus, Greece

Organizers

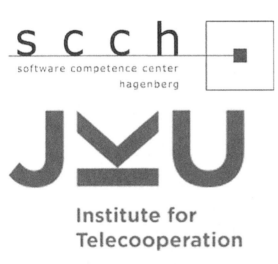

Contents

Privacy

Privacy and Machine Learning

Trust

Blockchain

Analysis of uPort Open, an Identity Management Blockchain-Based Solution

Andreea-Elena Panait[1] , Ruxandra F. Olimid[1,2,3] ,
and Alin Stefanescu[1,2(✉)]

[1] Department of Computer Science, University of Bucharest, Bucharest, Romania
`andreea-elena.panait@drd.unibuc.ro`, {`ruxandra.olimid,alin`}`@fmi.unibuc.ro`
[2] The Research Institute of the University of Bucharest (ICUB), Bucharest, Romania
[3] Department of Information Security and Communication Technology, NTNU -
Norwegian University of Science and Technology, Trondheim, Norway

Abstract. Recently, academics and professionals proposed a substantial number of identity management solutions based on blockchain technology. Among them, uPort appeared promising, being considered for both personal and administrative operations. This paper analyzes the open-source version uPort Open in terms of risk delegation and private key recovery of the mobile application, smart contract security of the uPort identity registry, and usage and on-chain transaction analytics.

Keywords: Identity management · Blockchain · Self-sovereign · uPort

1 Introduction

Technological development in the last years led to an increased number of digital entities that must be identified in an interoperable and efficient way. With the adaptation of 5G and mostly Internet of Things (IoT), identity and access management became a difficult issue to address. Papers like [10] propose ways to leverage blockchain for solving such problems. A recent identity management model, called the *Self-Sovereign Identity (SSI) model* makes the user be his/her own identity provider and fully responsible for his/her identity, thus eliminating the need of an external identity provider [13]. The blockchain technology has been considered to be a candidate solution to accommodate identity management while decreasing risks such as identity fraud or data leaks [13]. Among the identity-management solutions built on blockchain, uPort is currently one of the most known, targeting both personal and administrative operations [21]. uPort comes in two versions, one for public networks, called uPort Open, which is open-source, and one for closed ecosystems and consortia, called uPort Serto.

Contribution. Motivated to find the current status of open-source identity-management solutions, the paper analyses the security and usage of uPort Open, as a representative open-source solution. For simplicity, unless otherwise specified, we will further refer to uPort Open by simply uPort. We conduct our analysis in three directions: (1) a brief assessment concerning risk delegation

S. Gritzalis et al. (Eds.): TrustBus 2020, LNCS 12395, pp. 3–13, 2020.
https://doi.org/10.1007/978-3-030-58986-8_1

and private key recovery, (2) an automatic code analysis of the identity registry smart contract, and (3) uPort usage and on-chain transaction analytics. By looking into terms, conditions, and privacy policies, we found that for the mobile application, the risks are delegated to the user, with (almost) no responsibility on the uPort side. Concerning the code analysis, the used tools found possible vulnerabilities, which we have notified to the uPort team. Later in the paper, we will refer to the uPort team response to our notice. Their feedback assisted us in understanding better the purpose of their proposed solution[1]. Finally, we developed an application to collect and analyze the blockchain transactions made to the uPort identity registry, *EthereumDIDRegistry*. We found that the on-chain usage of the uPort identity is rather low, the identities did not make significantly usage of the offered features (i.e., changing owner, setting attributes) through its *EthereumDIDRegistry*. Moreover, advanced features such as delegation (i.e., granting the right to perform identity-related actions for a certain period to other addresses) are even more rarely used. However, this on-chain usage is somehow expected since the uPort identities are intended to be mainly used without any call to the *EthereumDIDRegistry*. In fact, changes in the owner or attributes and delegation are only possible using libraries, and not via the mobile application.

Related Work. Except uPort, several other identity management solutions have been proposed so far. More comprehensive lists are available at [8,13]. From those, we chose to investigate uPort because it is one of the most visible open-source solution[2] both in the academic literature and in the online setting. uPort is theoretically described and briefly analysed in several publications, including [2,4,13,14]. Nevertheless, they mostly analyze uPort only on general aspects. To the best of our knowledge, no similar results in terms of smart contract security and on-chain usage and transaction analytics exist.

2   Background

Identity Management on Blockchain. A *blockchain* is a type of decentralized distributed database with cryptographic enhancements. It is *distributed* because the data is stored on multiple *nodes* (each node stores a complete or partial copy of the blockchain), and it is *descentralized* because the storage decision is a result of a *consensus* protocol between the nodes [13]. Data is stored in *blocks*, which are basically collections of *transactions*. A user authenticates a transaction by signing it with the private key. The paired public key represents the user's address in the blockchain. A blockchain-based identity management solution implements selective storing of identities in the blockchain, where the identities are *attested* by authorities or other entities in the blockchain, usually by *verifiable claims* [13]. A *self-sovereign* solution eliminates the need for an external authority by transferring the full responsibility for creating and managing the digital identity and associated attributes to the user.

---

[1] We have notified the uPort team to their official address, *info@uport.me*.

[2] Maybe together with Sovrin [15].

Ethereum is a particular implementation of a blockchain, which is capable to store *smart contracts*. A smart contract is identified and referred to by an address (a public key) and provides a function-based interface that allows it to be executed. To execute a smart contract (changing its state), a user performs a transaction with the function signature and the input parameters as the data payload and the smart contract's address as the destination [19]. We differentiate between *direct* transactions, which directly call the smart contract and *indirect* transactions, which result from an execution of a smart contract that executes another stand-alone transaction[3].

uPort Open. uPort Open is an open-source identity management system built on Ethereum that claims to satisfy the self-sovereign property [21]. It has three main components: (1) the mobile application, which stores the user's public-private keys pair, and is used to perform different actions (e.g., create and manage the digital identity, authenticate to third parties, sign transactions), (2) the Ethereum smart contracts, and (3) protocols for signed messages and message flows, as well as libraries and interfaces necessary for integrating uPort with third-party applications [19,20]. The uPort identity has a Decentralized Identifier (DID) and a pair of public-private keys [20]. The management of the DIDs is done by the *EthereumDIDRegistry* smart contract that allows the *owner* of an identity to update the customized *attributes*. The *owner* is, in fact, an Ethereum address that has full control over the identity but accepts *delegates*. A delegate is an address that is delegated for some specific time to perform actions on behalf of an identity [20]. The *EthereumDIDRegistry* smart contract is deployed both on mainnet Ethereum blockchains (Mainnet, RSK, and Alastria Telsius) and on testnets (Ropsten, Rinkeby, Kovan, RSK Testnet, and Goerli) [20]. It is written in the Solidity programming language and provides several functions to manage identities: change identity ownership, set or revoke attributes, set or revoke delegates [20]. Some of these functions emit events that change the state of the contract. The event arguments are stored in a blockchain special data structure called *transaction log* that can be listen to through the Remote Procedure Call (RPC) interface of an Ethereum client. The *EthereumDIDRegistry* functions related to identity ownership emit the *DIDOwnerChanged* event, the functions related to identity attributes emit the *DIDAttributeChanged* event, and ones related to delegates emit the *DIDDelegateChanged* [20].

Analysis Tools. To check for vulnerabilities in the uPort registry smart contract *EthereumDIDRegistry* we looked into the static and dynamic tools listed in [3]. To analyze uPort transactions, we used *Etherscan.io*, which is a stand-alone web-based Ethereum blockchain explorer, but also provides access to the data stored in the blockchain by APIs. The APIs are provided as a community service and require the creation of a free *API-Key Token* [5]. We developed an application to extract data and store it in a SQL database. For this, we used *Swagger*, an open-source editor dedicated to OpenAPI Specification (OAS)-based APIs that help developers to make use of RESTful web services [16].

---

[3] For clarity, we avoid to refer to *normal* and *internal* transaction.

3   Results and Discussion

We further present and discuss our results. Since uPort is a solution under continuous development, note that our analysis is conducted based on the source code and transactions prior to Dec. 13th, 2019.

3.1   Risk Responsibility

The uPort mobile application is a credential wallet that does not manage all aspects of an decentralized identity, features that are included in the uPort libraries (e.g., *eth-did-registry* and *ethr-did* that uses [6]). The application can be used, for example, to register in decentralized applications.

We first look into how the uPort mobile application manages risks responsibility and private key recovery. For this, we have installed and inspected the uPort application that is freely available in Google Play and tested the application ourselves. To create an account, the user must accept the *Terms and Conditions* and the *Privacy Policy*, which delegate strong responsibility to the user and assume usage on the user's own risk. The agreements refer to risks in terms of cryptography and platform security, and also absolve uPort from bugs, errors, and defects by delegating the responsibility to the user. Although this might be seen as natural for an open-source solution, the users must fully understand the responsibility and risks in using the solution.

The *Terms and Conditions* specify that generation of the private key is possible from a potential leaked twelve-word seed and the impossibility of recovery of the private key or the twelve-word seed by other means but by user knowledge. After installation, uPort displays two options: *Get Started* and *Recover Identity*. While creating the account (*Get Started*), the user sets a twelve-word Recovery Seed Phrase that can be used for recovering the account: the words are selected from a list that becomes available after inputting two letters from a word. This restricts the available words to be part of a dictionary - BIP39 standard with 2048 English words [11]. The number of possible combinations is $2048^{12} = 2^{132}$, so 132 bits of security, which can be considered rather secure. The twelve-words passphrase is a widely used practice in applications such as crypto wallets. We note that while selecting the twelve words, the *Next* button remains inactivated. It becomes active only for a valid twelve-word phrase.

3.2   Code Analysis

We further present our findings after analyzing the *EthereumDIDRegistry* smart contract with several tools from [3]. The used tools and the found vulnerabilities are summarized in Table 1, together with suggested tool mitigation techniques and our notes. We looked into other tools from the above-mentioned list, but we were not able to use them due to various reasons.

The uPort Response. Regarding the upgrade to a 0.5.x version of Solidity, uPort admitted that the next contract deployment will be upgraded to a recent

Table 1. Code analysis: vulnerabilities exposed by different tools

SmartCheck [17]

(V1) Incorrect compiler version

Mitigation: Specify the exact compiler version used for test

Note: Not applicable for a consumption contract, such as the one analyzed [3]

(V2) Old Solidity compiler version

Mitigation: Upgrade to Solidity 0.5.x

(V3) Function *keccak256(arg)* will become deprecated

Mitigation: Change the function call to *keccak256(abi.encodePacked(arg))*

(V4) Data location for function parameters is not explicit

Mitigation: Specify data location

Note: This vulnerability is applicable after smart contract update to Solidity 0.5.x

Securify [18]

(V1) Recursive calls after a method call that is followed by a state change

Note: Not accurate, state changes are made after calling the predefined Solidity function *ecrecover* by the identity owner, otherwise no state change occurs

(V2) Insecure coding patterns when unrestricted write to storage

Note: Writing is restricted to identity owners only

(V3) Unexpected Ether flow (lock of Ether)

Note: The smart contract does not receive or deposit any Ether

MythX [9]

(V1) Possible overflow at the binary addition of current time with a *uint* validity

Mitigation: Use an assertion to catch the overflow

(V2) *Block number* considered a weak source of randomness

Note: Tool warning. The block number is used for logging triggered events, not as a source of randomness

(V3) Potential Denial-of-Service to block gas limit when using *keccak256* function

Note: Tool warning

ContractGuard [23]

(V1) *Block number* dependency

Mitigation: Not recommended to use, it can be manipulated by attackers

(V2) Timestamp dependency

Mitigation: Not recommended to use the current time

Note: Triggered by an event having a date that is an addition between the current time and a validity parameter of type *uint*

(V3) Using *require* assert without reason string attached

Mitigation: Suggested to add a reason string

Note: Tool warning

(V4) Misplaced order of smart contract functions

Mitigation: Recommended order: constructor, fallback, external, external const, public, public const, internal, and private functions

Note: Tool warning

Solidity version, but even though the *keccak256* function is deprecated in the recent versions, the function behaves as expected in the previous deployments. For the possible overflow of the binary addition of the current time with a validity of type *uint* (within the *addDelegate* and *setAttribute* functions) for future deployments, one can indeed use the assert statement. A possible overflow will only result in adding a delegate or an attribute that is already expired, but no other off-chain or on-chain changes will occur. Therefore, this would not be a problem from the uPort team's point of view. For the possible DoS attack that might occur because the first argument of the *keccak256* hash function might grow unbounded, the worst-case scenario would be that the transaction fails.

3.3   Advanced Usage and Transactions Analytics

Finally, we investigate the usage of uPort solution. We start by finding the number of mobile application downloads but then proceed to a more in-depth analysis concerning on-chain performed transactions.

Downloads. The first point in our numerical analysis addresses the number of downloads of the uPort mobile application. Although this cannot be a precise indication for the number of users (as for example the same user can download the application on several devices, or individuals can download the application but never create a digital identity), we consider this to be an acceptable indication of the interest towards the uPort mobile solutions. At the time of the writing, in Google Play there were 10,000+ downloads and only seven reviews [7]. This seems to indicate a low usage of the application, with many users that downloaded the application just by curiosity. Similarly, within the AppStore there were only three reviews, indicating the same low usage [1].

Transactions. Secondly, we focused our analytics concerning the analyzed smart contract's transactions on different networks. The address of the *Ethereum-DIDRegistry* smart contract in different blockchains can be found at [20]. At this step, we have used these addresses and found the number of transactions directly from the web interface. Table 2 shows the number of direct transactions made to the uPort smart contract for each blockchain network where it was deployed, together with other details. Note that some of these transactions can be with error (all transactions are included in the web interface), and the number of transactions always includes one transaction used for the contract creation. We deliberately exclude the Alastria Telsius testnet from our analysis, as it presents errors and does not correctly display the information extracted.

Transaction Types and On-chain Digital Identities. We further performed a more in-depth analysis concerning the networks with a significant number of transactions (Mainnet, Rinkeby, and Ropsten). This time, we extracted the transactions using the *Ethereum Developer APIs* [5]. To fulfill our goal, we developed a .NET Core simple web application for making the API requests through a Swagger frontend interface [16] and saved the transactions in a SQL Server Database. The sample project can be found at [12]. In order to find

Table 2. *EthereumDIDRegistry* direct transactions (from the web-platform)

Blockchain network	Blockchain type	Contract creation	First transaction	Last transaction	Direct trans.
Mainnet	Mainnet	Jun-15-2018 01:27:27 AM	Jan-11-2019 07:56:32 PM	Nov-09-2019 05:56:40 PM	2079
Rinkeby	Testnet	Jun-15-2018 01:05:09 AM	Aug-02-2018 01:28:52 PM	Dec-06-2019 11:24:32 AM	4106
Ropsten	Testnet	Jun-15-2018 01:07:19 AM	Oct-01-2018 08:45:27 PM	Nov-22-2019 02:41:49 AM	681
Kovan	Testnet	Jun-15-2018 01:01:44 AM	Dec-04-2019 02:27:44 PM	Dec-04-2019 02:27:44 PM	2
RSK	Mainnet	Jun-06-2019 04:41:33 AM	-	-	0
RSK Testnet	Testnet	Jul-24-2019 05:24:34 AM	-	-	0
Görli	Testnet	Dec-02-2019 01:57:27 PM	-	-	0

Table 3. Types of transactions and number of unique addresses grouped by network

Blockchain	Successful trans.	Direct trans. with error	Direct successful Trans.	Indirect successful Trans.	Unique addresses	Unique Addr. with > 1 trans.
Mainnet	2844	68	2010	834	2004	431
Rinkeby	7570	89	4016	3554	3805	3570
Ropsten	634	46	634	0	434	19

the number of uPort created identities that changed their owner, set identity attributes and/or revoked identity delegates, we used the *getLogs* API method. This is an Etherscan API method that provides the event type triggered when a specific uPort registry function is executed (for the event types, see Section 2). To exemplify, we give next a Rinkeby request for transactions belonging to blocks in a given interval (fromBlock - toBlock), where the address could correspond to the *EthereumDIDRegistry* smart contract and YOUR-API-KEY is the Api-Key Token: https://api-rinkeby.etherscan.io/api? module=logs&action=getLogs&fromBlock=2463641&toBlock=3224895& address=YOUR-ADDRESS&apikey=YOUR-API-KEY.

Table 3 shows the number of successful transactions, the number of error transactions, the number of direct and indirect successful transactions, the number of unique addresses that made transactions, and the number of addresses that made multiple transactions. Note that this time, the number of transactions excludes one successful transaction, which is the contract creation transaction. In Mainnet, the number of indirect transactions represents 26.93% from the total number of successful transactions, while for Rinkeby it represents 45.78%. This suggests that, on tests, the developers are more likely to send transactions to intermediar smart contracts before sending transactions to the uPort registry. In Mainnet, only 21.50% of the unique addresses made more than 1 transaction, for Rinkeby network 93.82%, whereas for Ropsten only 4.37%. The number of

Table 4. Transactions and unique addresses grouped by event type and year

Blockchain	Year	uPort event	No. trans	Unique addresses.	Unique addr. with > 1 trans.
Mainnet	2019	Owner	2002	2001	1
		Attribute	839	431	381
		Delegate	3	2	1
Rinkeby	2018	Owner	7105	3573	3525
		Attribute	137	71	21
		Delegate	70	10	5
	2019	Owner	2	2	0
		Attribute	225	170	18
		Delegate	31	8	4
Ropsten	2018	Owner	93	93	0
		Attribute	103	85	12
		Delegate	15	7	1
	2019	Owner	12	5	1
		Attribute	276	250	4
		Delegate	135	1	1

unique addresses is important as it reveals the number of identities in the network that made changes to their initial values, while the number of addresses with more than one transaction implies that some identities made several changes to their initial identity. The transactions with errors were not returned by the API requests because for an error transaction the events are not triggered. Hence, for each network of interest, we computed their number by the difference between the number of transactions in Table 2 and the number of direct transactions returned by API request. A high percentage of errors usually indicate a problem or an immature solution. We found a percentage of 2,39% errors in Mainnet. Overall, the numbers indicate that on-chain, the solution is mostly used for performing tests (Rinkeby), with no significant usage in real applications.

Digital Identity-Related Events. Table 4 splits the transactions on year and event type. For Mainnet, there are no transactions in 2018. The data shows that only one identity changed the owner more than once. 88.4% of the addresses triggered more than a single attribute event. This appears normal, as an identity should naturally set and change attributes corresponding to its identity. The delegation was mostly unused: with only 3 *DIDDelegateChanged* events, it is clear that the this was found to be an uninteresting feature. With respect to the test networks, we notice a significant number of creating or changing owners in 2018. This is natural for testing purposes. Moreover, we observed intense testing in owner change on Rinkeby (98.65% of the identities made at least a change in the owner). Concerning the total number of unique addresses per blokchain network, from Table 3 and Table 4, as well as from querying the database, it results that: for Mainnet 429 addresses made owner-related and attribute-related transactions, and 1 address made owner-related and delegate-related transactions; for Rinkeby 18 addresses made owner and attribute-related transactions, 6 addresses made owner and delegate-related transactions, and 5 addresses made attribute and delegate-related transactions. From this, 1 address made all three types of transactions; for Ropsten there were 7 addresses that made transactions related to owner and attributes.

Discussion. The measure of downloads and on-chain interaction with the uPort *EthereumDIDRegistry* does not entirely reflect the usage of this solution (uPort self-sovereign libraries), and we can not make a correlation between them, as initially thought: the uPort mobile application is a credential wallet and does not interact on-chain with the registry, whereas the on-chain interaction does not reflect the entire uPort usage. Identities can act themselves as public keys by using the *eth-did-resolver* library, which enables the Ethereum addresses to be self-managed Decentralized Identifiers [22]. This means that they need not to previous register to produce valid signatures (and prove their identity). Moreover, as the uPort team mentioned in their feedback, the identities are more likely not to use the changing owner, setting attributes and delegate features due to reasons of scalability, cost and in order to enhance their privacy. Lastly, uPort mentioned that the attribute and delegate changes are expected to be performed mostly by organizations that require multiple entities to have the power of signature without sharing the private keys with each entity. The ownership changes are to be performed even rarely in extreme events or when upgrading the identity model from a key pair to a multi-signature contract, the team specified.

4   Conclusions

Being quite visible online and in the academic world, we were interested in researching whether uPort Open is popular among users. Our analysis concluded that the on-chain usage of the uPort identities is not significant, but the solution is expected to be more used for off-chain interaction and valid signature signing. However, off-chain usage is difficult to be measured due to the privacy-by-design nature of the solution. The possible vulnerabilities encountered while analyzing the security of the *EthereumDIDRegistry* smart contract were reported to the uPort team, which responded to all our points. The uPort mobile application is a credential wallet and does not make use of advanced identity features. Finally, when using the mobile application, responsibility is fully delegated to the user.

Acknowledgement. This work was partially supported by a grant of Romanian Ministry of Research and Innovation project no. 17PCCDI/2018.

We thank Mircea Nistor, from the uPort team, for his valuable support.

References

1. Apple Store: uPortID (2020), https://apps.apple.com/us/app/uport-id/id1123434510#?platform=iphone
2. van Bokkem, D., Hageman, R., Koning, G., Nguyen, L., Zarin, N.: Self-sovereign identity solutions: The necessity of blockchain technology. arXiv preprint arXiv:1904.12816 (2019)
3. Consensys: Ethereum Smart Contract Best Practices - Security Tools (2020), https://consensys.github.io/smart-contract-best-practices
4. Dunphy, P., Petitcolas, F.A.: A first look at identity management schemes on the blockchain. IEEE Secur. Priv. **16**(4), 20–29 (2018)
5. Etherscan: Ethereum Developer APIs (2020), https://etherscan.io/apis
6. Foundation, D.I.: DID resolver for Ethereum Addresses with support for key management (2020), https://github.com/decentralized-identity/ethr-did-resolver
7. Google Play: uPort (2020), https://play.google.com/store/apps/details?id=com.uportMobile
8. Mire, S.: Blockchain For Identity Management: 33 Startups To Watch In 2019 (2020), https://www.disruptordaily.com/blockchain-startups-identity-management
9. MythX: MythX User and Developer Guide (2020), https://docs.mythx.io/en/latest
10. Nuss, M., Puchta, A., Kunz, M.: Towards blockchain-based identity and access management for internet of things in enterprises. In: Furnell, S., Mouratidis, H., Pernul, G. (eds.) TrustBus 2018. LNCS, vol. 11033, pp. 167–181. Springer, Cham (2018). https://doi.org/10.1007/978-3-319-98385-1_12
11. Palatinus, M., Rusnak, P., Voisine, A.: Bitcoin bip39 (2020), https://github.com/bitcoin/bips/blob/master/bip-0039.mediawiki
12. Panait, A.E.: uPort etherscan transactions (2020), https://github.com/apanait/EtherscanTransactions
13. Panait, A.E., Olimid, R.F., Stefanescu, A.: Identity management on blockchain-privacy and security aspects. Proc. Rom. Acad. Series A **21**(1), 45–52 (2020)
14. Roos, J.: Identity management on the blockchain. Network **105** (2018)
15. Sovrin: A protocol and token for self-sovereign identity and decentralized trust (2020), https://sovrin.org/wp-content/uploads/Sovrin-Protocol-and-Token-White-Paper.pdf
16. Swagger: API development for everyone (2020), https://swagger.io
17. Tikhomirov, S., Voskresenskaya, E., Ivanitskiy, I., Takhaviev, R., Marchenko, E., Alexandrov, Y.: Smartcheck: static analysis of ethereum smart contracts. In: Proceedings of the 1st International Workshop on Emerging Trends in Software Engineering for Blockchain. pp. 9–16 (2018)
18. Tsankov, P., Dan, A., Drachsler-Cohen, D., Gervais, A., Buenzli, F., Vechev, M.: Securify: practical security analysis of smart contracts. In: Proceedings of the 2018 ACM SIGSAC Conference on Computer and Communications Security. pp. 67–82 (2018)
19. uPort: A platform for self-sovereign identity draft version (2016-10-20) (2016), https://blockchainlab.com/pdf/uPort_whitepaper_DRAFT20161020.pdf

20. uPort: Ethereum registry for ERC-1056 ethr did methods (2020), https://github.com/uport-project
21. uPort: uPort (2020), https://www.uport.me
22. W3C: Decentralized Identifiers (DIDs) v1.0 (2020), https://w3c.github.io/did-core
23. Wang, X., et al.: Contractguard: defend ethereum smart contracts with embedded intrusion detection. CoRR abs/1911.10472 (2019), http://arxiv.org/abs/1911.10472 [4]

---

[4] All links were last accessed March 2020.

Cloud Security/Hardware

Cloud Computing Framework for e-Health Security Requirements and Security Policy Rules Case Study: A European Cloud-Based Health System

Dimitra Georgiou[(⊠)] and Costas Lambrinoudakis

Systems Security Laboratory, Department of Digital Systems, School of Information and Communication Technologies, University of Piraeus, Piraeus, Greece
dimitrageorgiou@ssl-unipi.gr, clam@unipi.gr

Abstract. The final few years, Information and Communication Technology (ICT) have delivered the concept of central enterprise model in e-health. Healthcare is increasingly being supported via IT functions and new technologies, such as Cloud Computing. But sharing sensitive private data in Cloud Computing can be risky, when an unauthorized person gets access to this information and uses this in a different way than those supposed by the Providers. Numerous nations are sharp to go their typical health care services to the modern innovation of Cloud Computing, in order to move forward the first-class of care and to limit the cost. In any case, these possibilities introduce new safety risks and require a special treatment of safety issues, which cannot be ignored. Our work focuses on analyzing the challenges when using Cloud Computing in e-health systems and on moderation of these risks. In this paper, we present a list of the main security requirements that have to be viewed when migrating an e-health system to a SaaS Cloud Computing environment by means of each Health-care Providers and Cloud Service Providers and at the same time we propose some basic provisions to mitigate the significant risks.

Keywords: Cloud computing · e-Health · Security · Requirements · Policy rules

1 Introduction - Information Privacy in Health Informatics

The healthcare environment is undergoing fundamental changes. The previous years, doctors and hospitals used to have many papers and envelopes to keep the health of their patients and every time that a patient used to change doctors, there were nothing about their history of their health. Nowadays, many countries in order to improve their services on e-health, incorporate new technologies into their traditional medicine care. Internet technologies try to protect patients' privacy and confidentiality of medical data, while at the same time improve the quality of care. The benefits provided by the Internet, however, come with a significantly greater element of risk to the integrity of information. Thus, information security and privacy remain a high concern for citizens regarding their

© Springer Nature Switzerland AG 2020
S. Gritzalis et al. (Eds.): TrustBus 2020, LNCS 12395, pp. 17–31, 2020.
https://doi.org/10.1007/978-3-030-58986-8_2

health data [1, 2]. Unfortunately, traditional security mechanisms are not appropriate to meet patients' requirements in new technological advances in e-Health Care services, so the creation of a general e-Health Cloud Security Policy that defines the security requirements for Cloud Computing e-health system is needed. To better understand the developments in terms of e-Health, it is necessary to understand what e-Health is and what exactly e-Health Security Policy is in the area of these new technologies. When we mention the term e-Health, we mean the use of information technologies across health related functions and activities [3].

An electronic Health service system, is a collection of components working together to implement the e-Health services. As data is processed into practical information by the system, authentication and authorization become the essential concerns of the e-Health service systems [4]. In addition, the European Commission defines e-Health very generally as *"The use of modern information and communication technologies that meet needs of citizens, patients, health care professionals, health care Providers, as well as Policy makers"* [5].

To use properly and effectively an e-health system, we need an appropriate Health Policy. A Health Policy has been defined as '*a set of statements, directives, regulations, laws, and judicial interpretations that direct and manage the life cycle of e-health*' [6]. In the area of health, the creation of an e-Health Policy that balances the need for access (authorization) with the needs and the rights of the citizens, is the biggest challenge. There are several examples of countries that have national e-Health strategies some of these are Italy, France, UK, while other has introduced the electronic health card, like Germany [7].

New technologies, such as Cloud Computing, could improve e-Health services to their patients. Health data will be more easily accessible by doctors thus supporting a better diagnosis and treatment for their patients. Cloud-based e-Health services could change the traditional Health environment and could bring a lot of advantages [8–10]. The industry may considerably improve the access to information and patients will have improved diagnosis, treatment and faster decision making responses from assigned medical professionals. However, despite the potentially high value of the new technological development of Cloud Computing, in the area of e-Health, the security of medical information, as well as data handling, is a serious issue [11–14]. In order to achieve the security levels in the medical environment, it is necessary to identify carefully the security requirements for this.

In our research, we study the protection of the confidentiality of patients' information and we facilitate the processes of the e-Health Cloud system with some suggestions for Health Cloud Providers. We analyze the security requirements of a Cloud-based System, from the perspective of the Service Provider, using as an example, the case study of an e-Health Cloud system in Europe. In particular, in this paper based on the list of threats published by our previous papers [15–17], we discuss how each category of threats can be linked to specific security requirements. Lastly we provide a set of security policy rules for the presented security requirements, that we consider significant for any growth methodology that supports the design of secure and private Cloud. Although, the list of the presented requirements is not the final, we believe that this list provides a good basis for any Developer that would like to consider inclusion of Cloud security and privacy analysis in their methodology.

Section 2 provides a brief overview of the background of Information Systems in Europe. Section 3 presents the Cloud Computing implementation issues with basic Cloud computing characteristics. Section 4 discusses the major categories of threats according to our Methodology and provides a clear linkage with a set of Security Requirements. Section 5 presents specific security policy rules related to the set of security requirements for every category of threats. Finally, Sect. 6 presents areas for future work and concludes the paper.

2   Case Study of Europe: e-Health Cloud-Based System

2.1   Background of the Information Systems in Europe

In Europe, the European Union (EU) has endeavored to promote the implementation of e-Health within the 27 Member States by making e-Health a key part of EU Health Policy [18–21]. The big challenge and the vision of the EU is to achieve the wide spread adoption of e-Health systems across Europe as part of the EU's Flagship initiative 'Digital Agenda for Europe' [22–24]. Also a key ambition of the EU Policy is the provision of better care services at the same or lower cost [25]. The 2004 EU e-Health Action Plan was the first initiative that set in motion the EU's plans to encourage European co-operation on Health Care issues [26]. In our research, we illustrate as an example application scenario, the European Union e-Health system and the implementation strategies that use across the EU and European Economic Area Member States.

So, in this paper, we will present an existing e- Health Information System, the system in Europe, that consists of 27 national e-Health programs, as the number of European Countries and illustrates the overall framework. Then, we will present how this Information System would be with the use of Cloud Computing, what the new Critical Security Requirements associated with the aforementioned threats are and what the proposed solutions for these Cloud Computing security requirements are. In this scenario, the approach of a European system conceptualizes the health-care system as a value system of a variety of Health Service Providers, each of which has to manage its own health system. As depicted in this research, this health system, which consists of individual health Service Providers, promotes good health and long-term care services, supports disease prevention and provides healthcare. The European Commission's e-Health Action Plan mentions the lack of awareness and confidence in new technologies among professionals and citizens as a barrier to adopt them [27].

The previous years, the European Commission (EC) has established working parties and expressed its intention for information development in all public health programmes [28–30]. Examples of the term of e-Health according to the European Commission's e-Health Taskforce are: clinical information systems, e-institutions, Telemedicine and Homecare systems, Integrated regional/national health information networks (Fig. 1), Secondary usage non-clinical systems [31]. Other examples also include: electronic health records, portable communicable systems including those for medical implants, health portals, and many other ICT-based tools assisting disease prevention, diagnosis, treatment, health monitoring and lifestyle management. This system makes it difficult to share information beyond organizational boundaries.

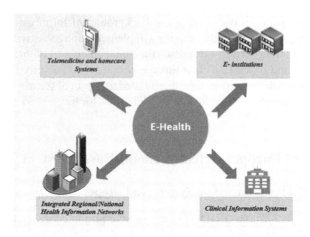

Fig. 1. e-Health example types

The increasing prevalence of ICTs can have transformative impacts on many industries, including health-care where ICTs can deliver citizen centrist health-care and foster a dyadic information symmetric physician-patient relationship [32].

3   e-Health Cloud Computing Implementations Issues

Cloud Computing has been widely recognized as the next generation's technology and it offers several advantages to its users. Cloud Computing can also offer many chances to expand health care services, due to its characteristics that are particularly appealing to the needs of Health-care Providers. On a Cloud-based-health system, the user does not manage or control the Cloud infrastructure, but mainly the software services are provided by the Provider to its end users, clinicians and patients [33–39].

In addition, Cloud Computing is characterized by consumers who use Cloud services as needed, who consume shared resources as a service and pay only for what they used and who access services over a networked infrastructure. Cloud adoption also provides the ability to exchange data between different and distinct systems. In health-care, it can be implemented as a way for maintaining or managing patient information, at different locations. In Fig. 2 we present a Cloud-based Health Information System that communicates with the following actors (doctors, patients, medical personnel) and hospitals via a lot of Clouds and via network connections. To provide consistent and coordinated care at a reasonable cost, Providers must be able to share patient's medical information freely while maintaining information security of their data.

The proposed e-Health Cloud-based system presents the end users (authorized Doctors, Medical Personnel and patients) that could take part in SaaS Cloud-based Health System. All the stakeholders are been navigated through the sharing hospitals and the whole Information systems. As we can understand, the most important component to this system is to ensure the security and to guarantee the confidentiality of the data, due to the fact that we have to deal with sensitive data and the protection of stored information comes as a top priority. And how can we succeed this? By defining, the assets that we want to protect, the possible security requirements of such a system and the

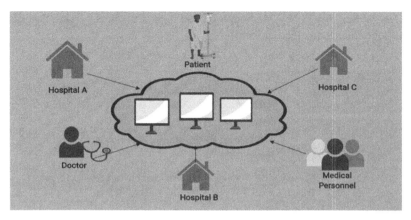

Fig. 2. A cloud-based health system

corresponding Security Policy Rules. The assets of such Information system, based on Cloud Computing, is described to ensure the availability, integrity, authentication, confidentiality of the service and the e-transformation of records. The security requirements and the proposed solutions for such a system will be analyzed in the next parts.

4 Major Security Requirements in Cloud-Based Health Systems

Whatever the choices of the organization or hospital are, there are some security challenges that need to be addressed, when somebody decides to implement a Cloud-based health system. This study aims to support the development of an EU Cloud-based Healthcare System by identifying the necessary key requirements relevant to build up a comprehensive system that supports health policy making.

At the proposed Methodology of our Security Policy, we presented all the Cloud security threats according to the list of threats published by Cloud Security Alliance [40], Gartner [41] other relevant literature and some new Cloud-specific security threats based on our research. Then we categorized threats in 4 Categories (Fig. 3) according to our Policy Methodology and finally we linked these Categories with the requirements related to critical areas.

This report contributes to the definition of a requirement Landscape, by providing an overview of current and emerging security requirements applicable to Cloud-based technologies. The goal of this report is to deepen our understanding into the security requirements that affect Cloud-based Health systems and to provide good practices and recommendations for those requirements that are considered important or emerging. In our research, we have decided to define a list of 19 different threats and only some of them are specific to Cloud Computing, while the rest can also be found in traditional distributed systems.

In addition, to support the challenges of Cloud-based Health Systems, we have defined a set of security requirements (specific for every category of threats), that an analysis and design methodology should support. It is worth mentioning that we only focus on a list of requirements related to modeling and analysis of security and privacy-related concern. In Fig. 3, we present the four Categories-Gates of threats that proposed in our General Security Policy Methodology and then at the next part we describe the security requirements involved in them.

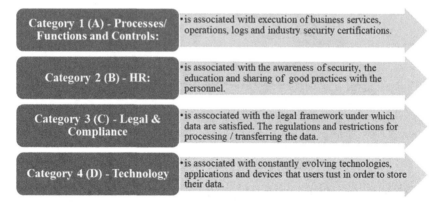

Fig. 3. Four categories of threats according to our security policy methodology

Understanding and documented the security requirements of an e-health Cloud System, gives a solution targeting to each threat and at the same time maps them with the provisions of the Cloud Security Policy. In each category of threats is necessary to ensure what security requirements are covered by the Cloud Provider according the following security measures. In the following analysis, while there are many security concerns in the cloud, this report focuses only on four specific related threats that are representative of every category of threats, according to our Security Policy Methodology. We selected the following threats, as representative threats of a Cloud-based Health System, because they are crucial for a Cloud Computing system and they have the maximum likelihood to occur:

Threat #1: The Abuse of Cloud Services - **Category 1 (A)**
Threat #2: Insufficient Knowledge - **Category 2 (B)**
Threat #3: Data Loss - **Category 3 (C)**
Threat #4: Back up Vulnerabilities - **Category 4 (D)**

In the Analysis that follows, we present the security requirements involved in a Cloud-based Health system (Fig. 4). Although that, there are different security tasks for every Service Model of Cloud Computing (IaaS, PaaS, IaaS), in our research we only focus to tasks that a Cloud Provider should implement for a SaaS Service Model.

Clouds face a multitude of requirements in Cloud-based systems. We have identified the following requirements associated with the aforementioned threats of **Category A (Processes/Functions & Controls) for Cloud-based health systems:**

- **A1. Data controls:** when health data are stored on Cloud, appropriate controls need to be in place. Data are at the core of security concerns for any e-health system, whatever form of infrastructure is used. The distributed nature of the cloud computing and the shared responsibilities that involves, bring the security considerations both to data at rest and also to data in motion, on the priority.

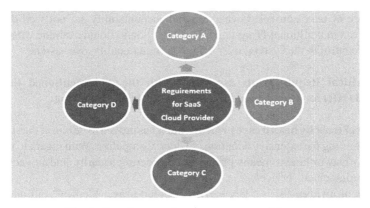

Fig. 4. Requirements for every category of threats

- **A2. Disaster recovery procedures:** Having Disaster recovery procedures in Cloud-based health system, reduces the need for data center space, IT infrastructure and IT resources, which leads to significant cost reductions, enabling smaller hospitals to deploy disaster recovery options.
- **A3. Unauthorized access by e-health professionals:** Cloud Providers are responsible for separating their clients in multitenant situation. Health data are of a sensitive nature, so a Cloud Provider may not allow direct access to information to everyone, without appropriate authorization.
- **A4. Ubiquitous network connectivity to the hospital:** consumers evaluate the external/internal network controls of a Cloud Provider. In a Cloud-based Health system, each user's requirements will be different, but it is recommended that users evaluate the internal network controls of a Service Provider such as: to protect clients from one another, to protect Provider's network, to monitor for intrusion.
- **A5. Quality of service and reliability:** one of the challenges posed by a Cloud-based health system is QoS, which is the problem of allocating resources to the application to guarantee a service level such as performance, availability, reliability.
- **A6. Data Centers - unauthorized entities:** According to the explanation of Cloud Computing by NIST [38], *resources refer to computing applications, network resources, platforms, software services, virtual servers and computing infrastructure.* It is a virtualization of resources, which the end user has on-demand access. In the e-Health Cloud System, the unlawful entities may obtain unauthorized access to the patients' data.
- **A7. Digital signatures/certificates:** A digital certificate is an electronic "passport" that allows a person, computer or organization to exchange information securely over the Internet using the public key infrastructure (PKI). Health-care professionals can gain access to health data using a digital certificate.
- **A8. Malicious insider (doctor, staff, family member):** A malicious insider is well known to most organizations, He could access the sensitive data, steal information, sell the data to other parties or perform number of malicious activities.
- **A9. Abuse of Cloud Services**: Cloud Computing Providers are actively being targeted, because their relatively weak registration systems facilitate anonymity and Providers' fraud detection capabilities are being limited.

- **A10. Lack of user control:** Ownership and accountability are not well defined or applied even in traditional IT systems. Thus, Providers should examine what they are trying to control in the system: over data, over functionality, over assets.

The Critical Requirements associated with the aforementioned threats of Category B (HR) for Cloud-based health system are the following:

- **B1. Lack of trust by health care professionals:** has proven to be one of the substantial barriers limiting the extensive adoption of Cloud Computing. With regard to the Cloud Provider trustworthiness means primarily considering security and privacy aspects when offering cloud services.
- **B2. Lack of awareness:** is a key barrier to Cloud usage. Medical staff and doctors are confused by the term Cloud Computing, which is preventing them from taking the necessary steps to implement the technology.
- **B3. Lack of Segregation of duties:** In the Health environment the staff believes that there is no need in segregation of duties in the technological environment
- **B4. Lack of Education in Information System and alertness:** Health professionals should be educated in the use of Information systems and their risks in order to be alert and respond to security incidents,
- **B5. Lack of Organizational Structure & Responsibilities:** Organizational structure creates the company hierarchy for authority and responsibility.
- **B6. Lack of Confidentiality agreement prior to being given information:** When drafted and used properly, confidentiality agreements are an effective way to protect confidential information. Parties should outline their respective obligations.
- **B7. Code of contact of proper use:** defines how a company's employees should act on a day-to-day basis. It is unique to the organization it represents.

The Critical Requirements associated with the aforementioned threats of Category (Legal Requirements & Compliance) for Cloud-based health system are the following:

- **C1. Loss of governance:** The cloud consumers need to be sufficiently in control of the IT systems.
- **C2. Data jurisdiction issues:** are mostly related to location of data and the specific laws that apply in that location.
- **C3. Intellectual property rights:** Cloud-stored data often transferred from country to country, some with weak Intellectual Properties laws or enforcement.
- **C4. Compliance with security policies:** Security policy provides Health organizations with a framework to operate its business and protect patients without interruption from bad incidents.
- **C5. Data protection:** used to protect stored, static and moving data. It is designed to implement data storage, protection and security methodologies.
- **C6. Data loss:** is any process or event that results in data being corrupted, deleted or made unreadable by a user, software or application. However, there are ways to minimize the risk of data loss and ensure the security of data in Cloud storage.

- **C7. Data Breach/data separation:** Cloud computing gives organizations the ability to run workloads and manage data anywhere without significant computing.
- **C8. Third party controls:** Using these controls can help to identify procedural errors which, if undetected could lead to the reporting of incorrect patient results.
- **C9. Lack of industry standards and certifications:** Without any industry cloud standards, vendors have the possibility to build cloud services on software stacks that are not compatible with the one used in public Clouds.
- **C10. International Regulations:** There are federal, international laws that impose responsibilities to both cloud computing tenants users and providers. Especially those related to the data you collect, store and process.
- **C11. Complexity to ensure compliance:** Decentralization, scaling and other characteristics in Cloud add further complexity to ensure the compliance.
- **C12. Control data:** means implementing policies of governance to ensure that the data are trustworthy, confidential and reliable.
- **C13. Compliance with legislative requirements.** All patients and Health organizations are required to comply with relevant legislation to which they are subject. This includes prescribed laws, regulations and by-laws for Health.
- **C14. Using DLP Data Loss Prevention Tools-software:** These tools are used to ensure that sensitive data is not lost, misused, or accessed by unauthorized users.

The Critical Requirements associated with the aforementioned threats of Category D (Technology) for Cloud-based health system are the following:

- **D1. Bugs in large-scale distributed cloud systems:** Unfortunately, guaranteeing Cloud services' dependability is challenging because these cloud services are supported by large distributed systems such as scalable data stores, data-parallel frameworks and cluster management systems.
- **D2. Support heterogeneous devices and networks:** a Cloud-based health system can support highly heterogeneous devices, as well as can provide interoperability and communication through the hospitals and the systems.
- **D3. Vendor lock-in:** is the result of proprietary technologies that are incompatible with those of competitors. It is the situation where patients are dependent on a single Cloud Provider implementation and cannot easily move in the future to a different vendor without costs, legal constraints, or technical incompatibilities
- **D4. Isolation failure:** Multi-tenancy and shared resources are essential characteristics of Cloud Computing. This risk category covers the failure of mechanisms separating storage, memory, routing, and even reputation between different tenants.
- **D5. Prohibition against cross border transfer:** In globalized world, there are large amounts of cross-border transfers of health data, which are sometimes stored on servers in different countries.
- **D6. Authentication and Trust** Cloud-based Health systems require extensive authentication and trust in their services.

5   Security Policy Rules for Every Category of Threats

As described in numerous relevant publications, a common practice to minimize the risk is to understand the internal control environment of a Cloud Provider and to analyze all the aspects, so we could identify possible contributing factors risks, including the definition of mitigation strategies. This is exactly what we present in our study. The proposed Methodology (Fig. 5) of our Security Policy can fulfill the entire list of Security Requirements of every Category of Threats that are covered by the following Security Policy Rules and provisions of our Cloud Security Policy Methodology.

Fig. 5. Processing of our Security Policy (Methodology)

Based on our analysis of threats in Cloud and the requirements related to these categories of threats, we have identified a number of security policy rules that make the integration of requirements into the development stages of a software systems development methodology considering Cloud-based Health System. These are the following tables (Tables 1, 2, 3 and 4).

Table 1. Security policy rules specific for the requirements of Category A

- **Security management:** should be based on risk assessment and should be active, surrounding all levels of participants' actions and operations.
- **Continual Reassessment**: making of suitable modifications to security policies, performs, measures and procedures.
- **Risk assessment:** should be adequately broad-based to include key internal and external factors, such as technology, physical and human factors, policies and third-party services with security implications.
- **Security Incidents Handling:** It is necessary to have the appropriate policies and procedures in order to handle effectively a range of security incidents.
- **Methods to Control Access:** the level of protection, the associated costs and the level of inconvenience that each option provides must be considered.
- **Technical measures for access control:** is based on the security that the physical barriers offer along with some additional means that permit access (a key).
- **Identifying Physical Assets:** The term includes the buildings, rooms, equipment a Cloud Provider is using.
- **Threat and vulnerability assessment:** Risk analysis method will reveal the potential threats against facilities, employees and clients.
- **Biometrics**: Biometric devices can provide some assurance that the person requesting entry is not using someone else's electronic access card or code.
- **Third Party:** Third party audits should be performed to monitor the Cloud Service Provider's compliance to agreed terms.

Table 2. Security policy rules specific for the requirements of Category B

- **Personnel security:** It is essential for the protection of information assets, especially since information systems and services are operated by people.
- **Awareness:** Is the first line of Defense for the security of Information Systems, including their information assets, computing and communication systems.
- **Responsibility:** All contributors are responsible for the security of information systems and networks. They should be responsible to their individual roles
- **Response:** Participants should act in a timely and co-operative way to avoid, detect and respond to security incidents, recognizing the interconnectivity of information systems/ networks and the potential for fast and widespread damage.
- **Security Organizational Structure:** Organization should adopt the appropriate security organizational structure with the appropriate roles and suitably trained staff in order to support the security policy.
- **On-going staff education, Security Culture and Education:** Organizations shall ensure that employees are properly informed about their rights, obligations and security policies and that they accept their security responsibilities.
- **Continuous Monitoring:** Organization shall ensure that information contained in employee records is up-to-date by establishing the necessary procedures, in accordance to the Public Service Law and relative regulations.

Table 3. Security policy rules for the requirements of Category C

- **Ethics:** Participants should respect the legitimate interests of others. They need to recognize that their action or inaction may damage others.
- **Categorized of Data:** Data should be categorized (Top Secret, Confidential, Sensitive, Reportable) in accordance with the protection they need, as this identified through the risk assessment or the assessment of the SP controller.
- **Localization of data:** In Cloud Computing data travels over the Internet to and from one or more regions where the data centers are. The user of Cloud must know: where the data are located, how the data are processed and by whom etc.
- **Identify the data sources, flow and destination:** This process must include data discovery and data fingerprinting that provides a better understanding, who, where, when and in what format the information is being generated.
- **Control Data:** In the absence of control data in a Cloud, no activity is recorded which modify or delete user's data. User should know how data is handled.

(continued)

Table 3. (*continued*)

- **Using DLP data loss prevention tool-software:** is a strategy for making sure that end users do not sent sensitive or critical information outside the corporate network and prevent them by monitoring and detecting
- **Security Data Management:** When an outside party owns and manages resources, users should be assured that data remain private, secure and that the provider offers strong key management.
- **Conformance to Technical Standards:** Provide specialized expertise on relevant National and International technical standards such as: ISO/IEC 27000 Series of standards, NIST SP 800 standards, ETSI Security Standards.

Table 4. Security policy rules for the requirements of Category D

- **Security design and implementation**: Security shall be a fundamental element of all products, services, systems and networks. A major focus of this effort is the design and adoption of appropriate safeguards and solutions.
- **General Configuration Guidelines:** Operating System configuration should be in accordance with approved Information Security guidelines.
- **Monitoring:** All security-related events on sensitive systems shall be logged and audit trails saved as follows: logs will be kept online for a minimum of 1 week. Daily incremental tape backups will be retained for at least 1 month. Weekly full tape backups of logs will be retained for at least 1 month. Monthly full backups will be retained for a minimum of 2 years.
- **Compliance:** Audits will be performed on a regular basis by authorized Organisations within the Cloud Provider and will be managed by the internal audit teams. Every determination will be made to stop audits from causing failures.
- **Malware Protection**: Never download files from unknown or suspicious sources. Never install unauthorized programs or applications. Choose and issue default anti-malware/anti-virus software.
- **Security of Software**: Changes to the software are approved prior to their implementation. Changes that affect - directly or indirectly.
- **Portable Computing:** Portable information assets shall be adequately protected wherever they are used, whilst being transported or stored and when being disposed of Provider's IT equipment shall only be used by authorized users.

---

6 Conclusions

In this paper, we presented a list of some basic security requirements and security policy rules for the deployment of Cloud-based Health System in an SaaS Cloud environment. Based on our analysis of the security and privacy threats in the Cloud and the categorization of these threats, we acknowledged an amount of security policy requirements and security policy rules that fulfill the provisions of every category of threats. Finally, we presented a proposed Model that provides a solution to the security challenges of Cloud Computing. The focus of this research, is, to minimize the risks that are presented in a Cloud-based health system and to present a Framework that offers the appropriate security to patients' data and achieves the required assurance level of protection. The proposed Cloud Model Service improves the security and integrity of the medical records without affecting data access functionality from a user perspective. Given the dynamic development in the area of Cloud Computing, the security recommended policy rules listed above, need to be regularly reviewed and adjusted, and additional requirements may need to be added.

We must keep in mind that, in order to address the challenges all parties involved need to work together to create uniform and interoperable solutions that will allow a better Cloud-based health System to exist. We believe priorities in e-Health may be mentioned as a national issue, so we hope this contribution will encourage an exchange of best practices and lessons learned in migrating public e-health systems to fully virtualized SaaS Cloud-based environments.

Acknowledgment. This research is co-financed by Greece and the European Union (European Social Fund- ESF) through the Operational Programme «Human Resources Development, Education and Lifelong Learning» in the context of the project "Reinforcement of Postdoctoral Researchers - 2nd Cycle" (MIS-5033021), implemented by the State Scholarships Foundation (IKY).

Ευρωπαϊκή Ένωση
European Social Fund

Operational Programme
Human Resources Development,
Education and Lifelong Learning
Co-financed by Greece and the European Union

ΕΣΠΑ
2014-2020
ανάπτυξη - εργασία - αλληλεγγύη

References

1. Goodwin, L., Courtney, K., Kirby, K.D., Iannacchione, M.A., Manley, T.: A pilot study: patients' perceptions about the privacy of their medical records. J. Nurs. Inf. **6**(3), 1–21 (2002)
2. Flynn, H., Marcus, S., Kerber, K., Alessi, N.: Patients' concerns about and perceptions of electronic psychiatric records. Psychiat. Serv. **54**(11), 1539–1541 (2003)
3. Silber, D.: (2003). http://www.openclinical.org/e-Health. Accessed 9 Nov 2018
4. Han, S., Skinner, G., Potdar, V., Chang, E.: A framework of authentication and authorization for e-health services 105–106 (2006). https://doi.org/10.1145/1180367.1180387
5. Oh, H., Rizo, C., Enkin, M., Jadad, A.: What is eHealth (3): a systematic review of published definitions. J. Med. Internet Res. **7**(1), e1 (2005)

6. Scott, R.E., Chowdhury, M.F.U., Varghese, S.: Telehealth policy: looking for global complementarity. Telemed. Telecare **8**, 55–57 (2002)
7. Gematik - gesellschaft fur telematikanwendungen der gesundheitskarte: http://www.gematik.de. Accessed 27 Nov 2017
8. Chatman, C.: How cloud computing is changing the face of health care information technology. J. Health Care Compliance **12**, 37–70 (2010)
9. Dudley, J.T., Pouliot, Y., Chen, R., et al.: Translational bioinformatics in the Cloud: an affordable alternative. Genome Med. **2**, 51 (2010)
10. Kabachinski, J.: What's the forecast for Cloud Computing in healthcare? Biomed. Instrum. Technol. **45**(2), 146–150 (2011). https://doi.org/10.2345/0899-8205-45.2.146
11. Meingast, M., Roosta, T., Sastry, S.: Security and privacy issues with health care information technology. In: Conference Proceedings, vol. 1, pp. 5453–5458 (2006). IEEE Eng Med Biol Soc
12. Shmatikov, V.: Anonymity is not privacy: technical perspective. J. Commun. ACM **54**, 132 (2011)
13. Reynolds, B., Venkatanathan, J., Gonçalves, J., Kostakos, V.: Sharing ephemeral information in online social networks: privacy perceptions and behaviours. In: Campos, P., Graham, N., Jorge, J., Nunes, N., Palanque, P., Winckler, M. (eds.) INTERACT 2011. LNCS, vol. 6948, pp. 204–215. Springer, Heidelberg (2011). https://doi.org/10.1007/978-3-642-23765-2_14
14. De Capitani di Vimercati, S., Foresti, S., Livraga, G., Samarati, P.: Protecting privacy in data release. In: Aldini, A., Gorrieri, R. (eds.) FOSAD 2011. LNCS, vol. 6858, pp. 1–34. Springer, Heidelberg (2011). https://doi.org/10.1007/978-3-642-23082-0_1
15. Georgiou, D., Lambrinoudakis, C.: Cloud computing security requirements and a methodology for their auditing. In: Katsikas, S.K., Sideridis, A.B. (eds.) e-Democracy 2015. CCIS, vol. 570, pp. 51–61. Springer, Cham (2015). https://doi.org/10.1007/978-3-319-27164-4_4
16. Georgiou, D., Lambrinoudakis, C.: Security policy rules and required procedures for two crucial cloud computing threats. Int. J. Electron. Govern. **9**(3/4), 385–403 (2017)
17. Georgiou, D., Lambrinoudakis, C.: A security policy for cloud providers the software-as-a-service model. In: Conference: ICIMP 2014: The Ninth International Conference on Internet Monitoring and Protection (2014)
18. Final European progress report. E-health strategies. www.ehealth-stragies.eu/report/report.html. Accessed 10 Nov 2018
19. European Commission SWD (2012) 413 final (2018)
20. Communication from the Commission to the Council the European Parliament, the European Economic and Social Committee and the Committee of the Regions, COM(2004) 356: e-Health—making health care better for European citizens: an action plan for a European e-Health Area {SEC(2004) 539}. European Commission, Brussels (2004)
21. European Commission SWD (2012) 414 final. On the applicability of the existing EU legal framework to telemedicine services (2018). https://eur-lex.europa.eu/LexUriServ/LexUriServ.do?uri=SWD:2012:0414:FIN:EN:PDF. Accessed 24 Nov 2018
22. Action77: Foster EU-wide standards, interoperability testing and certification of e Health: digital Agenda for Europe. http://ec.europa.eu/digital-agenda/en/pillar-vii-ict-enabled-benefits-eu-society/action-77-foster-eu-wide-standards-interoperability. Accessed 28 Aug 2018
23. EU activities in the field of e Health interoperability and standardization: an overview. European Commission (2013, press release)
24. Europe's Information Society eHealth portal. http://europa.eu.int/information_society/activities/health. Accessed 30 Sept 2019
25. European Commission. eHealth Action Plan 2012–2020 - Innovative healthcare for the 21st century (2019). http://ec.europa.eu/health/ehealth/docs/com_2012_736_en.pdf. Accessed 12 Dec 2019

26. European Parliament, Council of the European Union. Decision on adopting a programme of Community action on health monitoring within the framework of action in the field of public health (1997–2001) (1400/97/EC). Off J EurCommunities, vol. 40, pp. 1–10 (1997)
27. European Parliament, Council of the European Union. Decision on adopting a programme of Community action in the field of public health (2003–2008) (1786/2002/EC). Off J Eur Union, vol. 45, pp. 1–11 (2002)
28. European Parliament, Council of the European Union. Decision on establishing a second programme of Community action in the field of health (2008–13) (1350/2007/EC). Off J Eur Union, vol. 50, pp. 3–13 (2007)
29. eHealth Industries Innovation. What is e Health? e Health Industries Innovation (ehi2) Centre, http://www.ehi2.swan.ac.uk/en/what-is-ehealth.htm. Accessed 3 Apr 2014
30. European Commission. eHealth Action Plan 2012–2020 - Innovative healthcare for the 21st century (2012). http://ec.europa.eu/health/ehealth/docs/com_2012_736_en.pdf. Accessed 12 Dec 2018
31. Khazaei, H., Misic, J., Misic, V.: Performance analysis of cloud computing centers using M/G/m/m+r. queuing systems IEEE Trans Parallel Distrib. Syst. **23**, 5 (2012)
32. Wang, L., von Laszewski, G., Younge, A., et al.: Cloud computing: a perspective study. New Gener. Comput. **28**, 137–146 (2010)
33. Kleinrock, L.: Queueing Systems: Theory, vol. 1. Wiley-Interscience, Hoboken (1975)
34. Mao, M., Li, J., Humphrey, M.: Cloud auto-scaling with deadline and budget constraints. In: 2010 11th IEEE/ACM International Conference on Grid Computing (GRID), pp. 41–48 (2010)
35. Barham, P., Dragovic, B., Fraser, K., et al.: Xen and the art of virtualization. SIGOPS Oper. Syst. Rev. **37**(5), 164–177 (2003)
36. WMWare White paper http://www.vmware.com/pdf/virtualization.pdf. Accessed 25 Dec 2017
37. The Open Stack Project: Open Stack 'The open source cloud operating system'. http://www.openstack.org/software/. Accessed 30 Nov 2017
38. Grance, M.P.: The NIST definition of cloud computing Gaithersburg: NIST Special Publication 800-145, 20899-8930 (2011)
39. Georgiou, D.: PhD Thesis Security Policies for Cloud Computing (2018)
40. Cloud Security Alliance, Top threats to Cloud Computing v1.0. https://cloudsecurityalliance.org/topthreats/csathreats.v1.0.pdf. Accessed 15 Nov 2019
41. Heiser, J., Nicolett, M.: Assessing the Security Risks of Cloud Computing, white paper, Gartner Group, ID Number: G00157782 (2008). Accessed 10 Dec 2018

On the Suitability of Using SGX
for Secure Key Storage in the Cloud

Joakim Brorsson[1,2,3(✉)], Pegah Nikbakht Bideh[1], Alexander Nilsson[1,4],
and Martin Hell[1]

[1] Department of Electrical and Information Technology, Lund University,
Lund, Sweden
{joakim.brorsson,pegah.nikbakht_bideh,alexander.nilsson,
martin.hell}@eit.lth.se
[2] Combitech AB, Linköping, Sweden
[3] Hyker Security AB, Linköping, Sweden
[4] Advenica AB, Malmö, Sweden

Abstract. This paper addresses the need for secure storage in virtualized services in the cloud. To this purpose, we evaluate the security properties of Intel's Software Guard Extensions (SGX) technology, which provides hardware protection for general applications, for securing virtual Hardware Security Modules (vHSM). In order for the analysis to be comparable with analyses of physical HSMs, the evaluation proceeds from the FIPS 140–3 standard, the successor to FIPS 140–2, which is commonly used to assess security properties of HSMs.

Our contribution is twofold. First, we provide a detailed security evaluation of vHSMs using the FIPS 140–3 standard. Second, after concluding that the standard is designed for stand-alone rather than virtual systems, we propose a supplementary threat model, which considers threats from different actors separately. This model allows for different levels of trust in actors with different capabilities and can thus be used to assess which parts of FIPS 140–3 that should be considered for a specific attacker.

Using FIPS 140–3 in combination with the threat model, we find that SGX enclaves provide sufficient protection against a large part of the potential actors in the cloud. Thus, depending on the threat model, SGX can be a helpful tool for providing secure storage for virtualized services.

1 Introduction

Secret keys used in cryptographic operations need to be safeguarded. If they are leaked to an attacker, many defense mechanisms are rendered ineffective. In systems with high security demands, Hardware Security Modules (HSMs) are often used for secure storage and key management. An HSM can securely isolate sensitive data from other parts of a system using *trusted hardware*, providing guarantees for integrity, confidentiality and isolation of cryptographic keys.

This work was partially supported by the Wallenberg AI, Autonomous Systems and Software Program (WASP) and the Swedish Foundation for Strategic Research, grant RIT17-0035.

ⓒ Springer Nature Switzerland AG 2020
S. Gritzalis et al. (Eds.): TrustBus 2020, LNCS 12395, pp. 32–47, 2020.
https://doi.org/10.1007/978-3-030-58986-8_3

However, using HSMs comes with several drawbacks. First, they are expensive, since they contain specially designed hardware and require maintenance by trained personnel. Second, they are purpose built, with a fixed limited set of operations. Third, they are not easily virtualizable, i.e. incorporating them into a virtual cloud environment without making custom configurations is difficult.

Recently, many applications and services have migrated from on-premise solutions to pure or hybrid cloud environments. The main motivation is that the cloud can provide more functionality and practically infinite computing resources without delay. It is possible to build applications and services which can automatically scale up and down with system needs. The infrastructure is handled by the cloud provider, and application owners only pay for what is used.

This points towards a mismatch between using cloud services and using HSMs for data protection. The cloud provides virtualized services on shared infrastructure, while HSMs are physical, single-tenant units. Being purpose built, an HSM can also not easily be continuously updated with better features. This mismatch fuels a need for alternative solutions for secure storage of secret keys in the cloud.

Intel Software Guard Extensions (SGX) [4] can be considered as an alternative technology for secure key storage in a cloud environment. SGX, like HSMs, leverages hardware protection mechanisms to isolate data. Since SGX is not purpose built like HSMs, the technology allows for running general purpose code within a hardware protected *enclave*. Systems based on the technology can therefore be easily virtualizable and continuously updated.

While the cost and functionality benefits that can be gained from virtualizing HSMs are clear, the security properties of such systems are not yet fully investigated. We therefore wish to evaluate the effectiveness of the security measures of SGX for protecting sensitive data in a cloud environment, where there are multiple actors with different levels of trust and capabilities, ranging from restricted application users to system administrators with physical access to servers.

The rest of this paper is organized as follows: We present related work in Sect. 2. Then, the background including details on HSMs, Intel SGX and FIPS 140–3 is given in Sect. 3. An evaluation of SGX for key storage purposes in a cloud environment using FIPS 140–3 is given in Sect. 4. In Sect. 5 we provide a new model for using FIPS 140–3 that consider attacker capabilities and intents. Then, in Sect. 6 we use the new model in combination with FIPS 140–3 and get a more nuanced conclusion. Finally, conclusions are given in Sect. 7.

1.1   Contribution

This paper provides two main contributions. First, we use the Federal Information Processing Standard FIPS 140–3 [13], designed for evaluating the security of cryptographic modules, to evaluate to what extent SGX technology can provide *secure storage*. For each applicable requirement in the standard, we classify the fulfillment of the requirement for SGX based secure storage modules.

Second, we consider a more flexible model, incorporating both different levels of trust and expected capabilities of other cloud actors. Using this model, we evaluate system security capabilities, using FIPS 140–3 as the basis for requirement fulfillment. This model and analysis can thus be used to better understand real world security capabilities of a system using SGX for secure storage.

2 Related Work

The general problem of charting security threats has various proposals in the literature, e.g. the systematic threat modeling methods suggested in [2,22]. Such proposals are surveyed in e.g. [25]. The more specific area of charting security threats for services running in the cloud is surveyed in e.g. [10,20]. These surveys discuss aspects of cloud security addressed in this paper, such as trust, multitenancy and malicious insiders. While [10] takes an attack focused approach and suggests TPM based solutions for trusted computing, [20] suggests SGX as an emerging solution, and roots its analysis in the capabilities and roles for different actors in a cloud environment, making them a suitable starting point for our analysis. It should be noted that SGX was a very new technology at the time these surveys were published.

The use of SGX for protecting containerized applications is proposed in SCONE and PANOPLY [1,21]. Similarly to this paper, the work explores SGX as a technique for creating trusted remote entities. While SCONE and PANOPLY give methods for creating containerized SGX enclave services, neither of the works consider side-channel or physical attacks as within scope for their security models, and can therefore not provide a full attacker model evaluation.

There has also been various suggestions for securing more specific cloud services and distributed use-cases with the technology [12,16,19]. Although these suggestions are dependent on the security properties of SGX, none of them present an attack model which considers the full capabilities of an attacker such as exploiting side-channels and having physical access. This is unfortunate since the security properties of SGX depends on the capabilities of an attacker.

A categorization of security properties of SGX in context of known attacks is given in [14], which surveys and categorizes the attacks on SGX and concludes that while there might come more attacks in the future, it is possible to mitigate the known attacks. Lindell [11] surveys attacks on SGX and concludes that the technology is not suitable as a protection mechanism or as an HSM replacement. In this paper, we instead argue that the suitability of SGX for data protection is not black or white, but instead use-case and attack model dependent, i.e. that SGX is not a suitable solution for all use-cases, but perfectly adequate for many.

3 Background

3.1 Hardware Security Modules

HSMs are hardware units which provide cryptographic functionality. They have physical protection measures, such as tamper proof coatings and separated input paths. Strong physical security measures, combined with strong security requirements, provides a base for trusting them not to leak or mishandle sensitive data. Further, the security of HSMs is often certified by a third party. One of the most common certifications to aim for is the FIPS 140–x standards [13]. Examples of functions supported by HSMs are key generation, key storage and random number generation. These functions are typically wrapped by a software API, which is responsible for giving access to the cryptographic functions.

While HSMs can give strong, certifiable, security guarantees, they are usually expensive, do not easily allow for multi-tenant usage, and can not be virtualized.

3.2 Software Guard Extensions

SGX is a set of Intel CPU extensions that provide integrity and confidentiality for computations. SGX can run code and operate on sensitive data in *enclaves*, which are execution environments isolated from the outside software environment.

While isolated execution environments can also be obtained using virtualization, such isolation techniques rely on concepts such as address translation, which puts full trust in the hypervisor or OS-kernel to control what physical memory is accessed when reading or writing to a virtual address. In a cloud scenario, this means that the cloud provider is fully trusted. The SGX threat model eliminates this trust by not trusting anything outside the software enclave, including the kernel, hypervisor and BIOS. On the physical side, no trust is placed on any component outside the CPU die (such as RAM modules).

However, physical attacks against the CPU module itself are not considered in Intel's threat model, nor are so-called side-channel attacks [4]. SGX has recently been subject to several attacks compromising the hardware isolation of data and code, most of these being side-channel based attacks. Although the SGX security model [4] does not specify side-channels stemming from application code as in-scope, some of these attacks are based on side-channels present in the micro architecture of the processor [6, 23, 24] and we must consider them. Side-channels originating from an improper software implementation is not in-scope, however.

SGX further provides functionality for *remote attestation*, where a user can convince herself that the enclave is running on genuine unmodified hardware, and that the software inside the enclave is indeed the expected one. This functionality is advantageous when running on shared hardware, as is our scenario. One can note that remote attestation is also available through use of a Trusted Platform Module (TPM). A TPM, however, has the drawback that the OS-kernel must be included in the Trusted Computing Base (TCB) for the measurement.

3.3 FIPS 140–3

FIPS 140–3 [13], is a standard issued by the American National Institute of Standards and Technology (NIST). It supersedes FIPS 140–2 and came into effect in September 2019. The standard specifies security requirements for systems protecting sensitive information, which has made it a common standard for

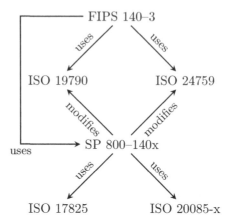

Fig. 1. Relationships between standards.

evaluating the security of HSMs. The new FIPS 140–3 standard is more detailed on side channel attacks compared to the older version.

The scope of the standard is defined by a set of security requirement areas, such as *authentication* and *physical security*. A *security level* is given as a measure of the quality of a security mechanisms. Depending on to what degree a system satisfies the *security requirements*, a system can be certified to *security level* 1–4.

FIPS 140–3 is not self contained, but consists of a series of other standards referencing each other. The relations between these can be seen in Fig. 1. FIPS 140–3 mandates the use of ISO 19790 [8] and ISO 24759 [9]. These standards specify, respectively, security requirements and test requirements for cryptographic modules. Not being fully satisfied with these ISO standards as-is, FIPS 140–3 also references a series of soon to be released NIST Special Publications, SP 800–140 A-F [15], which modify ISO 19790 and ISO 24759. They are currently available as drafts. These Special Publications in turn uses two other ISO standards as the basis for the modifications. These are ISO 17825 [7], which describes testing methods for side channel attack prevention mechanisms, and the soon to be released ISO 20085–1 and ISO 20085–2, which define test tool requirements.

To get FIPS 140–3 certified for a specific level, the system must comply with the requirements of that level as well as the requirements for lower levels.

Security **Level 1** is the basic security level with requirements analogue to those of standard production-grade systems.

Security **Level 2** adds physical security requirements through measures such as hard coatings, which will leave detectable traces of physical attacks, called tamper-evidence. Level 2 further requires role-based operator authentication.

In addition to tamper-evidence, **Level 3** requires *high* probability of tamper-detection and response, i.e. physical security that not only leaves evidence of abuse, but acts to prevent it. Further, identity-based authentication is required for operators, physical or logical separation is required for I/O ports for secret data, the system needs to protect sensitive data against compromise following environmental factors such as varying power supply or temperature, and it needs to provide protection against non-invasive attacks, i.e. side channel attacks.

Finally, **Level 4** requires *very high* probability of tamper detection with immediate and uninterruptible response, regardless if the system is connected to power or not. Further, multi-factor authentication for operators is required, the protection against environmental factors must be explicitly specified and tested, and there are higher testing requirements for mitigations of non-invasive attacks.

4 Evaluation Using FIPS 140–3

We use the following method to use FIPS 140–3 for determining (1) the security of a cryptographic module when applied to a certain scenario or use case, and (2) how the security depends on a given threat model.

1. Define the scenario.
2. Identify the FIPS 140–3 requirements that need particular attention for the given scenario, and evaluate the attainable security level.
3. Define the threat model in terms of attacker capabilities and intents.
4. Evaluate the identified FIPS 140–3 requirements in relation to the threat model and determine the security level attainable for each requirement.

Step 2 and step 4 in this process require interpretations of the FIPS 140–3 standard, taking both security and test requirements into account. Since we are interested in the attainable level, we also need to rely on assumptions on algorithms, protocols and implementations. Thus, it is important to clearly document these interpretations and assumptions in order to be transparent when determining the security level. In the following, we demonstrate how this methodology is used to evaluate the attainable security for using SGX for key storage in the cloud.

4.1 Scenario and Threat Model

This paper investigates whether virtualizable alternatives to HSMs can provide similar security features. Therefore, the evaluation considers the concrete scenario of a virtual HSM, hosted on a public cloud, implemented as an SGX enclave, and used for secure key storage. This scenario imitates a real public cloud system, and introduces the full set of present actors. The actors in this scenario are then: the cloud provider and its personnel, the application owner and users, and owners and users of other co-hosted services on the same cloud.

We used a system model as illustrated in Fig. 2 to evaluate our selected scenario explained above. We base this model on the findings in [20], which also discusses threat models for virtualized systems in a cloud environment. Note that the SGX protection mechanisms reside in the hardware layer, so that while an application runs in the guest layer, the protection mechanisms are rooted in hardware. The FIPS 140–3 security requirements do not take the trustworthiness or capabilities of potentially adversarial actors into account.

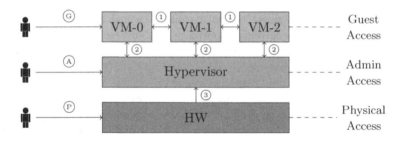

Fig. 2. Cloud System Model.

Therefore, our threat model does not differentiate between actors in this evaluation. We consider all actors potentially malicious and thus bring all FIPS 140-3 related security measures into scope. An extended model which differentiates between actors will be discussed later in Sect. 5.2.

4.2 Identifying FIPS 140–3 Requirements

FIPS 140–3 includes a lengthy set of *security requirements*, specifying things such as roles of operators, the finite state model of the system, etc. For the sake of brevity, we here limit ourselves to discussing the requirements which are of interest when comparing HSMs and SGX based systems for key storage.

Based on our interpretations while analyzing the requirements, we find the following sections for which the outcome can differ when applied to HSMs or SGX based solutions.

– **FIPS 140–3 Section 7.3: Cryptographic Module Ports and Interfaces.** These requirements handle separation of I/O ports.
– **FIPS 140–3 Section 7.7: Physical Security.** The Physical Security requirements address tamper-proofing, -evidence and -detection.
– **FIPS 140–3 Section 7.8: Non-invasive Security.** This section concerns mitigating passive side-channel attacks.
– **FIPS 140–3 Section 7.9: Sensitive Security Parameter Management.** These are requirements on input and output of sensitive data.
– **FIPS 140–3 Section 7.12: Mitigation of Other Attacks.** These requirements concern resistance towards attacks not specified in the standard. Depending on the type of attack, there might be differences in implementation.

We go through the selected requirement areas individually and discuss how an SGX based system can comply with the requirements. The standard also makes heavy use of *test requirements* which mandate how the security requirements are meant to be evaluated. These give great insight into how the security requirements are to be interpreted. In the following sections, these are only referenced implicitly. In our evaluation, for brevity, we focus on only security requirements.

4.3   Evaluating FIPS 140–3 Requirements

Cryptographic Module Ports and Interfaces: Level 1–2 requires logically distinct interfaces, which can be implemented as e.g. an API, and restriction of information flow to points identified as entry and exit. Different required interfaces are specified. There are also requirements for the specification of all interfaces and of all input and output data paths. For achieving level 3 there is a requirement to implement a *trusted channel* for protected input and output of sensitive data with physical or logical separation from other channels. This channel further needs to have identity-based authentication. Level 4 additionally requires multi-factor authentication for using a trusted channel.

Conclusion. Since the requirements allow for logical separation of interfaces, SGX is well documented, and authentication is implementation independent, we see no problem in implementing security up to level 4 using SGX. Note that attacks on trusted channels such as TLS is outside the scope of our threat model.

Physical Security: According to ISO 19790, software based cryptographic modules are not subject to requirements for physical security. The maximum allowed level for software based systems is level 2. For a hardware based system it is required for level 1 that there are production grade components. For level 2 physical tampering should leave evidence on an opaque enclosure. It is possible to reach level 3 if there is *environmental failure testing*, where fluctuations in environmental factors such as varying power supply or temperature is tested to not have any impact on the security. Level 3 also specifies that zeroization of sensitive data should occur in case of tampering. For level 4 the system must additionally provide *environmental failure protection* which includes active monitoring and immediate response to environmental changes. Additionally, protection against fault induction must be documented for this level.

Conclusion. Since Intel CPUs include glued-on heatsinks, which are difficult to remove, we conclude that level 2 ought to be attainable.

Depending on the requirements on the coating and fault injection, which are not clearly stated, SGX based modules will probably not live up to level 3. Regarding environmental failure testing and protection Intel SGX will not be able to reach level 3 or 4.

Non-invasive Security: For security level 1 & 2, it is required to document mitigation techniques used for non-invasive attacks, otherwise known as passive side-channel attacks. ISO-19790 does not in itself specify any list of approved non-invasive attack mitigation test metrics.

For security level 3 & 4, ISO 17825 should be used for evaluating the protection against non-invasive attacks. The standard specifies 3 main attack classes: Timing, Power-Consumption and Electro-magnetic emission.

Conclusion. Regarding non-invasive attacks (i.e. passive side-channel attacks) using *timing* information, it is possible to use standardized cryptographic libraries which are designed to be constant time. Note that for the SGX scenario, special care must be taken in order to also be secure against *cache*-timing and other microarchitectural timing-based attacks. Using an up-to-date and well vetted industry standard cryptographic library which includes these kind of attacks in its threat model should be sufficient to enable an SGX based system to pass the level 4 security requirements considering only timing based attacks.

For electromagnetic emission and power consumption based analysis, Intel SGX—which is implemented inside regular Intel CPUs—is not designed to protect against such attacks. Such attacks have been found, see for example [3,5]. For this reason we would not expect SGX to be resistant against these classes of attacks. However some work have been proposed which would allow for software based mitigations against these types of attacks [18]. It remains an open question whether such mitigations are effective in our proposed scenario. We are therefore hesitant to offer a clear conclusion of what FIPS 140–3 security level the certification process would ultimately end up with. We would like to point out however that it would not be unreasonable to argue that level 1 & 2 are passable since these levels only require documentation of reasonable protections, while 3 & 4 require vetting and extensive testing according to ISO 17825.

Sensitive Security Parameter Management: For security level 1, ISO 19790 specifies that input and output of sensitive data must be done through well defined and documented channels. See ISO 19790 Section 7.9.5. for more details. It also requires role-based authentication and that it is possible for a module operator to zeroize (erase) sensitive data independent of system operation.

To obtain level 2, the system must additionally perform zeroization of temporary or unprotected sensitive data if and when the data is no longer needed. Level 3 additionally specifies that input and output of sensitive data must be done either through a trusted channel or by using encryption. Further, an identity-based authentication method is required for level 3.

Level 4 requires multi-factor identity-based operator authentication for data input and output. Further, the system must be able to zeroize the above mentioned data without being interrupted and the process must be immediate.

Conclusion. Since it is possible for Intel SGX based systems to zeroize by overwriting all sensitive data, we judge that level 3 is obtainable in regard to the zeroization requirements. Level 4 is not obtainable in situations where the process can be interrupted and prevented from executing.

Mitigation of Other Attacks: For level 1, 2 & 3, the system under evaluation must provide documentation on mechanisms protecting against specific attacks not found elsewhere in the FIPS 140–3 standard. The documentation must include an enumeration of all possible known attacks against the implementation.

For level 4, the documentation additionally must include the methods used for testing the effectiveness of the mitigation techniques. One notable consequence of these requirements is that if no attacks are known then level 4 is reachable.

Table 1. Summery of level fulfillment according to FIPS 140–3 requirements

Requirement areas	Level 1	Level 2	Level 3	Level 4
Cryptographic Module Ports and Interfaces				✓
Physical Security		✓		
Non-invasive Security		✓		
Sensitive Security Parameter Management			✓	
Mitigation of Other Attacks			✓	

Conclusion. Because of the known attacks, SGX based systems will have to provide mitigations and documentations about these attacks. Since mitigations[1] exist for all attacks known to the authors (just to mention a few: [6,23,24]), we consider level 3 to be obtainable for these requirements.

It is unclear whether level 4 is reachable in practice, since many of the attacks and their mitigations are difficult to practically implement and test. Evaluating the level 4 security requirements listed in ISO 17825 requires performing a full FIPS 140–3 certification. Since ISO 17825 is used for evaluating the protections against non-invasive attacks, we theorize that it is possible to use it for evaluating the more invasive side-channel attacks as well. This would be reasonable since both attack classes depend on the same type of biases (timing, or otherwise).

4.4   FIPS 140–3 Evaluation Results

Building on the intermittent conclusions above we can summarize the level of fulfillment for the different requirement areas as illustrated in Table 1. It should be noted that we here summarize our most optimistic views and we refer back the respective sub-sections in Sect. 4 for further discussions.

We believe that an SGX based system can reach level 1 & 2 due to meeting the requirements of level 1 & 2 for all requirement areas. However level 3 & 4 are not reachable since the requirements are not fulfillable for all requirement areas.

5   A Threat Based Security Model

5.1   Motivation

Secure key storage in the cloud comes with a threat model which contrasts with on-premise solutions in that it introduces new actors (enumerated in Sect. 4.1).

To evaluate the security of a system, the evaluation requirements must be clear. We need an evaluation model that takes the system use case into account.

---

[1] For some cache-based attacks the mitigation must be implemented in the software implementation since Intel has not considered such attacks as in-scope for SGX.

Table 2. The attack model

	Honest	Curious	Malicious
Guest access	G+H	G+C	G+M
Admin access	A+H	A+C	A+M
Physical access	P+H	P+C	P+M

The FIPS 140–3 standard is good for evaluating the *capabilities* of a security system. However, we find that it needs complementing for evaluating a system with different levels of trust in different actors, which we argue is crucial for cloud use cases. In order to compare the security of SGX-based key storage to other methods, such as HSMs, we need a complementary security evaluation framework to be used with FIPS 140–3.

We suggest a model designed to address security in a cloud environment. It is based on a model where the threat from an actor is defined as a combination of *trust* in the actor in combination with its *capabilities* to perform an attack. The model can be used to complement FIPS 140–3, by allowing the security classifications to take the perspective of what threat model a service can handle, in contrast to only measuring inherent system capabilities directly. Thus, the suggested threat model allows for varying degrees of trust in different actors.

5.2   Model Description

Based on the motivation above, we define a two-dimensional attack model, taking into account that actors in a cloud scenario can have different *capabilities* and different levels of *trust* from the application designer. The attack model is given in Table 2. The *capabilities* are based on access levels and are defined as follows.

- **Guest Access (G).** A remote attacker with admin or user level access to a specific virtual service.
- **Admin Access (A).** An attacker with hypervisor-level remote administrative access to the physical machine hosting the VM.
- **Physical Access (P).** An attacker with physical access to the physical machine hosting the VM.

The second dimension specifies the *trust* that the application designer has in an actor. Trust is divided into three categories.

- **Honest (H).** The actor is expected to abide by any rules as agreed on with the application designer. This includes the expectation that this actor will not attempt any bypass of technical protection mechanisms.
- **Curious (C).** The actor is expected to try to circumvent rules and technical protection mechanism by mounting non-invasive or passive attacks.
- **Malicious (M).** The actor is expected to attempt all existing attacks.

In Fig. 2, the capabilities corresponds to the three horizontal layers. An actor has to interact with the system through the corresponding interface (Ⓖ, Ⓐ or Ⓟ). Further there are attack paths (①, ② and ③) to consider, where an attacker can traverse between different entities on the same access level (①), and jump between access levels (② and ③). For example, co-hosted services is an actor which has to be considered in the cloud. In [17], it is deemed feasible to get co-hosted with a cloud service of your choice, allowing attacks through ① or ② on neighbouring applications. Another attack vector, not present in on-premise systems, is a malicious service provider, i.e. a hostile cloud, which can access virtual services by an attack through e.g. ②. For further discussions of capabilities and possible attacks, we refer to [20].

By combining capabilities and trust, security requirements can be defined with more flexibility, allowing us to target more specific use-cases. An example of this is in the scenario where you trust the cloud provider to be *honest* but consider co-hosted VMs to be potentially *malicious*. In such a scenario, require-ments are different compared to if you had to abide by the lowest trust level (malicious) for all actors. Care must be taken when combining capabilities and trust in this manner. For example, an assumed honesty of co-hosted services is not sound in practice, but is included in our model as a theoretical baseline scenario.

The security model discussed here considers the confidentiality and integrity of data. The requirements for availability of systems are considered out of scope, which is consistent with the attack models for both Intel SGX and FIPS 140–3.

6   Mapping Our Security Model to FIPS 140–3

Using FIPS 140–3 for evaluating the suitability of a system does not take the specific scenario into consideration. Thus, in this section, based on our earlier evaluation of SGX using FIPS 140–3 in Sect. 4, we adapt the scope of FIPS 140–3 to a cloud scenario by taking the threat model into account.

6.1   Methodology

In order to map our threat model to FIPS 140–3, for each category in Table 2, we take the threat model into consideration when evaluating the relevance and fulfillment of a requirement. For example, if an actor is honest, the full set of requirements are out of scope, and if an actor does not have physical capabilities, requirements for physical security and non-invasive attacks based on power trace and EM are out of scope. From this we get a security level for each requirement category for each actor. This method is analogous to how FIPS 140–3 excludes its own requirements in physical security for pure software based cryptographic modules which implicitly renders the Operating System a trusted actor.

6.2   Mapping the Threat Model

The result of mapping our threat model onto the scenario can be seen in Table 3. The possible security level for each actor is based on the conclusions in the relevant requirement category in Sect. 4.

Table 3. Mapping FIPS 140–3 to our attack model

		G+C	G+M	A+C	A+M	P+C	P+M
Cryptographic module ports and interfaces		4	4	4	4	4	4
Physical Security		N/A	N/A	N/A	N/A	N/A	2
Non-invasive security for:	Timing	4	4	4	4	4	4
	Power/EM	N/A	N/A	N/A	N/A	2	2
Sensitive security parameter management		4	4	4	3	4	3
Mitigation of other attacks		4	3	4	3	4	3

For *Cryptographic Module Ports and Interfaces*, an SGX based implementation is capable of reaching level 4 for all actors considered.

For *Physical Security*, the only actors with the required capabilities are the physical actors (P+C and P+M). For these actors, only the malicious (P+M) has a possible intent to mount such an attack since it requires an active intrusion. As a result, level 2 can be achieved for (P+M). No other actors are relevant here.

For the *Non-invasive Security*, we split the timing related requirements from the ones related to EM and power emissions. For timing attacks, we find that level 4 is reachable for SGX based systems. For EM/power however, it is concluded that only level 2 is reachable. This is because the EM/power analysis attacks uses physical access. Therefore, here, we can consider the attack channel as not applicable for all actors except those with physical access. For both (P+C) and (P+M), the attacks are feasible since they are passive attacks.

In *Sensitive Security Parameter Management*, level 4 requires zeroization of data being uninterruptible. Considering different capabilities of actors, we can conclude that actors with guest level capabilities, e.g. co-hosted services, can not mount such attacks and can therefore achieve level 4. Further, curious actors are not expected to mount such invasive attacks. The system is therefore given level 4 with regards to those actors. Level 3 is obtainable for all remaining actors.

Finally, we consider *Mitigation of Other Attacks*. Curious actors are not expected to perform invasive or active attacks. By this reasoning level 4 is, by our estimate, achievable for all curious actors. There exists a small number of recently published attacks (for example, [23,24]) that ought to be achievable[2] from inside a malicious co-hosted VM (G+M), luckily they appear to have been mitigated by Intel microcode updates. Still, by the reasoning given in Sect. 4

---

[2] These attacks can leak secrets from VM and SGX boundaries. What is not clear however, is whether the combination of the two technologies would be a significant hindrance for an attacker. We have elected to use the most pessimistic interpretation.

("Mitigation of other attacks") we put level 3 as the maximum achievable level that can be obtained. For the remaining actors and capabilities (A+M, P+M), we reuse the same reasoning to achieve level 3 since there is such a broad range of attacks possible here. We would like to point out, however, that different conclusions might be drawn depending on the level of effort one put into the testing of the proposed mitigation that exist for the corpus of known attacks. Level 4 is not out of the question, especially not for the G+M combination which is affected by a far smaller number of attacks.

7 Conclusions

In this paper we have used FIPS 140–3 to evaluate the suitability of SGX as a method for keeping sensitive data secure in a cloud environment. While the standard is well suited to assess the capabilities of a system executing in an isolated environment, it is not sufficient to provide the nuanced judgment needed in a cloud scenario with actors of different levels of trust and capabilities.

When using our security model to complement FIPS 140–3, we reached a more nuanced view, where the scenario and threat model is taken into account when evaluating the security of a system.

Based on considerations in this paper, for systems with a threat model including a curious or malicious cloud provider attempting to illegally obtain sensitive data from the customer, SGX is deemed not suitable. The main reasons for this is due to our model and FIPS 140–3 classification of EM and power analysis as non-invasive attacks. These reasons led to the conclusion that an SGX-based system could not live up to FIPS 140–3 level 3 for Power/EM analysis in Non-invasive Security for actors with physical access, which is the lowest level requiring tested protections against these attacks. The same reasoning is applicable to the Physical Security requirements, where level 3 is the lowest level with active data zeroization requirements. If you consider those kind of attacks to be outside the scope of your threat-model then SGX would be a suitable choice of protection mechanism. Thus, HSMs can better protect against adversaries with physical access. However for all the other actors, including curious and malicious co-hosted services and attackers inside the same VM, SGX is deemed to successfully protect sensitive data from those actors.

Finally, we note that while our results are specific for SGX, the threat based security model proposed in Sect. 5 is applicable to other hardware protection mechanisms running in a shared environment, e.g. TPMs.

References

1. Arnautov, S., et al.: SCONE: secure Linux Containers with Intel SGX. In: OSDI, pp. 689–704 (2016)
2. Braz, F.A., Fernandez, E.B., VanHilst, M.: Eliciting security requirements through misuse activities. In: 2008 19th International Workshop on Database and Expert Systems Applications, pp. 328–333. IEEE (2008)

3. Callan, R., Popovic, N., Daruna, A., Pollmann, E., Zajic, A., Prvulovic, M.: Comparison of electromagnetic side-channel energy available to the attacker from different computer systems. In: IEEE International Symposium on Electromagnetic Compatibility, vol. 2015, pp. 219–223. IEEE, September 2015

4. Costan, V., Devadas, S.: Intel SGX explained. IACR Cryptology ePrint Archive 2016 086, 1–118 (2016)

5. Genkin, D., Pipman, I., Tromer, E.: Get your hands off my laptop: physical side-channel key-extraction attacks on PCs: extended version. J. Cryptogr. Eng. **5**(2), 95–112 (2015)

6. Huo, T., et al.: BlueThunder: a 2-level directional predictor based side-channel attack against SGX. IACR Trans. Cryptogr. Hardw. Embed. Syst. **2020**(1), 321–347 (2019)

7. ISO/IEC 17825:2016: Information technology – security techniques – testing methods for the mitigation of non-invasive attack classes against cryptographic modules (2016)

8. ISO/IEC 19790:2012: Information technology – security techniques – security requirements for cryptographic modules (2012)

9. ISO/IEC 24759:2017: Information technology – security techniques – test requirements for cryptographic modules (2017)

10. Khan, M.A.: A survey of security issues for cloud computing. J. Netw. Comput. Appl. **71**, 11–29 (2016)

11. Lindell, Y.: The security of intel SGX for key protection and data privacy applications. Technical report (2018). https://cdn2.hubspot.net/hubfs/1761386/Unbound_Docs_/security-of-intelsgx-key-protection-data-privacy-apps.pdf

12. Mokhtar, S.B., Boutet, A., Felber, P., Pasin, M., Pires, R., Schiavoni, V.: X-search: revisiting private web search using intel SGX. In: Proceedings of the 18th ACM/IFIP/USENIX Middleware Conference, pp. 198–208 (2017)

13. National Institute of Standards and Technology: Fips 140–3: Security requirements for cryptographic modules (2018)

14. Nilsson, A., Nikbakht Bideh, P., Brorsson, J.: A survey of published attacks on intel SGX. Technical report (2020). http://lup.lub.lu.se/record/a6d6575f-ac4f-466f-8582-48e1fe48b50c

15. NIST: SP 800–140F(draft): CMVP approved non-invasive attack mitigation test metrics: CMVP validation authority updates to ISO/IEC 24759:2014(E) (2019)

16. Priebe, C., Vaswani, K., Costa, M.: EnclaveDB: a secure database using SGX. In: Proceedings - IEEE Symposium on Security and Privacy, vol. 2018, pp. 264–278, May 2018

17. Ristenpart, T., Tromer, E., Shacham, H., Savage, S.: Hey, you, get off of my cloud: exploring information leakage in third-party compute clouds. In: Proceedings of the 16th ACM Conference on Computer and Communications Security, pp. 199–212. ACM (2009)

18. Saab, S., Rohatgi, P., Hampel, C.: Side-channel protections for cryptographic instruction set extensions. IACR Cryptology ePrint Archive 2016, 700 (2016)

19. Schuster, F., et al.: VC3: trustworthy data analytics in the cloud using SGX. In: 2015 IEEE Symposium on Security and Privacy, vol. 2015, pp. 38–54. IEEE, July 2015

20. Sgandurra, D., Lupu, E.: Evolution of attacks, threat models, and solutions for virtualized systems. ACM Comput. Surv. (CSUR) **48**(3), 1–38 (2016)

21. Shinde, S., Chua, Z.L., Narayanan, V., Saxena, P.: Preventing your faults from telling your secrets: defenses against pigeonhole attacks. arxiv.org (2015)

22. Sindre, G., Opdahl, A.L.: Eliciting security requirements with misuse cases. Requir. Eng. **10**(1), 34–44 (2005)
23. Van Schaik, S., Minkin, M., Kwong, A., Genkin, D., Yarom, Y.: CacheOut: Leaking Data on Intel CPUs via Cache Evictions, p. 16 (2020). cacheoutattack.com
24. Weisse, O., et al.: Foreshadow-NG: breaking the virtual memory abstraction with transient out-of-order execution. In: Proceedings of 27th USENIX Security Symposium (2018)
25. Xiong, W., Lagerström, R.: Threat modeling-a systematic literature review. Comput. Secur. **84**, 53–69 (2019)

Employment of Secure Enclaves in Cheat Detection Hardening

André Brandão$^{(\boxtimes)}$ ⓘ, João S. Resende ⓘ, and Rolando Martins ⓘ

CRACS/University of Porto, Porto, Portugal
andre.brandao@fc.up.pt
{jresende,rmartins}@dcc.fc.up.pt

Abstract. Over the last years, it has become clear that online games are one of the most used applications on the Internet. This increasing popularity has attracted an influx of players, with some of them trying to gain an unfair advantage for economic reasons, e.g., eSports tournaments, through the use of cheats and exploits. From a different perspective, it is of utmost importance to start analyzing attacks from a defensive perspective to create novel mechanisms that can stop such behaviors. In this work, we introduce a novel solution that extends current anti-cheat solutions through Intel SGX. Our solution moves the core cheat detection engine to a secure enclave provided by SGX while making use of a kernel module for the necessary primitives for system-wide protection. With this, we can prevent client-side tampering in both game code and configuration data by creating a trusted execution environment isolated from the hosting operating system. We are making it capable of preventing the attacker from modifying the cheat detection engine and associated game files. This solution blocks known attacks in games such as CS:GO while maintaining the performance, ensuring gameplay integrity and fairness.

Keywords: Intel SGX · Trusted execution environment · Anti-cheat

1 Introduction

It is usual for users to want to introduce modifications to their games in order to add extra functionalities. While these modifications are not harmful in single-player focused games, issues can arise when taken to multi-player/online games as these may lead to unfair advantages over other players. Those unfair advantages cause players to leave the game or seek similar modifications, often called game cheats. These advantages may diminish the popularity of a game resulting in financial losses for both game publishers and developers, especially in Freemium and "Free-To-Play" business models [3]. To prevent this, game developers must guarantee that everyone is on the same playing field by preventing modifications from third-party applications and punishing those who try to use them.

The solution to deter players from cheating this is often called an anti-cheat. It is an extension to the base game, and depending on what it wants to monitor,

S. Gritzalis et al. (Eds.): TrustBus 2020, LNCS 12395, pp. 48–62, 2020.
https://doi.org/10.1007/978-3-030-58986-8_4

it can run on the client, server, or even in both places. Since anti-cheats on the server-side are limited to analyzing the input sent by the client, it is common to deploy an anti-cheat at both ends. Alternatively, it can just be deployed on the client-side as it permits to monitor the client's behavior in more detail. The disadvantage of this option is that it exploited by misplaced trust [6] in the anti-cheat. The attacker often has full access to the device, to tamper with the running software, including but not limited to, the game code and the anti-cheat [7] itself. This full access can be used to bypass the implemented security checks in the anti-cheat, giving the illusion that nothing has been tampered.

Back in 2015, Intel introduced Software Guard Extensions (SGX) along with the Skylake micro-architecture [9], a hardware implementation of Trusted Execution Environments (TEE). SGX allows for code to execute in an isolated environment called an enclave while guaranteeing that the enclave memory regions can only be accessed by the enclave itself, disallowing all others, even the operating system's kernel, to access these secure allocated memory regions.

Furthermore, SGX guarantees that unauthorized parties have not modified the code that is loaded onto the enclave by attesting that the developer's key has signed the enclave's binary. This key, in turn, must be whitelisted either by Intel in SGXv1 or SGXv2 by a third-party trusted by Intel [9].

Considering the added hardware-based guarantees SGX provides, we propose a system that implements anti-cheat monitoring techniques within SGX, guaranteeing that our implementation cannot be modified.

1.1 Contributions

This work aims to minimize the impact of malicious software use to gain an unfair advantage in multiplayer online games through the following contributions:

- Analyze possible cheating opportunities in Counter-Strike: Global Offensive (CS:GO) and how cheats exploit these to accomplish the desired outcome;
- Monitor kernel space interactions: Usage of a kernel module to monitor file access, achieve debug prevention and unauthorized reads and writes on the game process;
- Application of anti-cheat monitoring techniques with Intel SGX;
- Creation and deployment of a prototype for a Linux system in a real-world scenario with a known cheat and measure the performance overhead introduced into the game;
- Definition of a threat model with security analysis.

1.2 Scope and Outline

SGX does not provide any mechanisms to prevent a Denial of Service on its initialization, as such we cannot guarantee that the remote system will load our enclave, although there is no way to prevent this attack, we can potentially flag users for further investigation if there was a change on the state of their SGX support, i.e., actively disabling it to prevent the anti-cheat engine from running.

Since our solution cannot be integrated with the tested game (i.e., given that Counter-Strike: Global Offensive is closed source), we rely on querying the operating system to discover additional information about the game. In this implementation, we assume that this information is trustworthy due to the lack of integration with the game's code.

Since an SGX enclave execute in user mode, it does not offer any protection nor includes any functionality of the operating system's kernel. Subsequently, the type of modifications we can detect solely from within the enclave is limited. In order to expand the range of detection of malicious modifications, we require a kernel module to help us detect additional attacks to the game's binary.

Outline
Section 2 presents state of the art with the systems related to our solution alongside with some common methods of attack used to redirect code from the game's executable within cheats.

In Sect. 3 a description of the implemented solution is given. Then Sect. 4 describes a security analysis along with a definition of the threat model with several attack scenarios, analyzing whether or not the attacks are effective against our approach.

Section 5 presents the results of the comparison of frame times and the game's load times between our solution and the base game. Finally, Sect. 6 presents the conclusions of this work.

2 Related Work

This section describes the technologies used in our proposed solution. It gives a brief overview of some methods used by attackers to control the game flow.

2.1 Background

We start by providing an overview of the background work used by our solution to provide a clearer and sufficient context.

Secure Runtime Environments
Sometime after the release of Intel SGX, Erick Bauman et al. [4] introduced a solution on to utilize SGX to protect computer games and at the same use it as a digital rights management (DRM) system.

The proposed protection model to prevent players from cheating requires some of the game's code and data to be moved to the enclave created by Intel SGX. As the Intel SGX Enclave Page Cache (EPC is limited at maximum to 128 MB of memory [9] and does not permit the usage of syscalls without first exiting the enclave. The game developer must first perform a careful analysis of the game's code not to exceed the EPC size to degrade performance beyond an unusable point. While this might be easy for games with a small code base, this task gets harder with the size of code that must be protected. As the code grows, the likelihood of game code that might leak data to and from enclaves will increase. While it might not seem an issue at first because tools such as Cheat Engine are still unable to read game data inside the enclave, it is not enough to defend from an application that might load additional code in the application [12,14].

Solution like Haven [1] and Scone [2] aim to run unmodified applications on secure enclaves, particularly within Intel SGX. In general, these solutions create an environment with a modified C library, so that system calls are intercepted and redirected to a kernel library or forwarded to untrusted code. We chose not to use these solutions as they give the application running inside the enclave, an isolated environment from the remaining system. To use these, we would need to load the game within the secure runtime environment, which would quickly exceed the maximum physical memory allocated to Intel SGX.

Known Attacks

Here we present some of the known methods to hijack the normal flow of execution by malicious software.

Flow of Execution Attacks: As operating systems usually have mechanisms that help, from userspace, to load code in almost any process, attackers often do not resort to typical buffer overflows or similar methods to take control of the executing application. Instead, this can be achieved by modifying the executing code of the running application, altering a thread's executing instruction, or even create a new thread. These can be accomplished by attaching a debugger to the process, or if available, through kernel provided APIs. After the attacker successfully loads the desired code into the game, it is often desired to change the way the game code behaves, as this can be accomplished in many ways and depends on the attacker's creativity we only cover a few possible solutions.

Binary Manipulation: One of the simplest ways to gain control of the game's code is to modify the byte code present in the executable section of the game. This can be accomplished by resorting to Kernel APIs that allow changing the allocated memory page permissions to permit writing to usually read-only sections of the binary.

Virtual Tables Tampering: One other popular way to achieve the principle mentioned above is to edit the virtual tables generated by the compiler for classes containing virtual methods. This can typically be accomplished in two ways, either by modifying the virtual table inside the read-only sections of the executable or by altering the pointer inside the instantiated object that points to the virtual table.

Forced Exceptions: Operating systems offer mechanisms to handle exceptions occurring in userspace code and signal these occurrences to the application, such as the Linux's *sigaction* API that allows the developer to handle signals. An attacker can, for example, take advantage of this by registering its handler for memory access violations or floating-point exceptions. Subsequently, the attacker can modify game data or memory page permissions to cause a registered signal to be raised and thus call the attacker's method.

2.2 State-of-the-Art Anti-cheats

To our knowledge, there does not exist a commercial anti-cheat solution that takes advantage of Intel SGX to implement cheat detection techniques. Current anti-cheats solutions work in diverse ways from just server-side monitoring to kernel space monitoring in the attacker's device. However, almost all typically rely partially on security by obscurity, probably with fear that attackers may more easily find exploits to circumvent these.

Battleye
Battleye [24] works by running code on the client's device and the server. With the main component being on the client's side, and using the servers only for reporting the cheater. It takes advantage of the client's device by running code in both user and kernel space to scan not only the running process but also other processes and impede code injecting on the game's process.

Easy Anti-cheat
Kamu. GG originally released and later acquired by Epic Games [25], Easy Anti-Cheat [23], works similarly to Battleye and achieves the same results in the same or similar fashion. Working in both kernel and userspace gives the anti-cheat access to the game process and others to monitor for unwanted activity. This anti-cheat will not load if specific Windows features that aid debugging of kernel code or loading non-signed windows drivers are enabled. Such options include disabling Driver Signature Enforcement, Kernel Debugging, using Windows Safe mode or disabling KKP (Kernel Patch Protection), Microsoft's solution to prevent patching the Windows NT Kernel.

Fairfight
Fairfight [22] by GameBlocks, LLC, is a non-intrusive, server-sided anti-cheat, that works much like a behavior-based Intrusion Detection System (IDS). The anti-cheat interprets game events of the player and uses them to compare against the rest of the players. The system may flag those who perform exceptionally well or in a weird way (e.g., pointing to other players through opaque objects) for manual review by the developers. The advantage of this type of anti-cheat is that it allows catching unknown or new types of cheats, but it might also not catch every cheater, especially the ones playing within what is considered 'normal' behavior.

3 Implementation

Our implementation tries to be the least intrusive by minimizing the amount of the game's code that needs to be modified. It stores information about the game in a secure environment rather than moving the entire game to the enclave. This change allows it to run efficiently inside the enclave as it does not exceed the physical memory limit imposed by Intel SGX. Similarly to current anti-cheat commercial solutions, the implemented enclave acts as an extra layer of security that will monitor changes to the game's code and data during runtime to guarantee that nothing has been tampered. An overview of this is Fig. 1, which shows that our solution (Protection Oversight) works in parallel with the game's code while performing integrity checks on itself and the game's code. With the help of a kernel module, it achieves additional monitoring of the game processes. The communication between the Protection Oversight and the kernel module uses Netlink [15].

The proposed implemented solution allows it to deploy on most games with no changes to its workings. It only requires modifications when the more generic type of checks does not catch game-specific attacks.

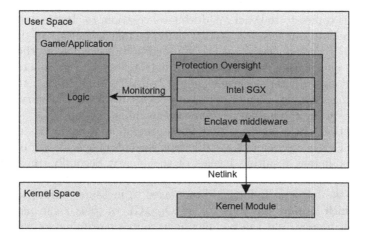

Fig. 1. Implemented architecture

3.1 Enclave Creation

In order to create the protecting enclave, we need to extract some information about the game. This section defines the type of information needed and how it is obtained in our solution.

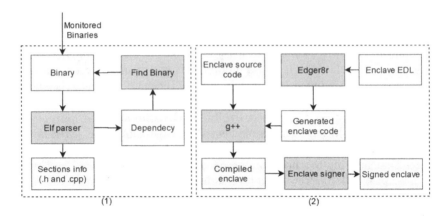

Fig. 2. Enclave generation - Existing flow to generated enclave with sections to verify.

Analysis of the Protected Application

We need to guarantee that the enclave during runtime is able to read the memory regions of the game and its dependencies. This poses a problem as the section table of an ELF binary is not needed by the program during runtime. This information is copied to the enclave, during its creation, to circumvent this issue so that the enclave can access it. Additionally, we take advantage of this process ((1) in Fig. 2) to create hashes of the mapped sections and store them on the enclave. The information gathered is saved onto the enclave by generating code to compile along with the enclave's code ((2) in Fig. 2). This way, the enclave is able, during runtime, to monitor the sections in loaded memory with the expected ones using the hashes of each corresponding section.

The selection of the binaries that need protection is not a trivial task for two reasons. Firstly, users may have different versions of specific libraries, which will lead to different resulting hashes of the binary. Secondly, there may be legitimate reasons for the modification of a binary's read-only data [12]. Two examples of the latter include the library used to measure performance of the game[19], which detours methods within OpenGL so that it can measure the time between frames, and the popular open-source streaming software "Open Broadcaster Software" in "game capture" mode, which uses a detour to capture the generated frame.

This process is repeated for the enclave's middleware binary which will also be monitored inside the enclave to ensure it has not been modified.

3.2 Runtime Protection

After we have collected the information as mentioned earlier, the enclave can now perform, during runtime, the integrity checks on the binaries. A description follows of the necessary steps required for the enclave to be aware of the application's memory space.

Enclave Middleware Address Discovery

Since SGX provides a way to allocate memory on the stack in the untrusted environment, we can use this to find the stack pointer and frame pointer used by the application that invoked the enclave. With this information, we can calculate, with the help of a disassembler, the offset at which the return address to the middleware is from the last known frame pointer.

With this data recovered, we can perform integrity checks on our solution (Protection Oversight in Fig. 1) within the enclave.

Application Address Discovery

In an ideal world, the application would link its dependencies, including the enclave's middleware statically. With this, the enclave could easily cover the game binary, as finding the middleware binary would imply finding the game binary. As statically linking every library is not practical, and since applications might load binaries through Operating System specific APIs (e.g. dlopen on Linux and LoadLibrary on Windows), parsing the Procedure Linkage Table (PTL) and the Global Offsets Table (GOT) sections of the loaded binaries might not yield all the required dependencies. As such alternative methods to find mapped binaries need to be used.

An alternative approach is to use TSX-based Address Probing (TAP) to discover the mapped memory regions in the game's process. TAP is a fault-resistant read primitive, introduced by Michael Schwarz et al. [8]. TAP leverages the Intel Transactional Synchronization Extensions (TSX) way of handling memory violations to stealthy query the virtual memory of the device without raising a memory access violation on the kernel.

Unfortunately, in the same paper, it is mentioned that TAP takes approximately 45 min on an Intel i7-6700k to scan the entire virtual address space. This makes it impractical as it would require a substantial amount of time to complete while requiring a considerable amount of resources, which might affect the performance of the game.

As it is not possible to modify the source code of the selected game, the enclave needs to temporarily leave the trusted execution environment SGX to query the mapped regions' operating systems. This does give us the advantage that it is significantly faster to retrieve the mapped regions, but it is also a source that is not considered trustworthy by Intel SGX's threat model. It also comes at the advantage of being a more 'universal' solution since not all CPUs that support Intel SGX, necessarily support Intel TSX.

Code and Data Integrity Checks

Once the addresses of the target binaries are acquired, the enclave can combine these with the information gathered in the first phase ((1) in Fig. 2) of the enclave's creation. The enclave can now monitor (as shown in Fig. 1) the game's memory for any unwanted changes. While the read-only data section should be straightforward to check, game-specific values might require the developer to create additional checks within the enclave.

A common code interception technique in CS:GO cheats involves modifying the objects' pointer to the virtual function table, as these objects need to be modifiable. They cannot stay in read-only memory regions meaning that the checks, as mentioned earlier, do not cover them. The enclave must know where the objects are in memory which must be specified by the developer, either by specifying a pointer path starting from a static address within the binary or by exporting symbols in the game code to allow the enclave to find the desired addresses, to protect against these types of attacks. This is ultimately the method used to detect the cheat tested during the evaluation of our results.

Kernel Space Aided Monitoring

Intel SGX is limited to run within user-space, thus limiting the surface area which we can monitor. To circumvent this, as suggested by Fig. 1, we load an optional kernel module that can communicate with the enclave middleware via Netlink. The kernel module, to monitor the application's interactions with the operating system, takes advantage of the *ftrace* framework to intercept system calls in the kernel [10].

With the function *sys_open* intercepted, it is possible to monitor file accesses on the file system. To monitor a particular application, the enclave first requests, through the middleware, the kernel module to start monitoring. Afterward, the kernel obtains the context of the process that wishes to be monitored and can start forwarding information to the enclave. This way, the enclave can be aware of all the file accesses the game makes and see if any additional files were loaded or modified. To reduce the number of events generated, we are strictly generating events for open requests with READ access (flags *O_RDONLY* or *O_RDWR*) to the file. The kernel module hashes the data and forwards the result along with the filename to the enclave to reduce the number of transitions between user space and kernel space instead of sending open events to the enclave.

To prevent external application, from reading and to write in the game application, *process_vm_readv* and *process_vm_writev* are also analyzed to deny access to the game process memory. Additionally, the access to the *ptrace* syscall is blocked when called against the game's process id to prevent debugging of the target application.

The enclave may also query the kernel for the permissions of the allocated pages, as showed SGX does not provide enough mechanisms to know if the pages have execution permission.

4   Security Analysis

In this section, we provide a security analysis of the proposed system. We identify potential threats and how an attacker may attempt to exploit the system.

Integrity Checker

In a typical scenario, the code that verifies the game's code should be in theory as easily modifiable as the game's code, assuming no extra obfuscation has applied to it. In this proposal we have moved this code inside a secure enclave with Intel SGX, this gives us a strong hardware guarantees that an attacker has not modified the code running.

Game Code Modification

An attacker can get code execution within the game code in two scenarios: through the operating system's API; or finding an exploit in the game executable. Then it can modify everything within the game's memory region, including its code by altering the permissions of the allocated memory regions. To mitigate this we perform integrity checks of the game during its runtime, and this means any modification made is visible to the enclave, and once the enclave is aware of it, it can take actions.

Malicious Hypervisor

As shown in SPIDER [16] by taking advantage of Intel's implementation of Second Level Address Translation (SLAT), Intel Extended Page Table (EPT), the hypervisor can split code and data views as seen by the guest operating system. With this, SPIDER manages to place a breakpoint on the guest's memory while keeping this change invisible to the guest operating system. The same technique was showed by Satoshi Tanda [18] to place invisible inline hooks, which allow to modify the execution flow of the guest's code to potentially malicious code.

As stated by Intel, memory regions outside of enclaves are considered untrusted. If the attacker modifies the game's code using this method, when our solution attempts to read code sections of the game, the EPT will cause a data view of the address to be read and not the code view. This will lead our solution to think that nothing has changed when that is not the case.

Such scenarios are possible to detect by side-channel information [13,17] that can be obtained by measuring the time taken to read or write to a memory region, as these will be significantly slower than unaffected memory regions. A different approach is to employ a solution that detects a hypervisor's presence and refuses to run under those circumstances. Igor Korkin [5] classifies four ways of identifying a hypervisor, signature-based, behavior-based, trusted hypervisor-based, and time-based.

Fault on Transitions To and From the Enclave

The attacker, if already executing code inside the game, may attempt to mark the libraries responsible for transitioning to and from the enclave as non-executable and register an exception handler to handle these situations.

With this, the attacker can know when the transitions to and from the enclave occur. We believe that achieving this after the enclave has been loaded does not accomplish meaningful results to the attacker besides unloading the cheat's modifications on enclave entry and loading them on enclave exit. This attack involves continuously altering the page permissions and exception handling, which comes at a relatively high cost, enough to be influential in the game's performance, increasing the time each frame takes to render and thus lowering the frames per second. Depending on how often the enclave transitions to and from user space (i.e., how often checks are made to the game) performance of the game could drop to an unplayable state (less than ten frames per second). While it would technically allow for the cheating to work successfully, the player will have an unsatisfactory game experience because it will feel jerky and slow, making it impractical.

5 Evaluation

In this section, we will show the test case used during the evaluation of our solution and show the obtained results. For this, we measured two metrics: The first test is the overhead associated with our solutions in the loading of the game; the second is the gameplay overhead associated with the middleware running. To test this, we ran the tests ten times with and without our implementations for each of the options.

During the game benchmark we measured the time taken to render each frame, also called the frame time, using *libperflogger* [19] so that we could take the average frame time of all the frames, the average frame time of the worst 1% and the average frame time of the worst 0.1%. With these metrics, we can see how bad the game performs in its worst-case scenarios, where a small number of frames take a relatively big time to render.

5.1 Methodology

Our evaluation machine runs Ubuntu 18.04 LTS with an Intel i7-6770HQ at 2.60 GHz with the corresponding integrated GPU for its video output, an Intel Iris Pro Graphics 580. The total memory installed on the system is 16 GB in dual-channel, with 128 MB reserved to Intel SGX.

Our game of choice to test our solution was Counter-Strike: Global Offensive along with the Open Source Linux cheat Fuzion [20]. To consistently measure the performance of the game, with and without our solution, we use an FPS Benchmark available in the steam workshop [21].

During our testing, the game used between 1 and 1.5 GB of memory. We have configured our enclave with a maximum stack and heap sizes to 256 kilobytes and 1 megabyte, respectively. As the generated binary's size is 862 kilobytes, we can conclude that our solution uses at most roughly 2.1 megabytes of the Intel SGX allocated memory.

As we used the integrated graphic card of the CPU, we decided to run the game at a resolution of 1920:1080 with the lowest possible quality settings with smoke grenades disabled. This is because we wanted the frame time to be CPU-bound as possible to test the impact of our solution.

We chose to monitor the game's executable, its *engine_client.so* dependency along with the array of global objects present in the exported symbol *s_pInterfaceRegs*, the enclave's middleware, and the SGX's dependencies. While it was possible to monitor all interdependencies of the game binary, it led to some false positives mainly because the library used to measure the game's performance, which, in order to do so, must intercept OpenGL functions. To counter this, we identified the binaries with functions of interest for the cheaters.

5.2 Results

Our enclave took on average 161.60 ± 45.05 ms to load while only marginally increasing the time taken to load the game from 23.75 ± 0.42 s to 24.12 ± 0.38 s.

Table 1. Comparison of the time each frame took, on average, to render

Frame time	No protection	Every second	Every 10 s
Avg (ms)	8.52 ± 2.38	8.60 ± 2.46	8.57 ± 2.40
Avg worst 1% (ms)	14.39 ± 1.08	14.75 ± 1.20	14.51 ± 1.12
Avg worst 0.1% (ms)	16.98 ± 1.08	17.56 ± 0.99	17.29 ± 1.10

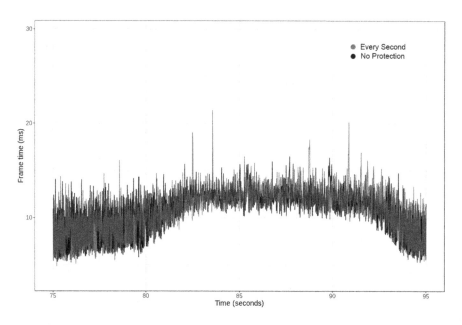

Fig. 3. A time interval of 20 s, with the frames per seconds of our solutions compared with the baseline

When looking at how the game performs, it is not enough to look at the average frame time of all the frames. It is essential to identify moments when frames take a relatively long time to render as these may cause sudden, short freezes during the gameplay. From the average frame time of all frames, it appears that our solution has a shallow impact on the gameplay's performance, while only marginally increasing the frame times of the worst 1% and 0.1% by 2.50% and 3.42% respectively (Table 1). In Fig. 3, we present a 20-s portion of the benchmark. This allows us to see the increase in frame time when our solution runs, and we can identify this by the sudden peaks in the graph.

When the enclave is not idle, i.e., it is performing the monitoring of the game code. We are able to detect the cheat Fuzion [20] successfully within 31.62 ± 2.47 ms. This time is dependent on the number of sections we are verifying. On average 5 MB of data takes 13.55 ± 0.58 ms to verify.

6 Conclusions and Future Work

This work presents a design and implementation that aims to move cheat detection techniques to a secure enclave in Intel SGX, giving the developers a reliable guarantee that the attackers do not tamper written code.

We were able to deploy our solution on an existing game successfully, CS:GO, a closed-source first-person shooter, without requiring changes to game code. We have also verified that while the proposed solution has a measurable overhead over the base game, we concluded that it does not significantly impact the game's performance.

The proposed system managed to detect the Open Source Cheat Fuzion without requiring a specific blacklist over the cheat's code. We identified the critical components in the game that the cheat required to work, which allowed us to perform additional checks and detect the cheat's modifications.

We have not implemented every known possible cheat detection method [14] in our solution but believe that the current implementation should cover many cases. However, we have built a framework that should allow developers to easily integrate new detection methods to the enclave, so implementation and testing time should lower.

With the interaction of the kernel module, our solution can protect the game process from attacks that otherwise would be unpreventable from the enclave alone.

The presented solution requires the executable game information to be present within the enclave binary, and future implementation could take Intel remote attestation service to guarantee a secure communication with game servers to load this information and also to inform if a player is cheating.

Due to the limitations imposed by Intel SGX, monitoring a program outside an enclave is not easy and described in Sect. 4 that our solution might be prone to some attacks that are undetectable in the current implementation. We are aware that communication between the kernel module and the enclave can be intercepted and tampered but this attack will only stop the detection of some new cheats that use techniques unknown to the enclave.

In the future work, we want to look at other types of games, measuring how adequate our solution is to each one of them. It can also be interesting for our solution to integrate with SGXElide [11] to enable code secrecy of the enclave's code, making it so the attacker can only see the enclave as a true black-box.

Acknowledgments. This work is financed by National Funds through the Portuguese funding agency, FCT - Fundação para a Ciência e a Tecnologia, within project UIDB/50014/2020. This work of João S. Resende was supported by Fundação para a Ciência e Tecnologia (FCT), Portugal, PD/BD/128149/2016. This work of André Brandão is also financed by National Funds through the Portuguese funding agency, FCT - Fundação para a Ciência e a Tecnologia within project CMU/CS/0042/2017 and by the EU H2020-SU-ICT-03-2018 Project No. 830929 CyberSec4Europe (cybersec4europe.eu).

References

1. Baumann, A., Peinado, M., Hunt, G.: Shielding applications from an untrusted cloud with haven. ACM Trans. Comput. Syst. (TOCS) **33**(3), 1–26 (2015)
2. Arnautov, S., et al.: SCONE: secure linux containers with intel SGX. In: 12th USENIX Symposium on Operating Systems Design and Implementation (OSDI 2016), pp. 689–703 (2016)
3. Davidovici-Nora, M.: Paid and free digital business models innovations in the video game industry. Digiworld Econ. J. (94), 2nd Q, p. 83 (2014). Available at SSRN: https://ssrn.com/abstract=2534022
4. Bauman, E., Lin, Z.: A case for protecting computer games with SGX. In: Proceedings of the 1st Workshop on System Software for Trusted Execution (SysTEX 2016), New York, NY, USA. ACM Article 4, 6 pages. https://doi.org/10.1145/3007788.3007792
5. Korkin, I.: Two challenges of stealthy hypervisors detection: time cheating and data fluctuations. arXiv preprint arXiv:1506.04131 (2015)
6. Yan, J., Randell, B.: A systematic classification of cheating in online games, pp. 1–9 (2005). https://doi.org/10.1145/1103599.1103606
7. Pritchard, M.: How to hurt the hackers: the scoop on internet cheating and how you can combat it. Inf. Secur. Bull. (2011)
8. Schwarz, M., Weiser, S., Gruss, D.: Practical Enclave Malware with Intel SGX (2019)
9. Intel: IntelR©64 and IA-32 Architectures Software Developer's Manual, Vol-ume 3 (3A, 3B & 3C): System Programming Guide (325384) (2016)
10. Rostedt, S.: Ftrace kernel hooks: more than just tracing. In: Linux Plumbers Conference (2014)
11. Bauman, E., Wang, H., Zhang, M., Lin, Z.: SGXElide: enabling enclave code secrecy via self-modification. 75–86 (2018). https://doi.org/10.1145/3168833
12. Berdajs, J., Bosnić, Z.: Extending applications using an advanced approach to DLL injection and API hooking. Softw. Pract. Exp. **40**, 567–584 (2010). https://doi.org/10.1002/spe.973
13. Tuzel, T., et al.: Who watches the watcher? Detecting hypervisor introspection from unprivileged guests. Digit. Invest. **26**, S98–S106 (2018)
14. Feng, W., Kaiser, E.S., Chluessler, T.: Stealth measurements for cheat detection in on-line games. 15–20 (2008). https://doi.org/10.1145/1517494.1517497

15. Cox, A., Kuznetsov, A., McHardy, P.: Netlink https://github.com/torvalds/linux/tree/master/net/netlink. Accessed 212 June 020
16. Deng, Z., Zhang, X., Xu, D.: SPIDER: stealthy binary program instrumentation and debugging via hardware virtualization (2013). https://doi.org/10.1145/2523649.2523675
17. Kyte, I., Zavarsky, P., Lindskog, D., Ruhl, R.: Enhanced Side-channel Analysis Method to Detect Hardware Virtualization Based Rootkits (2012)
18. Tanda, S.: DdiMon Github, 22 September 2018,. https://github.com/tandasat/DdiMon. Accessed 19 Sept 2019
19. libperflogger - Game performance logging library. https://github.com/Lurkki14/libperflogger. Accessed 19 Sept 2019
20. Fuzion - Open Source Linux Counter Strike: Global Offensive Cheat. https://github.com/LWSS/Fuzion. Accessed 19 Sept 2019
21. Counter Strike: Global Offensive benchmark map. https://steamcommunity.com/sharedfiles/filedetails/?id=500334237. Accessed 19 Sept 2019
22. GameBlocks, LLC. Fairfight server-sided anti-cheat. https://gameblocks.com/. Accessed 19 Sept 2019
23. Epic Games, Inc., Easy Anti-Cheat. https://www.easy.ac. Accessed 19 Sept 2019
24. BattlEye Innovations. BattlEye AntiCheat. https://www.battleye.com/. Accessed 19 Sept 2019
25. Cowley, D.: Epic Games Acquires Kamu, Game Security and Player Services Company, 8 October 2018. https://www.unrealengine.com/en-US/blog/epic-games-acquires-kamu-game-security-and-player-services-company. Accessed 19 Sept 2019

Economics/Privacy

SECONDO: A Platform for Cybersecurity Investments and Cyber Insurance Decisions

Aristeidis Farao[1(✉)], Sakshyam Panda[2], Sofia Anna Menesidou[3], Entso Veliou[3], Nikolaos Episkopos[4], George Kalatzantonakis[5], Farnaz Mohammadi[1], Nikolaos Georgopoulos[6], Michael Sirivianos[7], Nikos Salamanos[7], Spyros Loizou[7], Michalis Pingos[7], John Polley[1], Andrew Fielder[8], Emmanouil Panaousis[9], and Christos Xenakis[1]

[1] University of Piraeus, Piraeus, Greece
{arisfarao,farnaz,xenakis}@unipi.gr
[2] University of Surrey, Guildford, UK
[3] Ubitech Limited, Limassol, Cyprus
[4] Fogus Innovations & Services, Kaisariani, Greece
[5] Lstech Espana SL, Barcelona, Spain
[6] Cromar Insurance Brokers Ltd., Marousi, Greece
[7] Cyprus University of Technology, Limassol, Cyprus
[8] Imperial College London, London, UK
[9] University of Greenwich, London, UK

Abstract. This paper represents the SECONDO framework to assist organizations with decisions related to cybersecurity investments and cyber-insurance. The platform supports cybersecurity and cyber-insurance decisions by implementing and integrating a number of software components. SECONDO operates in three distinct phases: (i) cyber-physical risk assessment and continuous monitoring; (ii) investment-driven optimized cyber-physical risk control; and (iii) blockchain-enabled cyber-insurance contract preparation and maintenance. Insurers can leverage SECONDO functionalities to actively participate in the management of cyber-physical risks of a shipping company to reduce their insured risk.

1 Introduction

The SECONDO project addresses the question "How can we support decisions about cybersecurity investments and cyber-insurance pricing?" This is a crucial research problem as the rapid growth of cyber-attacks is expected to continue its upwards trajectory, causing fear to organizations due to potentially incurred losses: (i) *direct* losses by having their confidentiality, integrity and/or availability being compromised; or (ii) *indirect*, by having to pay vast fines as defined by the General Data Protection Regulation (GDPR). Hence, the growth of cyber-attacks presents a prominent threat to normal business operations and the EU society itself. In addition, a noteworthy finding is that an organization's computer systems may be less secure than a competitor's, despite having spent more

© Springer Nature Switzerland AG 2020
S. Gritzalis et al. (Eds.): TrustBus 2020, LNCS 12395, pp. 65–74, 2020.
https://doi.org/10.1007/978-3-030-58986-8_5

money in securing them [1]. Obviously, in the face of uncertainties, cybersecurity investment choices and cyber-insurance, are highly challenging tasks with serious business implications. SECONDO aims to impact the operation of EU businesses which often: (i) have a limited cybersecurity budget; and (ii) ignore the importance of cyber-insurance.

1.1   Motivation

Technological inventions and developments have started to become an integral part of any company's lifecycle. However, despite conferring significant advantages, they bring with them an enhanced cyber-physical risk of cyber incidents, and a subsequent growth in products and services aimed at combating the cyber-physical risks. In turn, the proposed solutions (products or services) come with a cost making cybersecurity investment which is a key problem for Chief Information Security Officers to tackle.

Importantly, the GDPR brings into force strengthened requirements for organizations, which process or store data as to build data protection and privacy into their organization and design, to notify the authorities of all data breaches that put individuals at cyber-physical risk. With high fines for GDPR violations (up to 20€ million or 4% of annual turnover), cyber-crime can no longer be considered an acceptable running cost of business. It provides a major impetus for organizations to proceed with optimal investments in cybersecurity solutions and procedures to minimize their cyber-physical risk exposure while transferring the residual cyber-physical risk to cyber-insurance.

1.2   Limitations

Considering the limitations discussed in [2] together with the importance of complying with GDPR and the rapid growth of cyber threats, there is an irrefutable need for developing new and automated tools to better explain and appropriately address existing and rising challenges not only through technical approaches, but also through the lens of economic analysis. Driven by market needs, SECONDO therefore proposes a unique, scalable, highly interoperable Economics-of- Security-as-a-Service platform that encompasses a comprehensive cost-driven methodology for: (i) estimating cyber-physical risks assessment based on a quantitative approach that focuses on both technical and non-technical aspects, (e.g.., users' behavior), that influence cyber exposure; (ii) providing analysis for effective and efficient cyber-physical risk management by recommending optimal investments in cybersecurity controls; and (iii) determining the residual cyber-physical risks as well as estimating the cyber-insurance premiums taking into account the insurer's business strategy, while eliminating the information asymmetry between the insured and insurer. Inspired by the above functionalities and our previous work [1,3–6], we will develop the SECONDO platform to establish a new paradigm in risk management for enterprises of various sizes, with respect to the GDPR framework, while it will enable formal and verifiable methodologies for insurers that require estimating premiums.

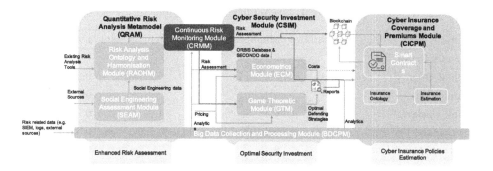

Fig. 1. Architectural components and integrated modules for SECONDO

The rest of the paper is organized as follows: Sect. 2 presents the SECONDO architecture and its components, whereas Sect. 3 describes a use case from the maritime sector and how SECONDO can be applied. Section 4 concludes the paper.

2   SECONDO Architecture and Components

In this section, we present the SECONDO architecture (see Fig. 1) along with its components and modules.

2.1   Quantitative Risk Assessment and Data Analytics

Information security management must start with a risk analysis [7]. The goal of SECONDO risks assessment is to identify: (i) relevant *threats* targeting the assets of an organization; (ii) *vulnerabilities*, both internal and external that these assets exhibit; (iii) *value-at-risk* of the organization that is equivalent to the value of assets (both tangible and intangible) being endangered by adversaries; and (iv) the likelihood that an attack will be launched against the assets. The risk represents the expected losses of an organization should one or more attacks compromise the asset affecting the confidentiality, integrity and availability of business critical services.

Asset Pricing - The SECONDO platform will adopt a combination of methods for pricing *tangible* and *intangible* digital assets from a cybersecurity perspective. The objective is to provide precise point estimates on valuations of assets considering both the tangible and intangible aspects such that they can be used to directly value insurance claims in a standard actuary framework.

The outcome of the valuation methods will contribute to the Econometrics Module (ECM) which provides estimates on all kinds of costs of potential attacks.

Risk Modeling - Utilizing a Quantitative Risk Analysis Metamodel (QRAM), SECONDO determine quantitative estimates of the exposed risk of an organization. It achieves this by defining methodologies for asset identification and

Table 1. Overall likelihood results

Actions	Contributor	Management	Upper management	Executives
Report Email	0	0	0	0
Email Opened	0.33	0.2	0.25	0.33
Email Sent	0.11	0	0.38	0.33
Link Clicked	0.11	0.3	0	0
Submitted Data	0.44	0.5	0.38	0.33
Attack Likelihood	0.55	0.8	0.38	0.33

valuation, and utilizing security metrics to quantitatively estimate risk exposure of an organization. QRAM is composed of two modules. The first, Social Engineering Assessment Module (SEAM) which is used to experimentally determine the likelihood of being exploited by social engineering attacks on different employee roles of an organization. Table 1 illustrates the results from our experimental study. The second, Risk Analysis Ontology and Harmonization Module (RAOHM) communicates with SEAM and existing risk analysis tools such as OLISTIC[1] to gather their output and harmonize through its unique vocabulary. It uses entity-relationship diagrams between threats, vulnerabilities, security controls, assets, and identified risks with an aim to identify assets to be used in the risk analysis process. Moreover, utilizing the risk analysis ontology will assist in gathering the heterogeneous information from all business areas to support the decisions of an organization regarding its cyber governance strategy. Currently, SECONDO is implementing this module.

Big Data Collection and Processing Module (BDCPM) - This module of SECONDO acquires risk related data either from internal organizational sources such as network infrastructure, Security Information and Event Management, log files, users' interactions, or external sources such as social media and other internet-based sources including Darknet with specialized crawlers. This module is yet to be implemented in the project.

The collected and processed data would be specified and quantified within a meta-model, and utilizing set of data mining and learning algorithms to perform sophisticated analysis.

2.2 Cyber Security Investments and Blockchain

This segment of SECONDO will build up on the above discussed modules to compute optimal cybersecurity investment strategies and deploy blockchain technology for secure storage, access and notification of security and privacy information of organisations. This segment consists of two modules:

---

[1] http://www.olistic.io/.

Continuous Risk Monitoring and Blockchain (CRMM) - This module will continuously assess the risk levels, including the performance of the implemented cybersecurity controls.

It will update the private blockchain with information regarding the security and privacy risk of cyber-insurance clients through smart contracts. Moreover, these will notify the involved parties (insurer and insured) when the insurance terms have violated or when an event has happened to activate the insurance. These are embedded in the distributed ledger and cannot be modified due to its immutability feature providing verifiable records.

Decision-Making for Cyber Investments - Security investment decisions with a limited budget is always a challenging task, even more in the presence of uncertainty, with massive business implications. There have been several studies [8] proposing cost-benefit approaches for selecting an optimal set of controls against cyber attacks. Along this line of work, the Cyber Security Investment Module (CSIM) aims at computing optimal cybersecurity investment plans utilizing the Econometrics Module (ECM) and the Game Theoretic Module (GTM). ECM will provide estimates about the costs of potential attacks as well as the costs of each possible security control using a set of existing econometric models. Utilizing the asset pricing method (detailed in the previous section), ECM will also determine the impact value of an asset. On the other hand, GTM will derive strategically optimal defending strategies expressed in the form of controls to be implemented by the organization. The interaction between players is modeled as a non-cooperative game in GTM where players compete against each other. Following the widely-cited work [1], the corresponding Nash Equilibria (NE), the solution of the game, for each available cybersecurity control will be computed and sent to CSIM to compute an optimal investment solution subjected to a budget while considering the financial cost of each NE.

2.3   Cyber Insurance and Smart Contracts

The core component of this segment is the *Cyber Insurance Coverage and Premiums Module* (CICPM). This module will provide insurance exposure assessment and estimates for insurance coverage and premiums based on the insurance policies of the underlying insurer. The insurance policies will be modeled using a common vocabulary and language of cyber-insurance policies by utilizing a cyber-insurance ontology. The ontology will empower the SECONDO platform to automatically incorporate policies. Moreover, the ontology will be based on a comprehensive survey and analysis of the cyber-insurance market and well-known insurance policies as discussed in [9–12].

CICPM will not only enable underwriters to incorporate their own strategy, as required by a competitive market, but also aim at minimizing the information asymmetry between insurer and insured by applying a verifiable and shared methodology that includes standard and enhanced procedures such as quantitative risk analysis using security metrics and optimal security investments for managing cyber-physical risk. In reconciliation with CRMM, CICPM will monitor conditions leading to non-compliance of the cyber-insurance contract agreements and assist with resolving claim disputes.

3 Use Case: Cyber-Physical Risk Transfer in Maritime

The Maritime Cyber Risk Management guidelines [13] highlights the importance of cybersecurity technologies in facilitating critical business functions and secure operation of the maritime industry. Regardless of the increasing cyber incidents, there has been no holistic approach to manage maritime cyber-risks [14]. Further, security procedures and policies are still being defined and determined to be practiced in maritime which further results to an increasing dependency on the insurance industry.

On the other hand, the insurance industry has particularly investigated the *affirmative risks* and *silent* cyber-physical risk [15] to facilitate suitable coverage. With regards to the affirmative cyber-physical risk, the Insurance Property and Casualty Policy [16] states that the insurer shall cover the costs of impact, either physical or digital, in case of data breach and/or network failure or attack.

Coverage capacity, cyber-physical risk estimation and appropriate solutions are difficult for insurers to manage, leading to a margin of the so called silent (unintended) cyber coverage. In this section, we summarize the applicability of the SECONDO platform in the maritime sector to achieve optimal cyber-insurance premium acknowledging both the insured's and insurer's perspective. In the recent past, physical attacks, such as piracy, was a common threat to the maritime sector.

3.1 Cyber-Insurance in Maritime

After the adoption of electronic systems such as sonar and IoT systems in both onshore and on-board environments, new cyber and cyber-physical vulnerabilities have emerged increasing the threat exposure of the sector. According to Alliance[2] more than 1,000 vessels have been hacked in the last five years. However, cyber losses quite often are excluded from an insurance coverage as the expected impact of cyber attacks may be considered too uncertain to be included in policy terms. Damages caused by cyber attacks or errors (e.g., damage to the vessel due to navigation system malfunctioning after being hacked) are not covered by non-cyber-insurance policies, due to a specific cyber attack exclusion clause ([10/11/2003] also known as Cl.380). According to this clause, insurers do not cover for damages caused by a cyber attack whether it includes physical harm, business interruption or property damage. Other exceptions may include terrorism-related attacks and the NMA2914 electronic data exclusion[3] creating a "cyber-insurance gap" which becomes an impediment for the maritime sector given the drastic increase of cyber incidents [17].

---

[2] https://maritimecyberadvisors.com/_files/200000086-a389ca4859/MaritimeCyber Insurnace052019.pdf.

[3] https://www.lmalloyds.com/LMA/Wordings/NMA2914A_C.aspx.

Although cybersecurity incidents in the maritime field increase, only few are being reported. Only major cyber attacks are made public and well-documented, such as the Maersk attack in 2017[4]. The lack of data regarding cyber attacks in maritime creates a "false sense of security" to maritime companies, making them to underestimate the expected cyber-physical risk inflicted by cyber attacks.

3.2 SECONDO Application

In this use case, we present the applicability of SECONDO in assisting a shipping company to effectively transfer its *cyber-physical risks* to an insurer provider. The risk transfer process is detailed in three different phases: (1) Cyber-physical Risk assessment; (2) Cyber-physical Risk management; and (3) Insurance exposure estimation, coverage and premium calculation.

Phase 1: The critical assets of a shipping company, as identified in [13], are vulnerable to cyber attacks inflicting cyber-physical impact and endangering the company's financial situation, reputation, property, crew's life, and the environment. This phase deals with undertake the cyber-physical risk assessment on a vessel's infrastructure and systems. It will utilize the CORAS language[5] to formalize threat models and cyber-physical risk scenarios. It will further involve in identifying assets, vulnerabilities and threats to compute the overall risk scores using the RAOHM (refer to Sect. 2).

The output will be a quantitative estimation of the cyber-physical risks of the shipping company's infrastructure, assuming known cyber and cyber-physical maritime threats.

Phase 2: This phase deals with the cyber-physical risk management utilizing the risk assessment results from Phase 1 and data gathered by BDCPM (refer to Sect. 2). The payoff functions and the optimal controls selection strategies are determined using the GTM and ECM (refer to Sect. 2).

The defending strategies will reveal a mapping between the Critical Internet Security (CIS) controls[6] and various threats of the shipping company. For each CIS control, a game will be defined and solved to obtain an optimal solution. The solution of each game will determine the optimal distribution of control implementation levels (Low, Medium, High) over all targets of this use case. The payoff functions will capture both the reduction of cyber-physical risk and the indirect costs of implementing each of the controls.

CSIM (refer to Sect. 2) will use the results of all these modules to derive optimal ways to invest in cybersecurity controls.

At the end, a smart contract will be set up between the insurance provider and the shipping company indicating the premium as well as the coverage derived from the optimal strategy.

---

[4] https://www.forbes.com/sites/leemathews/2017/08/16/notpetya-ransomware-attack-cost-shipping-giant-maersk-over-200-million/.

[5] http://coras.sourceforge.net/coras_language.html.

[6] https://www.cisecurity.org/controls/.

Phase 3: In this phase, CICPM (refer to Sect. 2) will be used to collect the results of the aforementioned modules to produce an optimal insurance premium and coverage protection. After the premium is set by the insurer, the broker communicates with the shipping company in order to analyze the contract. Along with the proposed contract terms, the shipping company must demonstrate its compliance with various information security guidelines such as BIMCO cybersecurity guidelines[7], the International Maritime Organization's Resolution on IT and OT systems [13], best practices and cyber-physical risk management, and ISO cybersecurity standards compliance. If the shipping company accepts the contract and exhibits compliance to industry and governance guidelines, then all three main actors (the shipping company, the broker and the insurer) strike an optimal deal with policies of the agreement being stored as a smart contract on a blockchain. During the smart contract lifetime, CRMM (refer to Sect. 2) is used to continuously monitor for possible violation of the agreed policies and to convey any discrepancies on behalf of the insurance provider and the insured shipping company.

3.3   Attack Scenario

In this section, we illustrate a cyber attack scenario illustrating the usefulness of SECONDO platform in effective post-incident management.

Malware Infection - Let's assuming that the shipping company is under attack by a ransomware called CryptoMarine.

Its payload encrypted the files of all hard disks and the back-up files. Moreover, the collected data from the sensors about tank levels, nitrogen oxide concentration, temperature, and other on-board parameters [18] are encrypted. Without these values, it is extremly challenging to detect potential failures which could lead to catastrophic accidents. Further, the navigation system and telecommunications including network communications have collapsed, not permitting the vessel to successfully communicate with the onshore infrastructure of the company. As a result, this attack affects the shipping company in several different ways, since its property, crew, and reputation are jeopardized, and its share price is in a downward trend while the attackers demand ransom in cryptocurrency to unlock the encrypted devices.

Company's Response Team - When an employee of the shipping company identifies the incident - the ransomware infection- and, according to the shipping company's *disaster recovery policy*, the responsible officers, e.g., the Cyber Security Operation Team, as well as the Insurance Company are contacted immediately. At the same time, the *business continuity plan* is activated. The Emergency Response Team is called to action, which then assembles: (i) a Disaster Recovery Team (DRT), which is responsible for key services restoration and business continuity; (ii) a Business Recovery Team (BRT) consisting of senior members

---

[7] https://iumi.com/news/news/bimco-the-guidelines-on-cyber-security-onboard-ships.

of the main departments and the management team, who are responsible for the company's operation's prompt recovery; and (iii) a Media Team, to be in contact with the media.

Insurer's Role - Besides, the insurer closely cooperating with the shipping company ensuring that immediate incident response actions are taken, the recovery plan has been initiated, and a dedicated team has been assign to assist the company with the cyber defense efforts. In parallel, Personal Relations assistance is also deployed to manage the communication with the shipping company's clients that have either been affected by the attack or information regarding them has been compromised in order to be compliant with regulations such as GDPR.

Response Actions - According to the Insurance Company's approach, paying the ransomware is the last option, given that alternative approaches have been planned beforehand. DRT and BRT, in collaboration with insurer's experts will work on the systems' restoration and attempt to disinfect them. First, the existing recovery plan must be applied. Existing back-up countermeasures, adopted by the shipping company prior to the incident (suggested by SECONDO), will be implemented to countermeasure the impact.

Smart Contract Updates - Since there is an active incident, the insurance provider initiates an immediate forensic investigation. The results of the investigation are input to the SECONDO smart contract, which automatically initiates its process to assess the damage and decide which actions will be executed. The actions will be recommended by cross-evaluating the security practices and postures recorded by CRMM and the insurance policies.

4 Conclusion and Future Work

In this paper, we present the SECONDO framework that can assist organizations with decisions related to cybersecurity investments and cyber-insurance. We present the architecture of the framework and its various components. In particular, we detail how SECONDO quantitative risk assessment effective risk management optimal cybersecurity investment strategies subjected to a budget constraint. Upon successful contract agreement, SECONDO facilitates smart contracts on a blockchain which could be used for transparency, monitoring and to verify compliance to agreed insurance policies in cases of discrepancies. At last, this paper presents an overview on SECONDO's applicability in a Maritime scenario. We envisage that the implementation of SECONDO will be a significant step towards standardization of a holistic cyber economics framework for organizations of any size and sector.

Acknowledgment. This research has been funded by the European Union's Horizon 2020 research and innovation programme under the Marie Sklodowska-Curie SECONDO grant agreement No. 823997.

References

1. Fielder, A., Panaousis, E., Malacaria, P., Hankin, C., Smeraldi, F.: Decision support approaches for cyber security investment. Decis. Support Syst. **86**, 13–23 (2016)
2. Panou, A., Ntantogian, C., Xenakis, C.: RiSKi: A framework for modeling cyber threats to estimate risk for data breach insurance. In: Proceedings of the 21st Pan-Hellenic Conference on Informatics. 1–6 (2017)
3. Fielder, A., König, S., Panaousis, E., Schauer, S., Rass, S.: Risk assessment uncertainties in cybersecurity investments. Games **9**(2), 34 (2018)
4. Chronopoulos, M., Panaousis, E., Grossklags, J.: An options approach to cybersecurity investment. IEEE Access **6**, 12175–12186 (2017)
5. Panda, S., Panaousis, E., Loukas, G., Laoudias, C.: Optimizing Investments in Cyber Hygiene for Protecting Healthcare Users. In: Di Pierro, A., Malacaria, P., Nagarajan, R. (eds.) From Lambda Calculus to Cybersecurity Through Program Analysis. LNCS, vol. 12065, pp. 268–291. Springer, Cham (2020). https://doi.org/10.1007/978-3-030-41103-9_11
6. Laszka, A., Panaousis, E., Grossklags, J.: Cyber-insurance as a signaling game: self-reporting and external security audits. In: Bushnell, L., Poovendran, R., Başar, T. (eds.) GameSec 2018. LNCS, vol. 11199, pp. 508–520. Springer, Cham (2018). https://doi.org/10.1007/978-3-030-01554-1_29
7. Oppliger, R.: Quantitative risk analysis in information security management: a modern fairy tale. IEEE Secur. Priv. **13**(6), 18–21 (2015)
8. Nespoli, P., Papamartzivanos, D., Mármol, F.G., Kambourakis, G.: Optimal countermeasures selection against cyber attacks: a comprehensive survey on reaction frameworks. IEEE Commun. Sur. Tutor. **20**(2), 1361–1396 (2017)
9. Böhme, R., Schwartz, G., et al.: Modeling cyber-insurance: Towards a unifying framework. In: WEIS. (2010)
10. Woods, D., Agrafiotis, I., Nurse, J.R.C., Creese, S.: Mapping the coverage of security controls in cyber insurance proposal forms. J. Int. Serv. Appl. **8**(1), 1–13 (2017). https://doi.org/10.1186/s13174-017-0059-y
11. Marotta, A., Martinelli, F., Nanni, S., Orlando, A., Yautsiukhin, A.: Cyber-insurance survey. Comput. Sci. Rev. **24**, 35–61 (2017)
12. Romanosky, S., Ablon, L., Kuehn, A., Jones, T.: Content analysis of cyber insurance policies: how do carriers price cyber risk? J. Cyber. Sec. **5**(1) (2019)
13. Organization, I.M.: Guidelines on maritime cyber risk manageme. http://www.imo.org/en/OurWork/Security/Guide_to_Maritime_Security/Pages/Default.aspx
14. Cimpean, D., Meire, J., Bouckaert, V., Vande Casteele, S., Pelle, A., Hellebooge, L.: Analysis of cyber security aspects in the maritime sector. (2011)
15. EIOPA: Cyber risk for insurers– challenges and opportunities. https://eiopa.europa.eu/Publications/Reports/EIOPA_Cyber%20risk%20for%20insurers_Sept2019.pdf
16. Balance small business, T.: What does a cyber liability policy cover? https://www.becyberawareatsea.com/awareness
17. SANS: Bridging the insurance/infosec gap: The sans 2016 cyber insurance survey. https://www.advisenltd.com/2016/06/21/bridging-the-insuranceinfosec-gap-the-sans-2016-cyber-insurance-survey/
18. Mrakovic, I., Vojinovic, R.: Maritime cyber security analysis - how to reduce threats? Trans. Marit. Sci. **8**(1), 132–139 (2019)

Are Sensor-Based Business Models a Threat to Privacy? The Case of Pay-How-You-Drive Insurance Models

Christian Roth[✉], Sebastian Aringer, Johannes Petersen, and Mirja Nitschke

University of Regensburg, Regensburg, Germany
{christian.roth,sebastian.aringer,johannes.petersen,mirja.nitschke}@ur.de

Abstract. Ubiquitous computing has also reached the insurance industry in the form of Usage Based Insurance models. Modern rates use sensor data to offer the user suitable pricing models adapted to his character. Our overview shows that insurance companies generally rely on driving behaviour to assess a user in risk categories. Based on the collected data, a new attack using kNN-DTW shows that, with the derived information, the identification of a driver in a group of all users of a vehicle is possible with more than 90% accuracy and therefore may represent a misuse of the data collection. Thus, motivated by the General Data Protection Regulation, questions regarding anonymisation become relevant. The suitability of standard methods known from Big Data is evaluated in the complex scenario Pay-How-You-Drive using both real-world and synthetic data. It shows that there are open questions considering the field of privacy-friendly Pay-How-You-Drive models.

Keywords: Pay-How-You-Drive · Privacy · Sensor data · Smartphone · Privacy enhancing technologies · Machine learning

1 Introduction

The willingness of users to share data is increasing. One reason for this according to Benndorf and Normann [2] is certainly monetary aspects. They further explain that this is especially the case when users trust the opposite instance or if the data—as marketed by insurers—is processed in anonymised form. Privacy threats are knowingly or unknowingly disregarded [6]. Thus, the majority of users is willing to disclose comprehensive information about their digital identity [7]. New types of insurance models promise customers usage-dependent rates that compensate them for cautious or restrained driving. These Usage Based Insurances (UBIs) are in line with the times and are now offered in many countries, including Germany, where data protection is of particular interest. Despite the lack of transparency of the models, they are enjoying increasing popularity.

The consequences of privacy violations are often unclear from the outset, so that this danger is partially disregarded. This work therefore raises the question

© Springer Nature Switzerland AG 2020
S. Gritzalis et al. (Eds.): TrustBus 2020, LNCS 12395, pp. 75–85, 2020.
https://doi.org/10.1007/978-3-030-58986-8_6

of the extent to which users are trackable in context of UBI. In fact, we contribute with a) an analysis of existing UBIs in Germany, b) a novel method for identifying drivers solely on the basis of information collected by insurance companies, c) an analysis whether existing protective measures from big data applications are applicable, and d) an evaluation of the identification and protection methods based on real-world and synthetic data.

The paper is structured as follows. We first analyse existing insurance models (Sect. 2). Section 3 explains the given scenario and Sect. 4 presents a novel approach to identify drivers. Section 5 applies traditional anonymisation techniques. Section 6 assess the performance of identification and anonymisation. The paper finishes with related work and a conclusion (Sects. 7 and 8).

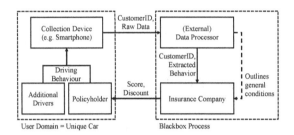

Fig. 1. Derived meta-modell after analysing 12 UBI rates.

2   Analysis of Usage Based Insurance Models

A field study was first carried out to get an impression of offered UBI rates with a focus on Germany. The rates were thoroughly analysed including general conditions (e.g. admitted participants), the information collected and the collection/processing process.

2.1   Metamodell of UBI Schemes

Privacy has been identified as an important criterion for insurance companies with regard to customer communication. Consequently, the insurance process was adapted to these requirements. After analysis of the 12 candidates (including Germany's largest insurers), a meta-model could be identified, which is represented in Fig. 1. Three parties are basically involved in the UBI process: Users (policy holders and other drivers, up to 10), an external data processor and finally the insurance company. In principle, a vehicle is insured in the rates, for the pricing of which the trip data of the users are used. A data processor receives the data, most of it being collected using an app provided by the insurance company. Together with a customer ID, which identifies the vehicle rather than the user, the data is transmitted to an external service provider, whereby several insurance companies generally use the same service provider. This service provider evaluates the data using non-communicated methods and extracts driving events, communicating them to the insurer. At this point, it is obvious that the data processor determines the structure of the results evaluation, since insurance companies that use the same processor transmit similar or identical information to customers. Insurance companies are therefore likely to outsource UBI technology. It has to be noted that, at least in Germany, the score criteria and the process of generation is a business secret and is not required to be published[1]. Feedback on the trip is given to the driver in the form of points or medals. Hence, trips of a day are aggregated independent of drivers in order to derive a vehicle's daily driving class, which, in turn, is the basis for the monthly assessment of the policy. Only Württembergische and CosmosDirekt consider negative consequences compared to a non-UBI rate.

Table 1. Overview of analyzed rates

Rate	Processor	Method		Features								
				PHYD					*PAYD*			
		App	Hardware	Braking	Acceleration	Cornering	Speed	Raw	Time	Roadtype	Dur./Dist.	Phone Usage
Aachen Münchener	MyDrive	X		X	X	X	X			X		
Allianz BonusDrive	IMS Inc	X	X	X	X	X	X		X	X		
AXA Drive	MyDrive	X		X	X	X	X					
CosmosDirect BetterDrive	MyDrive	X		X	X		X		X			
Friday	–		X[a]								X	
Generali	MyDrive	X		X	X	X	X		X			
HDI DiamondDrive	?	X		?	?	?		X	X		X	
HUK-Coburg Mein Auto	HDD	X	X	X	X	X	X					
Signal Iduna sijox AppDrive	Akquinet	X		X	X	X	X[b]		X	X		X
Sparkassen DV	Telefonica		X	X	X				X	X		
VHV Telematik-Garant	Akquinet		X[c]	X	X		X		X	X		
Württembergische	Vodafone	X		?	?	?	X[b]	X	X	X		X

[a]Via website　　　[b]Detection of speeding violations　　　[c]Local data processing

2.2 Overview of Rates

The analysis has shown that insurance companies usually use a form that is a mix of Pay-As-You-Drive (PAYD) and Pay-How-You-Drive (PHYD) in their UBI rates (83.3%) (see Table 1). The PHYD features are dominated by braking or acceleration manoeuvres and speed derived ones (relative to the permitted speed

---

[1] German Federal Supreme Court (Bundesgerichtshof, BGH), 2014, VI ZR 156/13.

or as a strict rule like "above 160 km/h is considered risky" (CosmosDirekt)). In some cases, the speed is also set in relation to the permitted speed limit so that speed violations are also included in the evaluation. From the point of view of the PAYD attributes, travel time is taken into account, as well as the distance covered. The street type also plays a role in some cases. Sometimes, it is considered whether the device is used by the driver while driving.

During the analysis, 6 data processors could be identified, of which 55% are not located in Germany, with some even being outside of the European Union. This aspect should be openly communicated with regard to transparency for and trust of each driver of a car, but was refused by insurance companies [16]. Furthermore, it is not apparent which data is exchanged between data processor and insurer, and thus can be considered a black box. Some companies are more specific in terms of collected data and its processing (e.g. expired Sparkasse rate) while others such as VHV state that they collect raw sensor data without specifying derived manoeuvres. Sometimes, it is not evident which data is extracted.

2.3   The Formulated Privacy Problem

The insurance company applies pseudonymisation techniques to convey a sense of security. It is evident and claimed by insurers (e.g. Allianz) that privacy is based (exclusively) on the outsourcing of data processing to an external service provider, who – not comprehensible for the customer – only passes on aggregated data to the insurer using the pseudonym (i.e. customer ID). In the interest of data economy and expediency, only data that actively allow pricing within the framework of a UBI rate should be collected by the insurer. If further information can be read out of the data, this should be viewed critically in the sense of privacy. Since UBI rates only insure a vehicle, not the individual person, a statement about the driver is not needed at all. However, this information can be used, for example to find out whether the vehicle is shared or to derive daily routines.

3   Scenario

A driver d transmits the data $\mathcal{X}$ describing a trip to the insurer after the trip is completed. For this work, we assume the following model: the insurer uses the data to assign d typically to 1 of 3 classes according to his business model with the help of an (unknown) classification function $h(\mathcal{X})$ to carry out pricing afterwards. For integrity reasons, the execution of h in the user domain is not accepted by the insurer. Cars are often shared in the household [3]; for the settlement of the rate it is sufficient to know the distribution of the 3 classes for a vehicle. The individual $\mathcal{X}$, however, also allows further conclusions about its originator d, such as the recalculation of the driven distance [17] or, as shown here, the identification of d in small groups $\mathcal{D}$ to derive movement patterns. Such illegal use of the data is to be prevented from an organisational and legal point of view by the General Data Protection Regulation (GDPR) in accordance with the paradigms *purpose limitation* and *data minimization* in Article 5.

We are of the opinion that technical methods are nevertheless required to protect the privacy of a user. Therefore, the claim is to anonymise the data accordingly with a method f in the trusted domain of the user to provide the insurer only with the amount of data required for pricing on the basis of h according to data minimization: $f : \mathcal{X} \rightarrow \mathcal{X}'$. It is assumed that a function a exists, which determines a driver $d \in \mathcal{D}$ on the basis of $\mathcal{X}$, while an attack on the basis of $\mathcal{X}'$ does not lead to a correct identification.

3.1 Data Set

A scenario-aware data set ds_R was collected 30 Hz using an Android 8 App to identify a driver d out of ds_R's 5 real drivers $\mathcal{D}$. For this purpose, three parameters, driving distance (over 500 km), driver (5) and vehicle (3), were alternated without restrictions (*3F scenario*). Each measurement s represents data from the accelerometer and gyroscope as well as GPS to calculate the speed v, forming a measurement series $\mathcal{S} \ni s = (acc_x, acc_y, acc_z, gyro_x, gyro_y, gyro_z, v)^2$.

In addition, a data generator based on polynomial regression was used to create synthetic drivers (6) with 21 trips based on the real trips. These trips were specially tailored to the parameters for the envisaged anonymisation function f and its evaluation. To create a generic model, manoeuvres were enriched with random scattering, compression and stretching.

3.2 Attacker Model

In summary, an attacker in the present scenario is an entity (e.g. insurer) that wants to uniquely assign the transmitted data $\mathcal{X}$ to a driver $d \in \mathcal{D}$ (closed-set problem): $a : \mathcal{X} \rightarrow d$. The attacker is able to intercept the data $\mathcal{X}$, but only after it has left the domain of the producing entity (e.g. driver). The attacker performs the identification *ex post* by using already assigned combinations $[((\mathcal{X}_{1,1}, \ldots, \mathcal{X}_{1,i}), d_1), \ldots, ((\mathcal{X}_{j,1}, \ldots, \mathcal{X}_{j,i}), d_j)]$. The form of $\mathcal{X}$ is determined by the insurance company, d follows this default; the attacker has no way to gather additional information. Metadata analysis is not considered in this paper.

4 Method for Driver Identification a

The attack a is limited to the environment (data & manoeuvres), which was identified after analysing different UBI rates in Germany (see Sect. 2).

4.1 Manoeuvre

We use the same manoeuvres $m \in \mathcal{M}$ as insurers do. This includes braking *bra*, accelerating *inc*, and cornering *cor*. δt_m denotes the length of a manoeuvre. They are extracted by looking for patterns (e.g. upwards speed trend for *inc*) in the recorded time series. One can use each sensor value to analyse a manoeuvre.

---

^{2} Vehicle axles: x: transverse axis, y: longitudinal axis, z: vertical axis; smartphone-to-vehicle alignment was carried out, otherwise correct identification is not possible.

4.2   Conversion and Interpretation

The proposed approach compares time series using Dynamic Time Warping (DTW). Thus, manoeuvres of different lengths must be resampled and translated into a relative perspective in order to be processable. Figure 2 makes clear that there are differences between the different drivers. Each manoeuvre defines a time span during which all sensors can be viewed for identification. Depending on the selected sensor, differences between drivers are more significant.

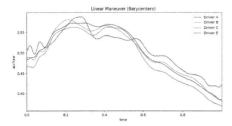   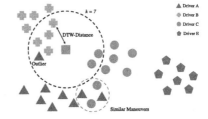

Fig. 2. Manoeuvres of four drivers, shown acc_x (average via SoftDTW).

Fig. 3. Construction of the manoeuvres allocation.

4.3   Detection

Figure 3 shows the idea of identifying a driver. The manoeuvre is described by a curve. A k-nearest neighbor (kNN) classifier uses DTW k to search for similar curves in the known and labeled data set (colored shapes) for the unknown curve (gray square). Manoeuvres that have a small distance according to DTW imply a high similarity to the unknown observation. The presumed driver is inferred by distributing k parts to the colored objects, where a person is considered more likely with increasing number of associated parts. This allows to create a gradation of the potential candidates for the manoeuvre. At this point, it becomes apparent that the assumption that a driver will perform many similar manoeuvres is implemented in the algorithm, while outliers are still handled.

5   Anonymisation Function f

f aims to ensure $|a(\mathcal{X})| > 1$, meaning d is no longer clearly identifiable in a group of other drivers. The goal of f is therefore to establish a certain degree of k-anonymity in the driver pool (c.f. [10]). To achieve anonymity in the context of Big Data, data modifying techniques are used [4].

Recent work [12,13] and the survey [5] present procedures that attempt to transfer the classical anonymisation methods to time series. The challenge is to maintain the information within the time series despite the insertion of disturbances, but at the same time to make it more anonymous. It turns out that the relationship between data protection and meaningfulness has to be carefully balanced and is more challenging compared to classical big data applications, which applies (as we will show) even more clearly to the PHYD scenario due to stricter requirements and more limited data sources. We will examine whether the classical anonymisation methods are sufficient as building blocks for f can be used:

- **Generalise.** Delete decimal places of a value with the start probability ρ_α
- **Change.** Randomly change a value with the start probability ρ_β
- **Suppress.** Randomly delete a value with the start probability ρ_γ
- **Insert.** Insert a dummy value with the start probability ρ_δ

5.1 Requirements

The scenario has special requirements that must be ensured when changing sensor data. Otherwise, the PHYD business model's integrity is at risk. Eventually, three core requirements can be identified:

$$① \ h(\mathcal{X}) = h(f(\mathcal{X})) \ ② \ a(f(\mathcal{X})) \neq a(\mathcal{X}) \ ③ \ \nexists g : g(f(\mathcal{X})) = \mathcal{X}$$

First, ① is necessary from the point of view of the insurance company, as it must still be possible to establish correct pricing based on the data. ② is driver-related as he wants to not be identifiable after anonymisation. Last, ③ ensures that there is no inverse function g to deanonymise $\mathcal{X}'$ in finite time.

5.2 Process

f, consisting of the described four operations, is executed for each value $x \in \mathcal{X}$ to generate a $\mathcal{X}'$. Following that, a feedback loop starts, which checks conditions ① and ②. If they are not met, f is executed with new parameters $\rho_\alpha, \rho_\beta, \rho_\gamma, \rho_\delta$ until a combination is found that meets the requirements (f optimises itself using a and h). In order to allow sufficient investigation, comparability and evaluation of the idea in the context of this work, the parameters were defined accordingly. Three strategies $\Sigma_1, \Sigma_2, \Sigma_3$ are defined, which reflect different parameterisations of sets $\rho_\alpha, \rho_\beta, \rho_\gamma, \rho_\delta$, where Σ_1 rarely makes changes and Σ_2 makes more frequent changes. In contrast, Σ_3 uses random values based on the other two strategies for each trip. $\Sigma_\emptyset$ forwards the raw data without anonymisation.

6 Evaluation

In the following, a is analysed on the real world data set and then f is evaluated. As h, a decision tree based categorisation with the 3 outcomes *aggressive*, *neutral* and *passive* is used. Three metrics were used to evaluate whether the attack a is still effective after f has been used:

- **F-Score** gives information about the quality of a; low values are aimed for.
- **Anonymity** measures how many manoeuvres of a driver are assigned to another user (*Number of trips* $*$ *Number of drivers*).
- **Standard deviation** of the prediction by a; low scatter is desirable.

Evaluation was done using 4x cross-validation with an 80–20 split and $k = 17$. Anonymisation was analyzed by using additional data sets: $ds_{1...4}$ contain 6 drivers with 21 different trips and with different class compositions. ds_3^L reduces ds_3 to 5 trips per driver. ds_3^D varies the number of trips per driver.

6.1   Identification

First of all, it shall be shown that with the help of a it is possible to identify a driver even under the real conditions of the data set ds_R.

Sensor Influence. The three most significant sensors for a manoeuvre which are robust to influences other then the driver were first identified and then used in the following.

Number of Drivers. Figure 4 shows that the drivers can be unerringly identified via the different test sets $|\hat{\mathcal{D}}|$ (random pairings) with probabilities always higher than guessing. Our approach applies more weight to manoeuvres which are more unique for a driver yielding better results.

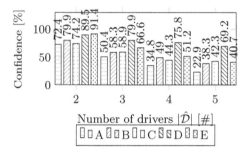
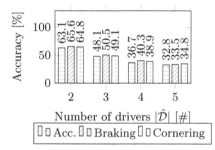

Fig. 4. Confidence [%] for different numbers of drivers (average after $l = 10$).

Fig. 5. Confidence [%] each experimental size (average after $l = 10$).

Table 2. Overview of the changes regarding anonymity.

	All drivers	4 Drivers/Class	3 Drivers/Class	2 Drivers/Class
max	ds_R Σ_1: 0.64	ds_R Σ_1 c2[a]: 0.475	ds_3^D Σ_1 c2: 0.667	ds_3^L Σ_1 c1: 0.45
min	0.0 *(repeatedly)*	0.0 *(repeatedly)*	0.0 *(repeatedly)*	0.0 *(repeatedly)*
Δ_{max}	ds_1 Σ_3: 0.2	ds_4 Σ_1 c2: 0.25	ds_3^L Σ_1 c2: 0.3	ds_3^L Σ_1 c1: 0.4
Δ_{min}	ds_1 Σ_1: 0.017	ds_R Σ_1 c2: 0.025	ds_2 Σ_1 c2: -0.067	0.0 *(repeatedly)*

[a]1 *Reading:* f was applied to record ds_R with strategy Σ_1. The value is the result of the a attack on class c2.

Accuracy per Manoeuvre. Figure 5 confirms that the derivable manoeuvres are all limited in their expression as the identification becomes harder with more drivers. Further, no manoeuvre is preferable due to the complexity of the *3F scenario*.

6.2 Anonymisation

Overview. It can be seen that anonymity is not high even after using f with different strategies. Nevertheless, in some cases a certain degree of anonymity has been achieved with no anonymisation strategy, having proven to be particularly preferable. However, it has been shown that by using any $\Sigma_{1,2,3}$ strategy, the confusion (and thus the anonymity) could be increased by up to 38.2%. The smaller the number of drivers per class, the smaller this increase is. Table 2 shows that drivers within their class become more anonymous, although this depends very much on the data set. The standard deviation as the third measure varies greatly between the individual tests with values between 0.037 and 0.195.

Strategy Selection. No strategy can establish absolute anonymity in the synthetic data sets $ds_{1,...,4}$ which is understandable from the point of view of data origin (polynomial basis). With ds_R the anonymity within the classes shifts only with a small increase of the overall anonymity. Even if ① is ignored, no strategy can deliver much better results. Hence, anonymisation results are partly by coincidence using these simple strategies without first adapting to the data set.

Conclusions. In general, no anonymisation strategy could be found that would give the best or even feasible results in the constrained PHYD scenario. A correlation between the f-value and anonymity could also not be found. It turns out that a low f-score is not sufficient because it is not the true prediction rate of a driver d_i that is decisive for anonymity, but rather the assignment of the false prediction rate from d_i to d_j that must be balanced. Only then, according to definition, are both drivers equally likely and therefore anonymous. Known anonymisation techniques hardly work here.

7 Related Work

PHYD is a rising trend, not only in the commercial sector but also in the academic world. In addition to the consideration of (privacy-threatening) driver recognition procedures (e.g. [8]) there is also a trend towards the investigation of UBI possibilities including model proposals (e.g. [1]) itself. Tselentis et al. [15] analyse existing theoretical models on the one hand, but also outline challenges associated with the widespread adoption of UBI tariffs on the other hand. Privacy aspects are not of interest in their consideration, but are nevertheless essential for user acceptance [2]. Existing anonymisation methods [11] for FPD are not appropriate in the existing context, while the threat is well-known [17]. In contrast to PHYD, privacy-friendly PAYD systems are already known [14], because often only the localisation is problematic here [9].

8 Conclusion

Based on a study of the UBI tariffs offered, this paper shows that identification is possible with our approach specially designed for the scenario. Provided protection measures as known from Big Data do not enable anonymisation here.

This has been demonstrated using synthetic and real-world data. The necessity for a transparent PHYD model that is comprehensible and controllable by users, including thorough protection of sensor data, becomes clear, since the question of the threat to privacy posed by sensor data can be clearly answered in the affirmative. Follow-up work should optimise the anonymisation f in the sense that the method is self-learning and at the same time uses intelligent anonymisation strategies to finally create k-anonymity. Furthermore, a balance between anonymity and integrity of the data must be found so that all stakeholders, especially the insurer, accept the changes.

References

1. Ayuso, M., Guillen, M., Nielsen, J.P.: Improving automobile insurance ratemaking using telematics: incorporating mileage and driver behaviour data. Transportation **46**(3), 735–752 (2018). https://doi.org/10.1007/s11116-018-9890-7
2. Benndorf, V., Normann, H.T.: The willingness to sell personal data. Scandinavian J. Econ. **120**(4), 1260–1278 (2018)
3. Eurostat: Household composition statistics (2019). https://ec.europa.eu/eurostat/statistics-explained/index.php/Household_composition_statistics#Household_size
4. Fung, B.C., Wang, K., Fu, A.W.C., Yu, P.S.: Introduction to Privacy-preserving Data Publishing: Concepts and Techniques. Chapman and Hall/CRC, Boca Raton (2010)
5. Hong, S.k., Gurjar, K., Kim, H.s., Moon, Y.s.: A survey on privacy preserving time-series data mining. In: 3rd International Conference on Intelligent Computational Systems, ICICS 2013 (2013)
6. Kang, R., Dabbish, L., Fruchter, N., Kiesler, S.: "My data just goes everywhere": user mental models of the internet and implications for privacy and security. In: Symposium on Usable Privacy and Security (SOUPS), vol. 2015, pp. 39–52 (2015)
7. Kreuter, F., Haas, G.C., Keusch, F., Bähr, S., Trappmann, M.: Collecting survey and smartphone sensor data with an app: opportunities and challenges around privacy and informed consent. Soc. Sci. Comput. Rev. 089443931881638 (2018)
8. Martínez, M.V., Echanobe, J., Del Campo, I.: Driver identification and impostor detection based on driving behavior signals. In: IEEE Conference on Intelligent Transportation Systems, Proceedings, ITSC, pp. 372–378 (2016)
9. Paefgen, J., Staake, T., Thiesse, F.: Resolving the misalignment between consumer privacy concerns and ubiquitous is design: the case of usage-based insurance. In: International Conference on Information Systems, ICIS 2012, vol. 3, pp. 2311–2327 (2012)
10. Pfitzmann, A., Köhntopp, M.: Anonymity, unobservability, and pseudonymity—a proposal for terminology. In: Federrath, H. (ed.) Designing Privacy Enhancing Technologies. LNCS, vol. 2009, pp. 1–9. Springer, Heidelberg (2001). https://doi.org/10.1007/3-540-44702-4_1
11. Schomp, K., Rabinovich, M., Allman, M.: Towards a model of DNS client behavior. In: Karagiannis, T., Dimitropoulos, X. (eds.) PAM 2016. LNCS, vol. 9631, pp. 263–275. Springer, Cham (2016). https://doi.org/10.1007/978-3-319-30505-9_20
12. Takbiri, N., Houmansadr, A., Goeckel, D.L., Pishro-Nik, H.: Matching anonymized and obfuscated time series to users' profiles. IEEE Trans. Inf. Theory **65**(2), 724–741 (2019)

13. Thouvenot, V., Nogues, D., Gouttas, C.: Data-driven anonymization process applied to time series. In: CEUR Workshop Proceedings, vol. 2029, pp. 80–90 (2017)
14. Troncoso, C., Danezis, G., Kosta, E., Preneel, B.: Pripayd: privacy friendly pay-as-you-drive insurance. In: Proceedings of the 2007 ACM Workshop on Privacy in Electronic Society, WPES 2007 (2007)
15. Tselentis, D.I., Yannis, G., Vlahogianni, E.I.: Innovative motor insurance schemes: a review of current practices and emerging challenges. Accid. Anal. Prev. **98**, 139–148 (2017)
16. Verbraucherschutz, P.d.A.W.: Telematiktarife im versicherungsbereich abschluss-bericht der projektgruppe der arbeitsgemeinschaft wirtschaftlicher verbraucher-schutz. Technical report (2019)
17. Zhou, L., Du, S., Zhu, H., Chen, C., Ota, K., Dong, M.: Location privacy in usage-based automotive insurance: attacks and countermeasures. IEEE Trans. Inf. Forensics Secur. **14**(1), 196–211 (2019)

Human Aspects

Microtargeting or Microphishing?
Phishing Unveiled

Bridget Khursheed[1], Nikolaos Pitropakis[1(✉)], Sean McKeown[1],
and Costas Lambrinoudakis[2]

[1] School of Computing, Edinburgh Napier University, Edinburgh, UK
40311221@live.napier.ac.uk
{n.pitropakis,S.McKeown}@napier.ac.uk
[2] Department of Digital Systems, University of Piraeus, Piraeus, Greece
clam@unipi.gr

Abstract. Online advertisements delivered via social media platforms function in a similar way to phishing emails. In recent years there has been a growing awareness that political advertisements are being micro-targeted and tailored to specific demographics, which is analogous to many social engineering attacks. This has led to calls for total bans on this kind of focused political advertising. Additionally, there is evidence that phishing may be entering a more developed phase using software known as *Phishing as a Service* to collect information on phishing or social engineering, potentially facilitating *microphishing* campaigns. To help understand such campaigns, a set of well-defined metrics can be borrowed from the field of digital marketing, providing novel insights which inform phishing email analysis. Our work examines in what ways digital marketing is analogous to phishing and how digital marketing metric techniques can be used to complement existing phishing email analysis. We analyse phishing email datasets collected by the University of Houston in comparison with Corporate junk email and microtargeting Facebook Ad Library datasets, thus comparing these approaches and their results using Weka, URL mismatch and visual metrics analysis. Our evaluation of the results demonstrates that phishing emails can be joined up in unexpected ways which are not revealed using traditional phishing filters. However such *microphishing* may have the potential to gather, store and analyse social engineering information to be used against a target at a later date in a similar way to microtargeting.

Keywords: Phishing · Email · NLP · URL Mismatch · Visual placement analysis

1 Introduction

The effectiveness of Digital marketing has developed significantly with online delivery via social media channels. Marketing campaigns can now be targeted at very specific groups and deliver very specialised, tailored, messages. The

© Springer Nature Switzerland AG 2020
S. Gritzalis et al. (Eds.): TrustBus 2020, LNCS 12395, pp. 89–105, 2020.
https://doi.org/10.1007/978-3-030-58986-8_7

campaign can even be customised and reactively modified in response to data gathered through this granular activity. This is known as *microtargeting*. Social awareness of microtargeting in social media, especially in the case of political advertisements, has caused increasing disquiet over its intentions [1].

Digital advertisements on social media operate in some ways that may be considered similar to phishing emails. Indeed, digital advertisements may themselves be used for phishing. For example after Brexit, it became clear that users had been encouraged to self-identify using an application named *thisisyourdigitallife* to receive direct messaging from the Leave campaign [2], which was intuited by clicking links tailored to their interests from previous interaction with data-gathering surveys. It is therefore prudent to explore existing marketing techniques and how their success is measured [3], and to explore if such analyses can be used as a preventative technique to stop users interacting with phishing emails [4]. Phishing damages and devastates business, both in terms of reputation and financial losses. If digital marketing operates in similar ways, it is essential to gain greater understanding of how online digital marketing operates and whether that understanding can be leveraged to reduce the success rate of phishing attacks.

Phishing email methodologies have made use of several approaches. Natural Language Processing (NLP) which uses data analysis to identify linguistic elements such as for example how grammar indicators can be used to assess phishing emails – use of imperatives, multiple verbs, intensifiers, time-related words, incorrect grammar, typos, lingo etc. [5]. Other social indicators can also be measured by NLP to identifying the sender of a *stereotypical phish* through, for example, foreign language identification, negative tone, demands and incorrect grammar [6]. URL mismatch is a key indicator that there is a likelihood of criminal intention in phishing email, which is often considered in terms of the destination website which may appear to be a well-known brand destination but links to a different site. This is known as domain squatting/combosquatting as criminals register domains, which, for example, are spelled similarly to a target legitimate site, acting as phishing destinations to entrap unsuspecting users [7].

To the best of our knowledge, our work is the first to expore the overlap between phishing and digital marketing. It compares online advertisements delivered via social media platforms to phishing emails and explores whether understanding digital marketing methods, such as microtargeting, can aid in phishing email analysis and identification. We also consider how phishing may work in similar ways to digital marketing in its use of stored user data to collect information and develop campaigns via *microphishing*. The contributions of our work can be summarised as follows:

- We explore the existing literature for a defined set of measurable visual placement marketing techniques and compare them with existing phishing analysis techniques which use NLP, URL mismatch and visual similarity.

- We set up an experiment using Weka [8] for our main analysis along with defined visual placement metrics derived from digital marketing. Our input datasets are Facebook Ad Library microtargeting advertisements [9] and phishing datasets from the University of Houston [10] and Corporate junk mail to compare these approaches and their results.
- We use the test results to compare the efficiency of selected phishing email identification techniques with those derived from digital marketing.

The rest of the paper is organised as follows: Sect. 2 explores the related literature and compares current digital marketing metrics, while Sect. 3 analyses our methodology and describes our experimental results. Section 4 evaluates and discusses our findings. Section 5, draws the conclusions giving some pointers for future work.

2   Related Literature

Phishing is a method of social engineering [11]. It exploits malicious email and/or websites to gain customer information. Emails are sent with the aim of encouraging users to follow URL links, with the result that the user gives away information such as credit card details or alternatively downloading files which may appear legitimate but have a malware payload. Phishing email is also used to gather information for social engineering attacks where the aim is a granular accumulation of data on a target company, potentially over a long time period. Phishing is a large-scale problem for companies as 55% of corporate emails in 2018 were identified as spam [12]. Spearphishing is a subset of phishing that contains genuine, targeted, information such as family details and/or visually authentic appearance to convince the target that they need to act [13]. Das et al. [14] recently published a survey which explored the existing phishing and spear phishing solutions e based on detection techniques for the known attack vectors (e.g., URLs, websites, emails).

Phishing software has become a commodity as phishing software kits sold by rogue developer are known as Phishing-as-a-service or PhaaS. PhaaS is a ready-made set of tools and resources to enable phishing often, featuring fake e-commerce sites and content for phishing campaigns over a variety of digital channels, including social networking posts, phishing email, sponsored social media network advertisements, etc. [15]. Ethical PhaaS has also been developed in response to phishing. It has two main purposes: *i)* pentesting an organisation; and *ii)* training users to recognise phishing emails. Many techniques are used to identify legitimate emails and separate them from phishing emails. These interventions can happen either as preventative measures or as offensive defence where, users are tested with phishing techniques as part of a controlled programme to identify phishing, where under-performing users are put on training courses. Table 1 details such techniques.

Table 1. Phishing detection techniques

Technique	Description	Effectiveness
NLP	Key words, parts of speech, jargon, typos, bad English etc. [10]	Successful if defined list is effective (cp whitelisting) but not zero day.
URL mismatch	Different URL to the one that is shown, URL that is almost correct, combosquatting; also used NLP [7]	Successful if implemented correctly, users can be trained to recognise this.
Sentiment analysis	Identifying phishing by picking up on emotion words e.g. urgency, intensity;also used NLP [6]	Provides a fine-tuning of NLP by picking out tone e.g. identifying rogue employees
Visual placement techniques	Looking at how the information is loaded in the email; breaking down the mail in terms of visible [16] sections/content ratio	Visual placement analysis and metrics techniques. Table 3
User training	Ethical PhaaS training to identify users who succumb to phishing and re-educate the [15]	Training an established part of corporate life but may train users to normalise phishing and underestimate its threat

Digital marketing is online sales promotion and brand support often used in social media campaigns. This channel very often employs, and some argue exploits, user data to promote their wares or message in an attractive way to a specific target audience. Digital marketing can take place in many forms: for example served as part of channel offerings on the likes of Facebook, YouTube, Twitter and most often targeted to a user's activity and likes etc.; but equally it can be seen within corporate websites where users can choose to click on promotional information to find out more about products or be served or suggested information based on cookies storing previous site activity. Online advertisements are measured in different ways depending on the aim of a marketing campaign, which are detailed in Table 2.

Microtargeting is a fine-grained online advertisement technique that is delivered across various digital channels alongside other more traditional methods such as targeted mail. Using information acquired from user data can enhance online advertisement success, for example by associating a particular individual's habits and data to enhance product placement. An example may be to analyse certain buying patterns using data mining techniques to identify that a user is pregnant, facilitating the promotion of associated items. Trust can be enhanced by making an ad's function explicit via onscreen messaging. This can be effective as long as it coincides with, rather than disrupts, a user's expectations and sense making [22]. There are inherent similarities between phishing and digital marketing: a) Phishing and digital marketing are developed and gather data using similar

Table 2. Online advertisement techniques

Approach	Concept	Techniques
UI granularisation	Positioning of information within the online ad, like UIs, online advertisement success can be improved depending on where on screen it is position [17]	Breakdown of advertisement into constituent measurable parts Eye-tracking studies can show how users interact with advertisements in great detail Heat charts are often used to visualise activity
Images	Effect of images, image size, colours etc. [18]	Use colour to highlight or diminish certain factors onscreen
Power words	Words considered strong tools for advertising messages [19]	Certain words are shown to be more effective than others at capturing user attention.
Information diffusion	Desire to share marketing information and its effect [20]	Call to actions that encourage viral spread of advertisement Buttons/links e.g. Share option
Homophily	Wanting to be like other people and how that effects user online advertisement response [21]	Aspirational image Relatable models Nowadays this might be called the influencer-effect
Microtargeting	Repetition of advertisement to gain detailed picture of target group [2]	Repeated serving of online advertisements to acquire detailed information on target allowing the serving of tailored advertisements Popular with political parties

methods, such as PhaaS and microtargeting, and could therefore deliver what might be termed *microphishing* to build a dataset for social engineering purposes; b) Users interpret and choose to respond based on similar trust decisions; and c) Phishing or online advertisement product message and purpose appear similar. Digital marketing and phishing can therefore both be considered as kinds of social engineering. Superficially, an online advertisement and a phishing email can look very similar as the latter often appears to sell a product or service.

Screen image placement has been researched in relation to software User Interfaces (UIs), websites and other online UIs such as mobile phones using testing techniques, such as eye tracking and screen tracking, to gather hotspot information on where users' eyes are focused on a screen during testing. Gathering eye tracking information showed a strongly consistent screen read and advert handling behaviour by both experienced and new users. Users have an intuitive sense of where the core page content resides, with their eyes barely straying to the footer, or bottom area, of a page, forcing relatively major design changes to draw their attention to a particular area [23]. When image analysis is focused especially on digital marketing and phishing emails, visual placement and use of image metrics may have some specialized applications and goals. Methods used to identify visual placement depend on factors such as the level of matching required, the aim of the match ranging from exact duplicate to rough comparison, computational resources required, and the match speed required. The latter two factors will affect choices made regarding the analysis depth as there must be a trade-off between investment and possible results. Common analysis techniques depicted in more detail in Table 3.

As previously discussed, digital marketing can be viewed in some ways as analogous to phishing. Our work describes the methodology used to explore how digital marketing metric techniques are used to enhance phishing email analysis. Our approach differs to previous work by exploring connections between digital marketing and phishing email by considering microtargeting and how it works and how that might be connected to PhaaS for example *textmicrophishing* where digital marketing and phishing overlap.

3   Experimental Design and Results

Our work explores and measures how online marketing microtargeting based techniques and metrics could be used as a complementary identification method for phishing. Three datasets were used in our experiments. The first, a popular email phishing dataset, was supplied by Professor Rakesh M. Verma from the University of Houston [10] and is available to everyone under request. The second dataset includes Corporate junk mail collected from a single company, received by the main author as part of an email group on Microsoft Outlook from June to August in 2019. The last dataset came from Conservative Party advertisements found in the Facebook Ad Library [9] which was active from 1st of August 2019 to the 14th of September 2019.

In relation to each dataset, further specific features were refined. Regarding the University of Houston phishing dataset [10] the features were confirmed and improved through reference to previous work and subsequently the Corporate junk mail set, for example, derived stopwords to improve results. The full list of our features is described in Table 4. For the Conservative Party advertisements we used features coming from the work of Fu et al. [26], as well as histograms. With regards to the Corporate junk mail dataset, a combination of the above methods would be used to experiment along with adapted methodologies using recurring blocks of HTML or style features. Our experimentation methodology in steps is illustrated in Figure 1 and described as follow: 1) Apply NLP on University of Houston dataset; 2) Apply image metrics to the Facebook Ad Library Conservative party ads; and 3) Apply the same training test model and further visual metrics to the Corporate junk mail dataset (HTML and image source).

Table 3. Visual Placement Analysis and Metrics Techniques

Source	Technique	Paper	Techniques	Limitations
Phishing	HTML analysis & similarity score	Wenyin et al. [16]	Identifying pages based on breaking HTML into 3 categories block level layout and overall style, a similarity calculation based on each element within each category provides alerts based on ranges	Webpage rather than email; won't work if graphic is used instead of code
	Cascading StyleSheet analysis & similarity score	Mao et al. [24]	Chrome extension measuring and alerting on key CSS analysis points text pieces including style, embedded and overall browser-rendered visual page appearance	Webpage rather than email; won't work if graphic is used instead of code
	Signature-based method using selected pages attributes	Medvet et al. [25]	Visual comparison using three page features namely text pieces and their style, images embedded in the page, and the overall visual appearance of the page as rendered by the browser	Webpage rather than email; won't work if graphic is used instead of code
	Low-spec rendering of images and measurement using EMD	Fu et al.[26]	Web pages are converted into low resolution images and images signatures are created using colour and coordinate features
EMD is used to pinpoint differences and is able to recognise and measure similarity rather than direct similarity	Webpage rather than email
	HTML page check & Machine learning	Fette et al. [27]	Spam filter approach based on machine learning technique measuring HTML elements	Minimal visual elements
Digital marketing	Online advertisement metrics to establish relative success	Rzemieniak et al.[28]	How online advertisements are measured to define relative success of strategy e.g. CPM, CPA, CPC, FF and combination approaches	Minimal visual specific elements considered
	Static versus dynamic creative content and its effectiveness	Bruce et al. [29]	Creative format, message content, and targeting on digital advertisement performance of static (GIF) and animated (Flash) display advertisement formats of various sizes analysing results from a major retailer and creating a dynamic model	Performance based analysis
	Using ghost advertisements or non-advertisements to judge online advertisement effectiveness and improve metrics	Johnson et al.[30]	Ghost advertisements, which are also compared to Public Service Announcements which have been used for the same purpose, are used to measure what users would do had they not seen the brand ad; in order to establish a baseline user metric of interaction outside a marketing campaign	Minimal visual elements
S.M Images	Visual comparison and techniques trained for usein for example sentiment analysis	You et al.[31]	Machine learning is used with the following process where images were cropped to uniform size, trained using Convolutional Neural Networks progressively in datasets from Flickr and then tested Twitter to analyse political images to predict election results	High time and resource commitment

Fig. 1. Experiment workflow

Weka [8] was used to explore the datasets. Several algorithms were evaluated in a preliminary study, where poorly performing algorithms such as REPTree were subsequently abandoned in favour of the best performing: IBk, J48, and NaiveBayes. These are commonly used as baselines for email spam classification [32,33], each taking a different approach: **IBk** is a lazy implementation of the k-nearest neighbours algorithm, where output classification is determined via consensus of the nearest node classes; **J48** is a Java implementation of the C4.5, entropy based, decision tree, where the splitting attributes are chosen based on the information gain ratio; and **NaiveBayes** is a simple probabilistic classifier which assumes feature independence. Bayes' theorem is applied to calculate the probability of the data matching each class, with the highest probability match resulting in the final classification.

Our experiments have a combination of results from NLP processing (of which URL mismatch was a subset) and visual placement analysis. The NLP model used a simplified breakdown of an established model [10] with significant additions taken from other factors such as image presence, sentiment analysis, urgency of request, foreign language usage and an emphasis on the imperative verb form. The attributes are described in more detail in Table 4.

URL mismatch is commonly considered in relation to spoofed sites. However for the scope of our work, the focus is more on a mismatch between the address as shown in the email sender field and the email that it is actually sent from or similar mismatch in any links in the body of the email. This is seen as a key indicator that the email is spam or phishing as described previously. URL mismatch via link or email address is largely pre-identified in the University of Houston dataset where the dataset is clearly divided into Legit and Phish, with the URL and sender details mostly stripped out. The Corporate junk mail dataset contained live junk mail and potential malware and it was therefore prudent to avoid following links and limit them to manual inspection. Our investigation became more interesting when further connections between emails were explored, as several emails were observed to be directly connected. These were not obvious mismatched URLs emails from the addressee; although they were all marked as spam by the spam filter using other heuristics.

Image, look, and feel are key to both digital marketing and phishing email effectiveness. Having identified microtargeting as the main area of interest because of its relationship to the social engineering of political campaigns, and its analogous behaviour to PhaaS output, the experiment centres on interpreting visual similarity. Our methodology examines three visual analysis techniques in more detail in the context of the datasets as follows: a) Signatures; b) Histogram

Table 4. NLP Attribute model breakdown

Attribute	Description	Type
Filename	Filename	Nominal
Word count	Amount of words in email	Numeric
Stopword count	Non-key words in email. Adapted from the Natural Language Toolkit	Numeric
Link y/n	Boolean	Numeric
Link number	Number of links	Numeric
URL mismatch	Boolean	Numeric
Spelling mistake	Number of spelling mistakes	Numeric
Grammar mistake	Number of grammar mistakes	Numeric
Punctuation mistake	Number of punctuation mistakes	Numeric
Code y/n	Visible code in email - Boolean	Numeric
Language OE	Email partially or entirely in a language other than English - Boolean	Numeric
Swear	Boolean	Numeric
Sentiment analysis	A – angry N – neutral H – happy	Numeric
Imperative verb	Instance of imperative verb form e.g. Click here or View now Boolean	Numeric
Urgency	Response urgency measured 0–5: 5 – immediate response required 4 - contact requested soon – e.g. meeting, appointment, action tomorrow or next week 3 – contact requested – e.g. meeting, appointment, action 2 – action suggested but no pressure 1 – descriptive e.g. affirmation or congratulatory email 0 – no response required as information only	Numeric
Image present	Image present or not. Only relevant to Corporate junk mail dataset	Numeric
Named entities	Count of proper nouns e.g. names of people, street names etc.	Numeric
Legit	Phishing email or not. Class attribute - Boolean	Nominal

comparison and c) HTML sections/code id using NLP techniques. A selection of advertisements was extracted from the Facebook Ad Library; the baseline focuses on a subset of these which centre on the former Conservative, now Lib Dem MP, Sara Wollaston. These were examined to provide an overview of what a microtargeting image set looks like. There was no accessible background provided by the Facebook Ad Library on the intended strategy changes behind each targeted advertisement. However it is possible to analyse the Facebook Ad Library political advertisements and draw some conclusions. In this case this is done by focusing on one set of advertisements on a similar message.

The experiment aimed to find similarities as potential evidence of *microphishing*. These results focus on the superficially similar footers in the following Corporate junk mail files. Footer areas can often be overlooked when a phishing email modifies an existing template, which, as noted in the literature [34], is often assumed by users (and developers) to contain no important information. In the author's own experience of developing an early company website for Digitext in 1995, the footer was discovered on a Canadian company who had borrowed the HTML source but not updated the footer; this then appeared in a Web search for company mentions for Digitext online as evidence of this adaptation.

The file footers were tested in the following ways: **Baseline MD5**: To emulate images the footer areas were cropped to exactly the same size. **Histogram Comparison**: Although the collected images were not suitable for providing a signature they can produce histograms which show a close similarity. Histogram

comparison produces clear results for the very similar microtargeted advertisements and can be refined further; techniques such as Earth Mover Distance
measurement can also be used to compare histograms by looking at the distance
required to move the pixels of the image or "earth" from one position to another
to measure difference.

We collected our results using the NLP model within Weka using the URL
mismatch and visual similarity information. In the first part of our experiment,
as depicted in Table 5(a), we had as input the University of Houston [10] sample
dataset. Overall, the IBk algorithm performed best with 99% Precision and 91%
Recall while J48 came second with 99% Precision and Recall and Naive Bayes
ranked third with 95% Precision and 96% Recall. It can be observed that the
performance difference between the lesser performing algorithms is not large.
Results for the Corporate junk mail dataset are depicted in Table 5(b). This
time both Naive Bayes and IBk ranked first with approximately 95% Precision
and Recall, while J48 came second with 93% Precision and Recall.

Table 5. Comparative Results of Individual Algorithms (10-fold cross-validation)

(a) Houston Dataset				(b) Corporate Junk Mail Dataset			
Algorithm	Precision	Recall	F Score	Algorithm	Precision	Recall	F Score
IBk	0.990	0.990	0.989	IBk	0.951	0.950	0.950
J48	0.951	0.960	0.954	J48	0.931	0.930	0.930
Naive Bayes	0.948	0.910	0.926	Naive Bayes	0.953	0.950	0.950

While investigating URL mismatches on the Corporate junk mail dataset, we
noticed that an email with the same, or similar, subject line containing similar
text and title in its body arrived from 5 different email addresses, as illustrated in
Fig. 2(a). Other correlations in apparently different spam email include the use
of repeat footer addresses. This could be a regular spam server but potentially
could also have the PhaaS capacity to record any responses in a more granular
way that could allow results analysis. This could be comparable to the way data
is recorded and stored in microtargeted adverts for example to allow the sender
to build a bigger picture of the company they are targeting.

The Sarah Wollaston Facebook Ad Library subset was explored in more
detail. Microtargeting data are being measured in very small variations in text,
colour weight and tone as, illustrated in Fig. 3(a). The comparable metrics were
set using histograms. Example histogram difference can be observed on Fig. 3(b),
which show how histograms highlight small distinctions in the microtargeting
data. Histogram comparison produces clear results for the very similar microtargeted advertisements and can be refined further.

4   Evaluation and Discussion

The primary aim was to develop a working NLP model that identifies phishing
methods based on the content of the email, which was shown to be effective in

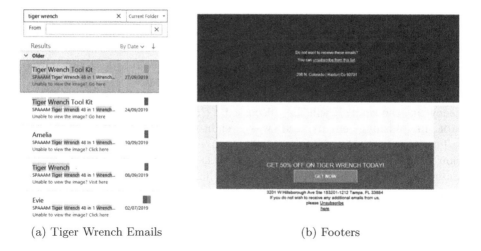

(a) Tiger Wrench Emails   (b) Footers

Fig. 2. URL mismatch examples

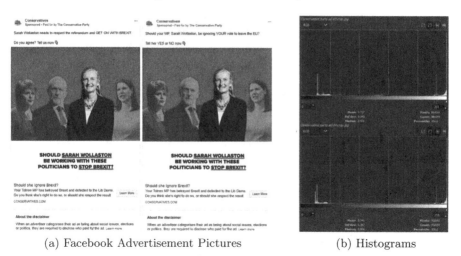

(a) Facebook Advertisement Pictures   (b) Histograms

Fig. 3. Visual similarity examples

Table 5 above. This section will discuss the feature and dataset performance in more detail. Following this, discussion pivots to the evaluation of visual elements of the email, via direct histogram comparison, cropped footer analysis, and NLP processing of the HTML code itself.

The NLP model was successful in that it was demonstrated to still be an effective method of categorising phishing and non-phishing emails. In a real life example, a build-up of match word knowledge can allow filtering out alongside tweaking known factors like a correlation between imperative words, such as Click and Unsubscribe, and the urgency of phishing emails can be used to alert to heightened risk. The visual metrics and the microtargeting example gave more scope to identify, perhaps in parallel in a real life system, what the implications of such persistent connections could be, i.e. some kind of *microphishing* technique run from a PhaaS software console gathering data on the target, to be analysed at leisure by the acquirers whether pentesters or criminals.

The results of different attributes used by the NLP model and their efficacy in the model will be discussed. *URL mismatch* was a constant factor in phishing emails and was weighted highly in the model. For *Spelling/Grammar/Punctuation mistakes*, there was a more noticeable correlation between phishing and language mistakes in the University of Houston dataset than in the contemporary Corporate junk mail dataset. Visible *code* in the email occurred in both datasets but did not appear to have a strong correlation with phishing email; emails with malicious code would be filtered out before hitting the Corporate junk mail mailbox. *Sentiment analysis* was explored firstly in terms of Happy/Neutral/Angry tones in the University of Houston dataset, but this category worked less well for the Corporate junk mail dataset which ended up being defined as largely neutral in tone. The *imperative verbs* facilitate a quick user response and were always present in phishing emails. They were usually in combination with the next attribute Urgency to push a quick unconsidered response. This was a weighted attribute to heighten the effectiveness of the model. There was also a strong correlation between phishing emails and *Urgency*.

J48 was noticeably more effective in the Corporate junk mail dataset compared to the University of Houston dataset samples; this is likely to be due to a more balanced sampling. URL mismatch was factored into the Weka model originally developed using the University of Houston dataset. There is an almost complete correlation between phishing and URL mismatch in the instances used from the Houston dataset as identified in the benign and phishing separation within the dataset. Having this clear identification made it easier to train the model. However the Corporate junk mail dataset had access to all header information and the experiment had to use resulting evidence to identify phishing email. Although URLs were only explored through manual inspection, as this dataset contained live potentially harmful emails, URL mismatch is a significant factor in assessing phishing email. For example, the clearest phishing with perhaps the most obvious malevolent intent spoofed the leading author's company.

Looking at URL mismatch on the basis of developing the model using the corporate junk mail dataset, and using visual similarity, it became clear that there were significant unexpected connections through almost 50% of the dataset contents coming from the same effective second level domain. Footer addresses reveal a connection between emails as they showed similar subject lines. Consequently, a simple assumption of URL mismatch as an indicator that an email was non-legitimate became more nuanced.

Visual Placement

Digital marketing relies heavily on images and that informed the selection of techniques and the way data was collected. A set of results were collected for visual placement using hashes, code snippets, and histograms from two of the datasets (excluding the University of Houston dataset which is text only and therefore could not be evaluated in this way). By examining the Sara Wollaston dataset information, it was possible to see microtargeting in action.

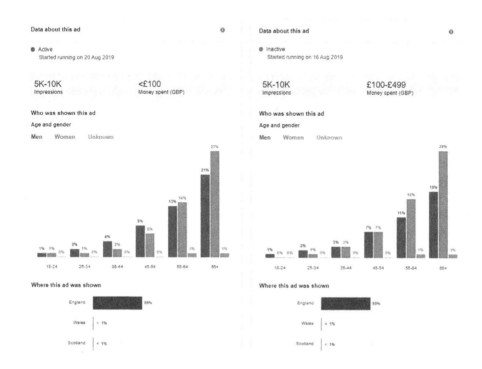

Fig. 4. Conservative party advertisement statistics

The voters targeted lived mostly in England but with small numbers in Wales and Scotland. The target of the advertisements is overwhelmingly statistically older men and women as illustrated in Fig. 4. Less than £100 was paid for all the advertisements targeting, with the exception of one which cost less than £499. Ad 23 had more money spent on it and was aimed predominantly at older women over 65 and achieved between 5000 and 1000 views. Only Conservative Party Ad 07 had similar impression numbers although less than £100 had been invested. It was primarily displayed to women over the age of 55 years old. Both of the most popular advertisements show the same image with the same text and calls to action. Conservative Party Ad 23 started showing on the 16th August and was inactive when the images were gathered; whereas Conservative Party Ad 07 started showing on the 20th August and was still active.

Although prior to testing the visual placement metric techniques seemed comparable to NLP, the results indicate that they appear less flexible and discriminative for longer-term use. This could mean it would be harder to evolve results as different factors are important in a fast-moving corporate analysis setting. The visual placement results show that some measurable activity can occur to identify phishing that may be connected to a larger, non-malicious, probing social engineering attack. However, without a large scale investment in image recognition it may be difficult to extract visual placement metrics from the ever-changing and Protean phishing email. However, visual similarities may be a factor that is usable to raise a low-level or complementary alert that may be of use to companies in facing a more general preparatory rogue activity that is hard to attack or pinpoint using traditional NLP methods. Visual similarity techniques could allow a more fuzzed approach that could centre on identifying multiple similar images produced by e.g. PhaaS software-based attack for the purposes of social engineering probing.

5   Conclusions and Future Work

A review of existing literature showed that there is a clear and identified correlation between digital marketing on social media and social engineering and also to phishing and social engineering. We also identified and gave greater significance to PhaaS, the organised data-gathering and analysed delivery of phishing. The experimental setup was able to compare the PhaaS method of phishing delivery to microtargeting, the digital marketing technique that allows a super-refinement of targets based on returned data. This comparison was explored in terms of how digital marketing metrics, as seen in online advertisement data-gathering techniques, could function in phishing analysis. So in effect a wider role of phishing as social engineering might be seen as, in its early stages, more interested in probing likely targets and understanding their behaviour prior to directly attacking them with phishing emails or other social engineering attacks. Using digital marketing metrics enables a measurement of how this works.

We were also able to observe through our experiments how the data gathering and reporting activities in digital marketing microtargeting can be seen to be mirrored in the reporting and analysis behaviour of ethical PhaaS and potentially in *microphishing*. In political advertisement terms the call to action would be the use of the microtargeted information to get the target to vote or perhaps not vote. In the same way basic and even already identified spam is a possible vehicle for data gathering. Both can be considered a kind of social engineering although one is currently most of the time still legitimate.

There is now continuing and urgent ongoing debate as to whether political advertisements should be permitted on Facebook and Google that has arisen since this work was carried out. Twitter has already banned such advertisements. Our work provides further evidence that collated results from phishing analogous to microtargeting are used in PhaaS which strengthens its connection to the negative association of social engineering; it also shows that connections between phishing emails that may be missed using for example an NLP model alone or in combination with URL mismatch are more likely to be picked up by adding visual placement analysis techniques. The comparison of the three techniques and experiment delivers a potential enhancement to phishing identification in that further information could now be gathered and a greater understanding of how phishing works and its wider aims and strategy can be gained.

The next steps for this work would be to explore the results by looking at more real world datasets or of phishing email collected in a corporate environment with the aim of establishing how prevalent connections within phishing emails are, and whether there are discernible patterns of microphishing targets that reveal a development of a social engineering campaign analogous to microtargeting in digital marketing. As PhaaS extends the possibilities for an organised campaign and its associated risk to a company or organisation, a methodology could also then be developed to provide the architecture for the automation of the processes used in our work. The visual analysis techniques could then be developed as part of an existing tool or as a plugin addon. As understanding of microtargeting, for example in the areas of its use in 2019 United Kingdom general election is only now coming to the attention of legislators, politicians and the general public, further exploration analysing microtargeting data mining goals and techniques especially in the area of granular level analysis metrics. In this context, similarity ratings could then become more pertinent as evidence of larger scale probing by rogue actors.

References

1. Cosentino, G.: The post-truth world order. Social Media and the Post-Truth World Order, pp. 1–31. Springer, Cham (2020). https://doi.org/10.1007/978-3-030-43005-4_1
2. Cadwalladr, C., Graham-Harrison, E.: Revealed: 50 million Facebook profiles harvested for Cambridge analytica in major data breach. Guardian 17, 22 (2018)
3. Gordon, B.R., Zettelmeyer, F., Bhargava, N., Chapsky, D.: A comparison of approaches to advertising measurement: evidence from big field experiments at Facebook. Market. Sci. 38(2), 193–225 (2019)
4. Goldman, M., Rao, J.: Experiments as instruments: heterogeneous position effects in sponsored search auctions. EAI Endorsed Trans. Ser. Games 3(11), e2 (2016)
5. Park, G., Taylor, J.M.: Poster: Syntactic element similarity for phishing detection (2015)
6. Kandias, M., Stavrou, V., Bozovic, N., Mitrou, L., Gritzalis, D.: Can we trust this user? predicting insider's attitude via Youtube usage profiling. In: IEEE 10th International Conference on Ubiquitous Intelligence and Computing and 2013 IEEE 10th International Conference on Autonomic and Trusted Computing, pp. 347–354. IEEE (2013)
7. Kintis, P., et al.: Hiding in plain sight: a longitudinal study of combosquatting abuse. In: Proceedings of the 2017 ACM SIGSAC Conference on Computer and Communications Security, pp. 569–586. ACM (2017)
8. Hall, M., Frank, E., Holmes, G., Pfahringer, B., Reutemann, P., Witten, I.H.: The WEKA data mining software: an update. ACM SIGKDD Explor. Newsl. 11(1), 10–18 (2009)
9. Silva, M., de Oliveira, L.S., Andreou, A., de Melo, P.O.V., Goga, O., Benevenuto, F.: Facebook ads monitor: an independent auditing system for political ads on Facebook. arXiv preprint arXiv:2001.10581 (2020)

10. Egozi, G., Verma, R.: Phishing email detection using robust NLP techniques. In: IEEE International Conference on Data Mining Workshops (ICDMW), pp. 7–12. IEEE (2018)
11. McDowell, M.: Avoiding social engineering and phishing attacks (2004). http://www.us-cert.gov/cas/tips/ST04-014.html
12. Symantec, I.: Internet security threat report. Broadcom (2019)
13. Krombholz, K., Hobel, H., Huber, M., Weippl, E.: Advanced social engineering attacks. J. Inf. Secur. Appl. **22**, 113–122 (2015)
14. Das, A., Baki, S., El Aassal, A., Verma, R., Dunbar, A.: SOK: a comprehensive reexamination of phishing research from the security perspective. IEEE Commun. Surv. Tutor. **22**(1), 671–708 (2019)
15. Meijdam, K.: Phishing as a service: designing an ethical way of mimicking targeted phishing attacks to train employees (2015)
16. Wenyin, L., Huang, G., Xiaoyue, L., Min, Z., Deng, X.: Detection of phishing webpages based on visual similarity. In: Special Interest Tracks and Posters of the 14th International Conference on World Wide Web, pp. 1060–1061 (2005)
17. Vanderdoncktf, J., Ouedraogo, M.: A comparison of placement strategies for effective visual design. People Comput. **IX**, 125 (1994)
18. An, D.: Advertising visuals in global brands' local websites: a six-country comparison. Int. J. Advert. **26**(3), 303–332 (2007)
19. Myers, G.: Words in Ads. Edward Arnold, London (1994)
20. Stieglitz, S., Dang-Xuan, L.: Emotions and information diffusion in social media–sentiment of microblogs and sharing behavior. J. Manage. Inf. Syst. **29**(4), 217–248 (2013)
21. Halevi, T., Lewis, J., Memon, N.: Phishing, personality traits and Facebook. arXiv preprint arXiv:1301.7643 (2013)
22. Kim, T., Barasz, K., John, L.K.: Why am i seeing this ad? The effect of ad transparency on ad effectiveness. J. Consum. Res. **45**(5), 906–932 (2019)
23. Djamasbi, S., Siegel, M., Skorinko, J., Tullis, T.: Online viewing and aesthetic preferences of generation Y and the baby boom generation: testing user web site experience through eye tracking. Int. J. Electron. Commer. **15**(4), 121–158 (2011)
24. Mao, J., Li, P., Li, K., Wei, T., Liang, Z.: BaitAlarm: detecting phishing sites using similarity in fundamental visual features. In: 5th International Conference on Intelligent Networking and Collaborative Systems, pp. 790–795. IEEE (2013)
25. Medvet, E., Kirda, E., Kruegel, C.: Visual-similarity-based phishing detection. In: Proceedings of the 4th International Conference on Security and Privacy in Communication Netowrks, pp. 1–6 (2008)
26. Fu, A.Y., Wenyin, L., Deng, X.: Detecting phishing web pages with visual similarity assessment based on earth mover's distance (EMD). IEEE Trans. Dependable Secure Comput. **3**(4), 301–311 (2006)
27. Fette, I., Sadeh, N., Tomasic, A.: Learning to detect phishing emails. In: Proceedings of the 16th International Conference on World Wide Web, pp. 649–656 (2007)
28. Rzemieniak, M.: Measuring the effectiveness of online advertising campaigns in the aspect of e-entrepreneurship. Procedia Comput. Sci. **65**, 980–987 (2015)
29. Bruce, N.I., Murthi, B., Rao, R.C.: A dynamic model for digital advertising: the effects of creative format, message content, and targeting on engagement. J. Market. Res. **54**(2), 202–218 (2017)
30. Johnson, G.A., Lewis, R.A., Nubbemeyer, E.I.: Ghost ads: improving the economics of measuring online ad effectiveness. J. Market. Res. **54**(6), 867–884 (2017)

31. You, Q., Luo, J., Jin, H., Yang, J.: Robust image sentiment analysis using progressively trained and domain transferred deep networks. In: Twenty-Ninth AAAI Conference on Artificial Intelligence (2015)
32. Shi, L., Wang, Q., Ma, X., Weng, M., Qiao, H.: Spam email classification using decision tree ensemble. J. Comput. Inf. Syst. **8**(3), 949–956 (2012)
33. Li, W., Meng, W., Tan, Z., Xiang, Y.: Design of multi-view based email classification for IoT systems via semi-supervised learning. J. Netw. Comput. Appl. **128**, 56–63 (2019)
34. Schroeder, W.: Testing web sites with eyetracking. Eye for design (1998)

Privacy

Privacy-Preserving Service Composition with Enhanced Flexibility and Efficiency

Kevin Theuermann$^{(\boxtimes)}$, Felix Hoerandner, Andreas Abraham,
and Dominik Ziegler

Institute of Applied Information Processing and Communications, Graz Technical
University, 8010 Graz, Austria
{kevin.theuermann,felix.hoerandner,andreas.abraham}@egiz.gv.at
dominik.ziegler@tugraz.at

Abstract. Service compositions are implemented through the interplay between actors of different organizations. Many composition systems use a middleware, which coordinates the service calls according to specified workflows. These middlewares pose a certain privacy issue, since they may read all the exchanged data. Furthermore, service compositions may require that only selected subsets of data that was initially supplied by the user are disclosed to the receiving actors. Traditional public key encryption only allows encryption for a particular party and lack of the ability to efficiently define more expressive access controls for a one-to-many communication. Besides privacy-preserving requirements, it may be necessary for participants in service compositions to be able to verify which actor has modified or added data during a process to ensure accountability of performed actions. This paper introduces a concept for efficient, privacy-preserving service composition using attribute-based encryption in combination with outsourced decryption as well as collaborative key management. Our concept enables end-to-end confidentiality and integrity in a one-to-many communication using fine-grained access controls, while minimizing the decryption effort for devices with low calculation capacity, which enables to use smartphones at the client side. The feasibility of the proposed solution is demonstrated by an implemented proof-of-concept including a performance evaluation.

Keywords: Confidentiality · Integrity · Privacy · Efficiency

1 Introduction

Service composition is the combination of multiple atomic services to achieve a more complex service. These atomic services can be offered by the public or private sector. The advantages of service composition stem from the services' modularity: Atomic services that can be reused in various use cases, which reduces the complexity of building new process flows or adapting existing flows. Furthermore, some use cases dictate that multiple services need to be integrated, e.g., if the involved data is governed by different organizations. Our work focuses on

S. Gritzalis et al. (Eds.): TrustBus 2020, LNCS 12395, pp. 109–124, 2020.
https://doi.org/10.1007/978-3-030-58986-8_8

service orchestrations where a middleware coordinates requests to sub-services within the process flow. Forwarding the users' requests through a middleware raises privacy concerns, as this middleware is able to read the requests' data content or learns from it. Additionally, in many cases, not all actors of a composite service need access to the whole data-set of an initially transmitted request because they only require selected parts. Finally, end-to-end integrity generally represents a challenge in service compositions, as sub-services within the process flow or the middleware in service orchestrations itself could alter message parts. A fully trusted middleware may evaluate privacy policies and only selectively disclose necessary attributes to the different services (c.f. Ma et al. [1]). This enables fine-grained access controls by the middleware and thus enhances the users' privacy with respect to information exposed to the sub-services. However, this approach requires full trust in a central party (i.e., the middleware), which still learns the users' (sensitive) data. Alternative work aims to reduce risks of a curious middleware by providing end-to-end security through applying public-key cryptography (c.f. Singaravelu and Pu [2]). In this approach, a sender encrypts message fields for each service. Disadvantages of this concept are the required knowledge about recipients and their public keys, poor efficiency, a high number of needed encryption keys and message overhead by having multiple encryptions of the same attribute for different services.

Contribution. In this paper, we **propose a service composition architecture** that tackles the before mentioned issues by leveraging the capabilities of Ciphertext-Policy Attribute-Based Encryption (CP-ABE) [3] in combination with collaborative key management as well as outsourced decryption [4]. Our main contributions are:

- Our proposed architecture **preserves the users' privacy** against both, the different sub-services as well as the middleware, by applying advanced cryptographic mechanisms (c.f. CP-ABE) to our service composition protocol. This end-to-end encryption further **reduces trust requirements** into the middleware, as it only handles ciphertext.
- Additionally, our proposal **enhances flexibility** for service composition. With attribute-based encryption, the sender does not need to know the identity (e.g., public key) of all receiving participants of the service composition. Instead, the sender encrypts message parts for attributes that can be derived from the message's content (e.g. sensitivity), while the middleware can combine and replace sub-services holding sufficient decryption rights to fulfill the use case.
- The applied cryptography enables **efficient one-to-many communication**, as the decryption policy of one message part may be satisfied by multiple receivers. In contrast to other approaches, our architecture is efficient in the sense of computational effort (e.g., outsourced decryption) as well as message size overhead (e.g., no duplicate encryption of the same message part for different receivers).
- This work further supports **end-to-end integrity** and accountability by integrating digital signatures into the service composition protocol.

– To **evaluate** our proposed concept, we **present a case study** that describes a possible use-case within an e-Health context. In this case-study, we define the actors and show in detail the interactions as well as the data flows including cryptographic computations. In addition, we have **implemented and benchmarked a proof-of-concept**, which not only demonstrates the feasibility of our concept but also highlights its efficiency in real-world scenarios.

The remainder of this paper is structured as follows. Sections 2 and 3 provide information about the related work as well as the cryptographic background applied in our proposed concept. Section 4 describes the system model including the involved actors and our defined security objectives. The novel privacy-preserving service composition protocol is introduced by Sect. 5. Finally, Sect. 6 provides an evaluation of an implemented proof-of-concept, followed by a conclusion in Sect. 7.

2 Related Work

Privacy in Service Compositions. Recent work has focused on solving privacy concerns towards the different services that receive and process data. The work of Ma et al. [1] tries to solve privacy concerns by introducing a Privacy-Proxy Service (PPS), which is a fully trusted middleware that receives all the user's data and only discloses the needed data to the services. Even though this work solves privacy concerns regarding data receiving services there are still privacy and trust concerns towards the middleware. In contrast, the work of Khabou et al. [5,6] addresses privacy concerns in service compositions by proposing a framework that defines privacy models and policies. This work introduces services that agree on a privacy model and policy between a client and data processing services via a middleware. Therefore, these concepts raise privacy concerns regarding the middleware. The work of Carminati et al. [7] solves this privacy issue of an untrusted broker in service compositions. However, this concepts uses public keys of actors for encryption, which requires a sender to know the recipients. We want to guarantee encryption, where senders do not need to know anything about recipients at message generation time, to enable a highly flexible composition in the background. Our proposed concept tackles privacy concerns towards a centralized trusted party or a set of trusted parties as well as towards data processing services by utilizing CP-ABE.

Policy Language and Systems. In the past, the OASIS eXtensible Access Control Markup Language (XACML) [8] was specified aiming to increase privacy. The work of Kaehmer et al. [9] defines an Extended Privacy Definition Tool (ExPDT) trying to solve privacy concerns by using a policy language. Several issues emerge with the use of policies to achieve stronger privacy such as the policy enforcement, required knowledge of recipients as well as the inflexibility with respect to changes of the service composition flow by adding, removing or replacing services. Our proposed system tackles these issues by utilizing a novel combination of CP-ABE outsourced decryption and a collaborative key management system. With the utilization of these cryptographic primitives, our system reflects a privacy-preserving system, which simultaneously provides high flexibility in terms of defining the process flows and involved services.

End-to-End Integrity. The work of Singaravelu et al. [2] focuses on end-to-end integrity within service compositions by applying public-key cryptography. In this concept, different message parts are encrypted for various service providers intended to decrypt them. This approach requires the client to know the included service providers and their corresponding public keys as well as their required data parts. This way, data that is transmitted to multiple receivers are contained in a service request redundantly, since the same data are encrypted for different service providers. Consequently, this approach suffers from issues regarding the required knowledge of involved service providers as well as an increasing message size overhead. We tackle these issues by using Ciphertext-Policy Attribute-Based Encryption in our concept, which does not require the client to have knowledge about involved service providers and their public keys and does not transfer data redundantly.

Cryptographic Primitives. Bethencourt et al. [3] first introduced Ciphertext-Policy Attribute-Based Encryption (CP-ABE), which enables the definition of access control policies through a set of attributes. While this cryptographic primitive enables a client to define complex access rules, it still raises concerns especially regarding the key revocation, key escrow and poor performance, because it is based on expensive bilinear pairings. This inefficiency becomes problematic, especially for client devices with limited computational power such as smartphones. To solve the performance problem in CP-ABE, concepts integrating outsourced decryption [10–12] were proposed. Lin et al. [4] proposed a solution for many of the issues related to CP-ABE by introducing a collaborative key management protocol. This protocol tackles the key escrow and key exposure problem and additionally reduces the decryption overhead of clients significantly through the application of outsourced decryption.

3   Background

Our concept for privacy-preserved service composition relies on cryptographic mechanisms. This section provides a description of applied technologies to understand the proposed solution.

3.1   Attribute-Based Encryption

Sahai and Waters [13] first introduced Attribute-Based Encryption (ABE), which represents an encryption mechanism that goes beyond traditional one-to-one public key encryption types. Instead of using the public key of a party to encrypt a message, a sender only has to know the attributes of the receiver in an ABE system. This way, the sender can encrypt a message, which is only decryptable by receivers owning the specified attributes. The main advantage over conventional one-to-one encryption is that ABE enables one-to-many encryption. There are two types of ABE: Firstly, in Key-Policy Attribute-Based Encryption (KP-ABE) [14], the trusted authority attaches policies (i.e., access structures) to the issued keys, while the senders specify a set of attributes when encrypting the message. A ciphertext can only be decrypted if the key's access structure is satisfied by the ciphertext's attributes. Secondly, in Ciphertext-Policy Attribute-Based Encryption (CP-ABE) [3], the user defines the access policy and attaches it to the ciphertext during the encryption process. The trusted authority assigns a set of attributes when issuing the key material to users. As we want the client to be able to determine access policies, we use CP-ABE for our concept and give background information below. When encrypting a message, the user specifies an associated access structure over attributes of a given attribute universe U. These access structures are defined by attributes using conjunctions, disjunctions and (k, n) threshold gates, which means that k out of n attributes must be present. For example, let us assume an attribute universe $U = \{A, B, C, D, E\}$, a private key PK^1 to the attributes $\{A, B, C\}$ and a second private key PK^2 to the attributes $\{D, E\}$. A ciphertext that was encrypted with the policy $(A \wedge B) \vee (A \wedge E)$ would only enable the PK^1 to decrypt it.

Definition 1 (CP-ABE). We recall the definition of CP-ABE as suggested by Rouselakis and Waters [15]. CP-ABE consists of several algorithms defined as follows:

$\mathsf{Setup}(1^\kappa) \to (\mathsf{params}, \mathsf{MSK})$: The setup algorithm only takes the security parameter $\kappa \in \mathbb{N}$ as input[1]. The output of this function is represented by the public parameters params containing a description about the attribute universe U and a master secret key MSK.

$\mathsf{KeyGen}(\mathsf{MSK}, S) \to \mathsf{PK}$: The key generation algorithm takes the master secret key MSK as well as an attribute set S as input and outputs a private key PK corresponding to the given attribute set S. The generated private key can be used to decrypt a ciphertext, if its corresponding attribute set is an authorized set of S.

$\mathsf{Encryption}(\lambda, \mathsf{params}, m, \mathbb{A}) \to \mathsf{CT}$: The algorithm to encrypt a message requires as input the security parameter λ, the public parameters params, a message m, and a corresponding access structure $\mathbb{A}$ on the attribute universe U and generates a ciphertext CT.

$\mathsf{Decryption}(\mathsf{PK}, \mathsf{CT}) \to m$: The decryption algorithm takes the private key PK and the ciphertext CT. Finally, it outputs the message m in plain text.

A CP-ABE scheme is correct if a decryption private key on the attribute set S correctly decrypts a given ciphertext of an access structure $\mathbb{A}$ according to the decryption algorithm, when the attribute set S is an authorized set of access structure $\mathbb{A}$.

---

[1] Algorithms of CP-ABE take as input the security parameter κ (unary representation), which represents an input size of the computational problem indicating the complexity of cryptographic algorithms.

3.2 Outsourced Decryption and Collaborative Key Management

A collaborative key management protocol for Ciphertext Policy Attribute-Based Encryption (CKM-CP-ABE) has been introduced by Lin et al. [4] to extend upon CP-ABE. In this model, an actor's private key is split into three key parts: 1) for the key authority (KA), 2) for a re-encryption server (RS), and 3) for the client (CL). Using these key parts, the key authority and re-encryption server can reencrypt and partially decrypt a ciphertext for the client, thereby performing the most expensive calculations. Finally, the client applies her private key part to decrypt the prepared ciphertext, which usually requires less computational effort. Their model also allows for updates of the key material by using attribute group keys, which represent a collection of actors sharing the same attribute. If an attribute has been revoked from an actor, this actor is removed from the respective attribute group. The reencryption algorithm in this concept takes all attribute group keys and a ciphertext as input and updates decryption keys in case of a revocation. Below, we recall the cryptographic definitions from Ziegler et al. [16], which we slightly adapted for readability. We omit the public parameters params $\leftarrow \{\text{params}_{\text{base}}, \text{params}_{\text{KA}}, \text{params}_{\text{RS}}\}$ as input for the algorithms.

Definition 2 (CKM-CP-ABE). Collaborative key management protocol in CP-ABE (CKM-CP-ABE) consists of the following algorithms:

BaseSetup$(1^\kappa, S) \rightarrow$ params$_{\text{base}}$: This algorithm takes a security parameter κ and a an attribute set S as input and outputs the base system parameters params$_{\text{base}}$.

KASetup(params$_{\text{base}}) \rightarrow$ params$_{\text{KA}}$: This algorithm takes the base system parameters and outputs the key authority parameters params$_{\text{KA}}$.

RESetup(params$_{\text{base}}) \rightarrow$ params$_{\text{RS}}$: This algorithm takes the base system parameters as input and outputs the reencryption parameters params$_{\text{RS}}$.

KeyCreation$(S) \rightarrow \text{IK}^{\text{KA}}$: This algorithm takes a client's attribute set S as input and generates the initial key IK^{KA}.

KeyUpdate$(\text{IK}^{\text{KA}}) \rightarrow (\text{PK}^{\text{KA}}, \text{PK}^{\text{RS}}, \text{PK}^{\text{CL}})$: Given the initial key IK^{KA} of a user, this algorithm outputs an updated version of a user's three private key parts for the corresponding actors, $(\text{PK}^{\text{KA}}, \text{PK}^{\text{RS}}, \text{PK}^{\text{CL}})$.

Encryption$(\mathbb{A}, m) \rightarrow \text{CT}^{\text{init}}$: To encrypt a message, this algorithm takes an access structure $\mathbb{A}$ as well as a message m as input. It outputs an initial ciphertext CT^{init}.

ReEncryption$(\text{CT}^{\text{init}}, [\text{Key}_{\text{AG}}]) \rightarrow \text{CT}^{\text{re}}$: This algorithm, given an initial ciphertext CT^{init} and a collection of attribute group keys $[\text{Key}_{\text{AG}}]$, generates a reencrypted ciphertext CT^{re}.

PartialDecryption$(\text{CT}^{\text{re}}, \text{PK}^{\text{KA}}, \text{PK}^{\text{RS}}) \rightarrow \text{CT}^{\text{ulti}}$: Given a reencrypted ciphertext CT^{re} and the private key parts of the key authority PK^{KA} and the reencryption server PK^{RS}, this algorithm partially decrypts CT^{re} and creates a final ciphertext CT^{ulti}.

Decryption$(\text{CT}^{\text{ulti}}, \text{PK}^{\text{CL}}) \rightarrow m$: The decryption algorithm takes the final ciphertext CT^{ulti} and the private key part of the client PK^{CL} as input. This algorithm outputs the plaintext message m.

4   System Model

This section describes the involved actors including their related trust assumptions as well as the data flow of a composite service in our service composition architecture. Based on this trust model, we derive several security objectives, which serve as motivation for our proposed composition architecture and protocol.

4.1   Actors and Data Flow

The system architecture for our service composition system consists of the actors explained in the following paragraphs.

Client. The client represents a device used by a user, who wants to consume a composite service. The client does not need to know anything about actors participating in a composition to define a confidentiality policy. Hence, it is not required to know recipients at message generation time, which enables a highly flexible service composition in the background. Since smartphones must considered at client side, also devices with limited computational power have to be considered. One-time transmissions of data-sets reduce the communication steps for clients in service compositions. Therefore, clients must be able to protect the privacy of their data in a one-to-many communication.

Middleware. The middleware consists of several engines providing the functionality needed to coordinate the service calls and to handle the cryptographic mechanisms (e.g., reencryption and partial decryption of ciphertexts). As the coordination of service requests is performed by the middleware, it acts as a service registry and defines the workflows of composite services. Therefore, the middleware also provides the functionality to register services of service providers in the composition network by collaborating with the key authority. To protect the privacy of the users' data, it must be impossible for the included engines to read any data contents, which are exchanged in a composition. The middleware is semi-trusted and only receives encrypted messages.

Service Provider. Service providers are actors providing one or more services that can be used for service compositions. Each service provider has to perform an initial authentication against the key authority in order to participate in the service composition network. In the course of this authentication, a service provider can apply for a set of desired attributes. On a successful authentication and validation of authorizations, these attributes are assigned to the respective applicant. To guarantee confidentiality in our system model, service providers must not be able to read data contents, which are not intended for them. Additionally, since an initial data set may be altered by any service provider in a process sequence, every actor in a composition must be able to verify which party has modified data. This is necessary to be able to attribute responsibilities to actors regarding the output of a service.

Key Authority. The key authority (KA) is a semi-trusted component and responsible for the creation and update of decryption keys together with the reencryption server and a client. Furthermore, it is also responsible for the registration of new actors who want to participate in the service composition network. However, the type of authentication itself is not in the focus of this work. During registration, every applicant has to generate an asymmetric key-pair needed for signing. After successful registration, the KA issues a certificate for the public key of an applying actor, which is based on a PKI. The KA is authorized to grant or revoke attributes and is allowed to add attributes to the existing attribute universe. Furthermore, the KA must agree on updating a decryption key of any actor and is primarily responsible for key revocation management. In most of the concepts for ABE [3,4,17], the KA requires full trust, as it is able to generate any decryption key on its own and is, therefore, able to decrypt every ciphertext. To ensure the privacy of exchanged data in our system model, the KA must not be able to read any data contents. Thus, the KA must not be able to generate decryption keys on its own. For this purpose, we apply collaborative key management, where the KA cannot create decryption keys alone and is only able to create a decryption key together with a decryption server and a client. This way, full privacy can be ensured against the KA as well, even if this component is compromized by any adversary, which decreases the required trust. Even if the decryption server and the KA collude, they are not able to fully decrypt a ciphertext, as the client must also be included. When creating a decryption key, neither the KA nor the decryption server gets access to the final decryption key, they only contribute to its generation.

4.2   Security Objectives

This section summarizes our security objectives in the following paragraphs based on our system model and the actors' trust assumptions.

Objective 1: End-to-End Confidentiality. Intermediate actors such as the middleware or the key authority in our introduced system model are not sufficiently trusted to read the users' data. Therefore, the first security objective is end-to-end confidentiality between communicating actors.

Objective 2: End-to-End Integrity. In service compositions, the output of one service may serve as input for another service in a sequence. Hence, an (intentionally) incorrect result of a service may affect subsequent service and may cause a critical impact on a user (e.g., prescribed wrong medication). Attackers could try to change the output of a previous service to manipulate the final outcome of a composite service. For this purpose, every actor must be able to verify which data has been modified or added by which actor during a process to ensure end-to-end integrity. Also, this makes it possible to clarify accountabilities.

Objective 3: Fine-Grained Access Control. The actors (e.g., service providers) have different information requirements and are also only trusted to learn different subsets of the data. Therefore, every actor in our system model must only be able to read data contents, which are intended for them. Our system model empowers clients to determine authorizations of actors to read desired message parts. This can be achieved by separating a message into several parts and encrypting them into fine-grained access rules. As clients in our system model do not necessarily need to know the actors of a composite service, it must be possible to encrypt message parts without knowing the specific recipients at message generation time.

Objective 4: Secure One-to-Many Communication. Parts of the same message might be required by multiple service providers. By applying one-to-one encryption to achieve confidentiality, such message parts need to be encrypted multiple times, for different recipients, which leads to a transmission overhead. Thus, our fourth security objective is encryption for one-to-many-communication to reduce the communication overhead by only transmitting an encrypted data-set once, where message parts are protected by individual access controls.

5   Composition Architecture and Protocol

This section describes architectural components and introduces our protocol for service compositions, which demonstrates the interplay between actors and achieves our defined security objectives.

5.1   Components

The middleware consists of the following four components:

Orchestration Engine. The orchestration engine (OE) coordinates the sequence of service requests. Information about available services is collected in a service registry. The OE determines the workflow of a composite service depending on the desired use case. Since this middleware receives all data transmitted by actors of a composite service, these data must be end-to-end encrypted.

Reencryption Server Engine. The reencryption server engine (RSE) reencrypts the ciphertext using the reencryption algorithm introduced in Sect. 3. Besides, the RSE is also needed for the generation of the system parameters and transmits its part of the user's private key to the decryption server engine to enable partial decryption. Since the RSE only receives and outputs ciphertext without learning the plain text intermediately, the privacy of sensitive data is guaranteed.

Decryption Server Engine. The decryption server engine (DSE) provides the functionality to partially decrypt ciphertexts. For the partial decryption, the DSE requires two parts of the user's private key: one part of the key authority and another of the reencryption server engine. It performs the computationally expensive operations of the decryption algorithm and outputs a final ciphertext. This final ciphertext requires less computational effort at client-side. The DSE only receives encrypted information and is not able to fully decrypt a ciphertext.

Service Registration Engine. This Service Registration Engine (SRE) is necessary to provide a registration mechanism for service providers applying to participate in the service composition network. The key authority informs the SRE after successful registration of a service provider about the approved attributes and transmits the issued certificate for the signing key material. The SRE validates the certificate and adds the respective services to the service registry.

5.2   Protocol for Privacy-Preserving Service Composition

This section describes a novel privacy-preserving service composition protocol offering end-to-end confidentiality and integrity. In this protocol, a user initially sends a request to the orchestration engine that forwards this request in sequence to multiple service providers $(SP_1, ..., SP_n)$, which operate on the received data and modify the data for the next actor. This process continues until the service composition is finally completed, and (optionally) a response for the user is generated. Below, we describe the protocol's steps as an iteration from a sender i to a receiver $i + 1$, which becomes the next sender and starts the iteration again.

① The sender i splits the message m_i into multiple message parts $m_{i,j}$, if different requirements regarding the confidentiality for distinct message fields are necessary. The sender encrypts the message parts $m_{i,j}$ for an appropriate attribute set $\mathbb{A}_{i,j}$ which produces a ciphertext $CT^{init}_{i,j} \leftarrow \{\mathsf{Encryption}(\mathbb{A}_{i,j}, m_{i,j}) : \forall j\}$. Next, a session key $SymKey$ is generated for the creation of a HMAC for each message part $HMAC(m_{i,j}, SymKey)$, which are added to the message parts and signed with the private signature key SK_i of the pre-registered key-pair of the sender $\sigma_{i,j} \leftarrow \mathsf{Sign}(\mathsf{SK}_i, m_{i,j}, HMAC_{i,j})\forall j$. The HMAC avoids that the signature of the individual message parts gives any oracle about the plain text, which is especially important if data inputs can only embrace limited values. The sender also encrypts the session key $CT_{SymKey} \leftarrow \{\mathsf{Encryption}(\mathbb{A}, SymKey)\}$. Also, another signature is generated for the whole initial data set $\sigma_{initData} \leftarrow \mathsf{Sign}(\mathsf{SK}_i, m_i)$. CT^{init}_i, CT_{SymKey} and the signatures $\sigma_{initData}$, $\sigma_{i,j}$ are transmitted to the orchestration engine.

② The orchestration engine receives the service request including all parameters and forwards $CT^{init}_{i,j}$ together with information about the next actor $i + 1$ to the reencryption server engine to perform a reencryption of the ciphertext.

③ The reencryption server engine receives the initial ciphertexts $CT^{init}_{i,j}$ and performs the reencryption algorithm. With multiple message parts $m_{i,j}$, this reencryption process is performed for each individual part, resulting in the reencrypted ciphertexts $CT^{re}_{i,j} \leftarrow \{\mathsf{ReEncryption}(CT^{init}_{i,j})\forall j\}$. Next, the reencryption server engine verifies, if the next actor of the composite service is still authorized to possess her attribute set, or if any attribute has been revoked for this actor. In case of revocation, the reencryption server engine updates the corresponding set of attribute group G keys. For reencryption, we used the attribute group-based algorithm of Hur [18]. Thereafter, the reencryption server engine returns the reencrypted ciphertext CT_i^{re} to the orchestration engine.

④ The orchestration engine receives the reencrypted ciphertext CT_i^{re} and forwards it to the decryption server engine.

⑤ The decryption server engine receives the decryption query with CT_i^{re} from the orchestration engine. First, it retrieves two of three private key parts of the receiver, i.e., PK_{i+1}^{KA} and PK_{i+1}^{RS} from the key authority and the reencryption server engine, respectively. With those key parts, the decryption server engine partially decrypts the individual ciphertext parts $CT_{i,j}^{ulti} \leftarrow$ PartialDecryption($CT_{i,j}^{re}, PK_{i+1}^{KA}, PK_{i+1}^{RS}$). The reencryption server engine outputs the final ciphertext CT_i^{ulti}, which is returned to the orchestration engine.

⑥ The orchestration engine forwards the final ciphertext CT_i^{ulti} together with all the received signature values to the next actor according to the process sequence.

⑦ The next actor receives the partially decrypted ciphertext CT_i^{ulti} and applies her private key part PK_i^{CL} to finally decrypt the message parts $m_{i,j} \leftarrow$ Decryption($CT_{i,j}^{ulti}, PK_i^{CL}$). If the user has sufficient attributes, she is able to successfully perform this decryption. Next, she verifies the signature value of each message part Verify($VK_i, \sigma_{i,j}, m_{i,j}$) as well as the signature of the whole message Verify(VK_i, σ_i, m_i). This way, she can verify changes of message parts. Afterwards, she performs her business logic on the plaintext, giving m_{i+1}. This actor may now take on the role of the sender and repeat the process with the next actor, which is coordinated by the orchestration engine. If the actor changes or modifies any data of a message part $m_{i+1,j}$, she has to sign this message part with her pre-registered private signature key SK_{i+1}, giving $\sigma_{i+1,j} \leftarrow$ Sign($SK_{i+1}, m_{i+1,j}$). Furthermore, she also has to generate a signature for the whole data set to enable a verification against integrity for the following actor $\sigma_{i+1} \leftarrow$ Sign(SK_{i+1}, m_i).

6 Evaluation

This section illustrates a case study for a telemedical service, presents a proof-of-concept implementation, evaluates the performance, and discusses various aspects.

6.1 Case Study

To demonstrate the feasibility of our proposed concept, let us assume an example use-case representing a telemedical service that offers an alert system, as shown in Figure 1. This composite service consists of three web services:

Ⓐ The first service validates a heart rate against abnormalities and verifies motion-data to detect unusual movements. If the heart rate is abnormal and the movement is unusual (e.g. patient fell down), it adds a validation result indicating a case of emergency. This service is provided by a health service provider.

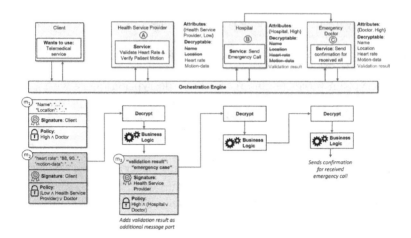

Fig. 1. Use-case of a medical drug prescription service

The second service verifies the validation result and transmits an emergency call including all information to any available doctor in case of emergency. This service is operated by a hospital.

Ⓒ The final service sends a confirmation to the client, when the emergency call has been received. This service is operated by an emergency doctor.

The attribute universe $\mathbb{U}$ for this scenario includes the following attributes: $\mathbb{U} = $ {Low, High, Health Service Provider, Hospital, Doctor}, whereby the attributes 'Low' and 'High' indicate a security level. The initial message transmitted by the client consists of the name, location, heart rate and motion-data of the patient, which are transmitted to the client device by sensors. The data set is split into two message parts and encrypted to different confidentiality policies as given by Fig. 1. Service A extends the initial message by adding the validation result based on the heart rate and motion-data. This services has to ensure authenticity, integrity and confidentiality of the added message field. Thus, this service provider signs the respective data field and encrypts it. In this use-case, any service provider encrypts a received message part to the same access structure, which was required to decrypt it.

6.2   Implementation and Performance

We have implemented the introduced use-case with Java-based web services as well as an Android app. These actors are based on the collaborative key management protocol for CP-ABE introduced by Lin et al. [4]. We have implemented this cryptographic scheme by using the IAIK Java Cryptography Extension (IAIK-JCE)[2] as well as the IAIK ECCelerate elliptic curve library (See footnote 2),

---

[2] https://jce.iaik.tugraz.at.

which provides cryptographic functionality for bilinear pairings. For our evaluation, we choose a security parameter of $\lambda = 256$ bits, providing long-term security according to NIST's recommendation [20].

Table 1. Execution times in milliseconds (ms) ("–" denotes unnecessary operations)

Sender → Receiver	Setup	Key Creation	Message Part	Encryption	ReEncryption	Partial Decryption	Decryption
Client ↓ HSP	26	47	1	18	95	140	–
			2	24	101	102	15
HSP ↓ Hospital			1	–	–	–	14
			2	24	111	106	13
			3	19	104	118	–
Hospital ↓ Doctor			1	18	115	135	15
			2	26	109	116	13
			3	29	106	142	18

Message Format. To encode the messages, we have chosen JSON Web Tokens (JWT). The sender (i.e., user or service provider) first structures the data as JSON documents and then attaches a signature generated with its private signing key. If an actor modifies the payload of a JWT or adds a new message part, it has to sign the token again, which enables to trace who has edited data. Finally, all the JWTs are encrypted to a desired access structure $\mathbb{A}$. The use of JWT allows for lightweight communication, which offers suitable performance for our use case.

Test Setup. The collaborative key management protocol algorithms are performed by three web services running on a Lenovo Thinkpad T460s, which has an Intel i5-6200U dual-core processor and 12 GB RAM. Since we also want to consider smartphones at client-side, we use a HTC U11, which has a Qualcomm Snapdragon 835 quad-core processor with 2.45 GHz each and 4GB RAM.

Performance for Case Study. The smartphone starts the process by initially encrypting the two generated JWT with different symmetric 256-bit AES session-keys. Afterwards, these keys were encrypted to different confidentiality policies as defined in Sect. 6.1. One web service represents the orchestration middleware and takes over the service call coordination and performs the reencryption algorithm. The second web service performs the partial decryption algorithm, which is normally performed by a powerful decryption server. To provide reliable results, we have conducted the test 50 times and used the median of these performance values. Message parts that are not decrypted by an actor do not need to be encrypted, reencrypted or partially decrypted for the next actor in the sequence. These unnecessary operations are denoted as "–" in Table 1. The test results demonstrate that our choice of cryptographic mechanisms provides practically-efficient execution time for service compositions. Especially, the needed execution time for decryption at client-side demonstrates a perfectly suitable approach to be used on devices with limited computational power such as smartphones. The execution time of the partial decryption can be further decreased by using of powerful hardware for the decryption server, rather than our Lenovo Thinkpad T460s.

General Performance of CKM-CP-ABE. According to Ambrosin et al. [19], a reasonable scenario in ABE comprises about 30 attributes, which can lead to highly complex policies. Ziegler et al. [16] performed a comprehensive evaluation of CP-ABE with outsourced decryption. They investigate the execution times for a varying number of attributes as well as the impact of different security levels with security parameters of $\lambda = 80$ bits to $\lambda = 512$ bits. Their results show, that applying CKM-CP-ABE to a service orchestration system enables practical efficiency.

6.3 Discussion

Fine-Grained Access Control. By applying ciphertext-policy attribute-based encryption to our concept, senders are to define fine-grained access controls to message parts. During encryption, the sender specifies a confidentiality policy based on attributes. Only receivers who hold attributes that satisfy this policy are able to decrypt the message parts.

Flexibility. The use of attribute-based encryption enables actors to encrypt data without requiring any specific knowledge about the intended recipients. This improves flexibility regarding the composition in the background, because the service registry can change workflows by simply replacing a service and does not need to inform actors in the service composition system about any alterations.

Reducing Trust Requirements. By employing a collaborative key management protocol, our proposed system avoids a common problem of ABE systems: Even the key authority in our concept is not able to create decryption keys on its own in order to fully decrypt a ciphertext, which ensures privacy against this party and represents a major advantage compared to other ABE systems.

Efficient One-to-Many Encryption. Our concept also supports efficient as well as secure one-to-many communication, as multiple services may hold sufficient attributes to decrypt the same message parts. Such one-to-many communication reduces the communication overhead in comparison to systems that have to encrypt the same message multiple times for different receivers.

Performance. The integration of outsourced decryption in combination with a collaborative key management protocol represents a suitable mechanism to ensure sufficient performance on smartphones. Although we did not perform the partial decryption on a powerful server, the algorithm' execution time was already satisfying and can be further reduced by using more powerful hardware.

7   Conclusion

In this paper, we have introduced an architecture and protocol for efficient, flexible, and privacy-preserving service composition. The proposed concept enables end-to-end encryption and fine-grained access controls in a one-to-many communication by combining ciphertext-policy attribute-based encryption with outsourced decryption and a collaborative key management protocol. Such attribute-based encryption also improves flexibility, as senders do not need to know the final recipients, which allows middlewares to change or replace the services within the process flow on demand. While secure one-to-many communication reduces the transmission overhead, little computational effort is required of clients (e.g., smartphones) as outsourced decryption enables to outsource large parts of the decryption efforts to powerful servers. Additionally, our protocol offers end-to-end integrity for exchanged messages, which allows to trace modifications to the message parts and therefore provides accountability. The feasibility of this concept is highlighted by a proof-of-concept implementation, which demonstrates practical efficiency of the used cryptographic mechanisms.

References

1. Ma, Z., Manglery, J., Wagner, C., Bleier, T.: Enhance data privacy in service compositions through a privacy proxy. In: Sixth International Conference on Availability, Reliability and Security, pp. 615–620 (2011). https://doi.org/10.1109/ARES. 2011.94
2. Singaravelu, L., Pu, C.: Fine-grain, end-to-end security for web service compositions. In: IEEE International Conference on Services Computing (SCC 2007), pp. 212–219 (2007). https://doi.org/10.1109/SCC.2007.61
3. Bethencourt, J., Sahai, A., Waters, B.: Ciphertext-policy attribute-based encryption. In: IEEE Symposium on Security and Privacy (SP 2007), pp. 321–334 (2007). https://doi.org/10.1109/SP.2007.11
4. Lin, G., Hong, H., Sun, Z.: A collaborative key management protocol in ciphertext policy attribute-based encryption for cloud data sharing. IEEE Access **5**, 9464–9475 (2017). https://doi.org/10.1109/ACCESS.2017.2707126
5. Khabou, I., Rouached, M., Abid, M., Bouaziz, R., Enhancing web services compositions with privacy capabilities. In: Proceedings of the 17th International Conference on Information Integration and Web-based Applications & Services, iiWAS 2015, Brussels, Belgium, pp. 57:1–57:9 (2015). https://doi.org/10.1145/2837185. 2837240
6. Khabou, I., Rouached, M., Bouaziz, R., Abid, M.: Towards privacy-aware web services compositions. In: 2016 IEEE International Conference on Computer and Information Technology, CIT 2016, Nadi, Fiji, December 8–10, pp. 367–374 (2016). https://doi.org/10.1109/CIT.2016.26
7. Carminati, B., Ferrari, E., Tran, N.H.: Secure web service composition with untrusted broker. In: IEEE International Conference on Web Services, pp. 137–144 (2014)
8. Organization for the Advancement of Structured Information Standards (OASIS): Extensible Access Control Markup Language (XACML), Identity, v.1.1. (2006)

9. Kaehmer, M., Gilliot, M., Mueller, G.: Automating Privacy Compliance with ExPDT. In: 2008 10th IEEE Conference on E-Commerce Technology and the Fifth IEEE Conference on Enterprise Computing, ECommerce and E-Services, pp. 87–94 (2008). https://doi.org/10.1109/CECandEEE.2008.122

10. Zuo, C., Shao, J., Wei, G., Xie, M., Ji, M.: CCAsecure ABE with outsourced decryption for fog computing. Future Gener. Comput. Syst. **78**, 730–738 (2016). https://doi.org/10.1016/j.future.2016.10.028

11. Wang, Z., Liu, W.: CP-ABE with outsourced decryption and directionally hidden policy. Secur. Commun. Netw. **9**(14), 2387–2396 (2016)

12. Green, M., Hohenberger, S., Waters, B.: Outsourcing the decryption of ABE cipher-texts, pp. 34–34 (2011)

13. Sahai, A., Waters, B.: Fuzzy identity-based encryption. In: Cramer, R. (ed.) EURO-CRYPT 2005. LNCS, vol. 3494, pp. 457–473. Springer, Heidelberg (2005). https://doi.org/10.1007/11426639_27

14. Goyal, V., Pandey, O., Sahai, A., Waters, B.: Attribute-based encryption for fine-grained access control of encrypted data. In: Proceedings of the ACM Conference on Computer and Communications Security, pp. 89–98 (2006). https://doi.org/10.1145/1180405.1180418

15. Rouselakis, Y., Waters, B.: New constructions and proof methods for large universe attribute-based encryption. In: Proceedings of the ACM Conference on Computer and Communications Security, pp. 463–474 (2013). https://doi.org/10.1145/2508859.2516672

16. Ziegler, D., Sabongui, J., Palfinger, G.: Fine-grained access control in industrial Internet of Things. In: Dhillon, G., Karlsson, F., Hedström, K., Zúquete, A. (eds.) SEC 2019. IAICT, vol. 562, pp. 91–104. Springer, Cham (2019). https://doi.org/10.1007/978-3-030-22312-0_7

17. Oualha, N., Nguyen, K.T.: Lightweight attribute-based encryption for the Internet of Things. In: 2016 25th International Conference on Computer Communication and Networks (ICCCN), pp. 1–6 (2016). https://doi.org/10.1109/ICCCN.2016.7568538

18. Hur, J.: Improving security and efficiency in attribute-based data sharing. IEEE Trans. Knowl. Data Eng. **25**, 2271–2282 (2013). https://doi.org/10.1109/TKDE.2011.78

19. Ambrosinet, M., et al.: On the feasibility of attribute-based encryption on Internet of Things Devices. IEEE Micro **36**, 25–35 (2016). https://doi.org/10.1109/MM.2016.101

20. National Institute of Standards & Technology: Recommendation for Key Management, Part 1: General (Rev 4). SP 800-57 (2016)

An Empirical Investigation of the Right to Explanation Under GDPR in Insurance

Jacob Dexe[1,2]($\boxtimes$) (ID), Jonas Ledendal[3] (ID), and Ulrik Franke[1,2] (ID)

[1] RISE Research Institutes of Sweden, 164 29 Kista, Sweden
[2] KTH Royal Institute of Technology, SE-100 44, Stockholm, Sweden
{jacob.dexe,ulrik.franke}@ri.se
[3] Lund University, PO Box 117, 221 00 Lund, Sweden
jonas.ledendal@har.lu.se

Abstract. The GDPR aims at strengthening the rights of data subjects and to build trust in the digital single market. This is manifested by the introduction of a new principle of *transparency*. It is, however, not obvious what this means in practice: What kind of answers can be expected to GDPR requests citing the right to "meaningful information"? This is the question addressed in this article. Seven insurance companies, representing 90–95% of the Swedish home insurance market, were asked by consumers to disclose information about how premiums are set. Results are presented first giving descriptive statistics, then characterizing the pricing information given, and lastly describing the procedural information offered by insurers as part of their answers. Overall, several different approaches to answering the request can be discerned, including different uses of examples, lists, descriptions of logic, legal basis as well as data related to the process of answering the requests. Results are analyzed in light of GDPR requirements. A number of potential improvements are identified—at least three responses are likely to fail the undue delay requirement. The article is concluded with a discussion about future work.

Keywords: GDPR · Trust · Meaningful information · Transparency · Insurance

1 Introduction

The European General Data Protection Regulation (GDPR) gives people the legal ability to delve deeper into automated decision making that involves their own data. Specifically, it grants individuals the right to request "meaningful information about the logic involved" in "automated decision-making" based on their personal data, and data controllers are required to hand this information

This research was partially supported by Länsförsäkringsgruppens Forsknings- & Utvecklingsfond, agreement no. P4/18.

S. Gritzalis et al. (Eds.): TrustBus 2020, LNCS 12395, pp. 125–139, 2020.
https://doi.org/10.1007/978-3-030-58986-8_9

over, measures that help customers ensure that processing is done in a manner that follows the law, and might therefore trust data controllers to a larger extent.

In 2018 the GDPR became applicable in all EU Member States [3]. The new rules, which replaced the EU Data Protection Directive from 1995 [2], aim at increasing transparency and strengthen the rights of data subjects to build trust in the digital single market. This is manifested by the introduction of a new principle of *transparency*, which requires that all processing of personal data should be transparent in relation to the data subject [3, Article 5]. However, such a requirement implicitly already existed under the Directive, since obtaining data secretly and without the data subjects knowledge was considered contrary to the principle of fairness [1, p. 33]. Although, obligations to inform the data subject have become stricter under the Regulation, such obligations also existed under the Directive [2, Articles 10 and 11]. This includes a right to access to personal data that is the main focus of this study [2, Article 12]. The Directive did, however, not explicitly contain any requirement for data controllers to explain the logic behind automated decision-making. This may be an important development going forward.

Because there are (legitimate) limitations to what companies can disclose, it is not apparent what this right means in practice. First, there is an ongoing discussion about how to properly interpret the GDPR requirements; a debate that also will, in due time, be informed by court decisions. Second, there is a more practical empirical question of what the practice actually looks like: What kind of answers can be expected to GDPR requests citing the right to "meaningful information"? It is this second question that is addressed in this article. More precisely, the following research questions are investigated:

RQ1. What do insurance companies disclose when consumers ask about the logic behind automated decisions?
RQ2. How does the practice of answering such queries align with requirements proscribed by the GDPR?

These RQs were investigated by making actual consumer requests to 7 insurers, collectively covering some 90–95% of the market for home insurance in Sweden.

The GDPR applies to all industries, but the insurance industry offers a particularly interesting case study. First, insurance industry professionals often claim that they are in the business of trust: since their product is intangible and delivered only in the future, successful customer relations critically depend on earning consumer trust that pricing is fair, losses will be adjusted, and indemnities paid. To earn and keep this trust, the insurance industry thus has every incentive to be forthcoming in explaining to customers how data processing is done, what it means for the costumer and what the rights of the customer are in any given case—a need to be transparency in order for consumers to be able to judge if the companies are being just and fair [20]. Second, about 40% of Swedes trust how insurance companies handle digital personal information [6]. While this is not a majority, it was the third highest number in the poll, second only to banks

(68%) and the public sector (46%). This suggests that the insurance industry could be a role model for less trusted industries.

The GDPR also applies across the EU, Norway, Iceland and Lichtenstein. However, there are reasons why Sweden is an interesting case study. Sweden regularly scores high in international country rankings on digitalization. For example, it was ranked second in the EU Digital Economy & Society Index (DESI) 2019 [8] and "among the leading countries in the diffusion and use of digital technologies" according to an OECD Review of Digital Transformation from 2018 [16]. Thus, it can be expected that Swedish companies in general are in the upper cohorts when it comes to digital maturity and, reasonably, also when it comes to managing GDPR requests.

It is important to note that the only explicit claim as to whether the replies comply with the GDPR is made regarding the time limits in Article 13(3). As for complience in other areas we present what information the answers given contain, and some estimate of the validity of that information. As described in Sect. 3, the purpose of giving "meaningful information" is to give a data subject the ability to judge whether any processing is in line with the legislation. Making the legal analysis to be able to judge if such requirements are met is outside of the scope of the answers we collected in this article. There could be other ways to asses whether the information is indeed meaningful. Some proposals to be able to do this are presented in Sect. 7.

The rest of this article is structured as follows. Section 2 discusses related work, putting the contribution into context. Section 3 gives a legal background on the right to explanation in the GDPR. Section 4 explains the method used, before Sect. 5 summarizes the results. These results are further analyzed in Sect. 6, before Sect. 7 concludes the paper.

2   Related Work

The GDPR is relatively new and since legal scholarship tends to study the law as it is (*de lege lata*), e.g. once legislation has been adopted or case law has developed, it is not surprising that the legal literature concerning the new data protection regulation is still rather sparse. Temme is one of few legal scholars that focus on the new so-called "right to explanation" in the GDPR [19]. The study finds that despite being highly complex, algorithms can be made more transparent when efforts are made to better address transparency requirements. However, the study also criticizes the regulation for insufficiently addressing challenges to render algorithms more transparent. It finds that it only directly addresses two key issues, that is, algorithmic illiteracy and trade secrecy. Temme also casts doubt on the legal basis of the right, and pointing out that even if it were legally binding, restrictions and carve-outs render its scope very limited.

The transparency requirements in the legislation are not meant to be valuable in and of themselves. As also remarked in Sect. 3, the goal of transparency in the GDPR is to be able to evaluate whether the processing is reasonable and lawful, not just to get access to the information. A similar sentiment is described by Turilli & Floridi when arguing that transparency is not an ethical principle but rather a pro-ethical condition in that transparency can enable ethical principles that necessitate information, such as accountability, informed consent and safety [20]. Furthermore, transparency can enable ethical principles by regulating information—promoting privacy, anonymity and freedom of expression by informing about the rules of the game.

Wauters et al. tackle the necessity of improving users understanding of terms and conditions by means of transparency, taking into account that human rationality is not only limited by what information we have access too, but also how much we can process [22]. Wauters et al. propose that companies adopt visualization techniques such as labelling, multi-layered policies and presenting information in its proper context. Similarly, Rossi & Palmirani investigate the use of icons to properly visualize data protection [17].

The requirements in GDPR Article 15, i.e., how to inform about use of data that has already taken place, could also be described as ex-post transparency. Fischer-Hübner et al. (2016) develop and test TETs (Transparency Enhancing Tools) that help users understand ex-post information [10], more of which can be found in the co-authors PhD dissertation where the article is also included [12]. How to implement good ex-post transparency is complicated by a paradox stating that the users most interested in transparency are also the users least likely to want to share information in the first place, as described and investigated by Awad & Krishnan, who also note that while privacy policies are rated as important by consumers, they are rarely read and thus effort has to be made elsewhere to increase trust in the service [5].

Concerning rights to explanations, Wachter et al. claim a right to explanation does not exist [21], and should be talked about as a right to be informed, while Edwards & Veale opt for a right to better decisions [7]—and Selbst & Powers advocate a return to "meaningful information about the logic involved" as stated in the GDPR text [18]. Kaminski gives an overview of the right to explanation in an American context [11].

To conclude, there is much conceptual discussion about the GDPR right to meaningful information, but little empirical evidence published in the literature. Thus, this article makes a novel contribution by its empirical investigation of the Swedish insurance market.

3   Legal Background

The Data Protection Directive of 1995, as mentioned above, did not contain any right to explanation. The GDPR introduces such a requirement as part of the data controller's obligation to inform the data subject about processing of his or her personal data. Pursuant to the new stricter rules the controller is obligated to inform the data subject about the existence of automated-decision making, including profiling, which produces legal effects concerning him or her or similarly significantly affects him or her. The requirement only applies when decisions are made based solely on automated processing. In those cases, the controller must also give a meaningful explanation about the logic involved, as well as the significance and the envisaged consequences of such processing for the data subject. This information shall be provided without request before the data is collected [3, Article 13] or when it is received from a third party [3, Article 14]. Such information should be easily accessible and can, for example, be included in the controller's privacy policy that is made available on the organization's web site [3, Article 12]. It shall also be provided on the request of the data subject, as part of his or her right to access [3, Article 15].

The Article 29 Working Party has adopted guidelines on how to apply and interpret the obligations of transparency in the GDPR, including the requirement to explain the logic behind automated decision-making [4]. These guidelines have been endorsed by the European Data Protection Board (EDPB), which have succeeded the Working Party [9]. The guidelines are not binding, but are nevertheless an important tool for the interpretation of EU data protection law, considering that the Board consists of the heads of the data protection supervisory authorities of each Member State as well as Norway, Iceland and Lichtenstein, and the European Data Protection Supervisor. At least in the absence of case law from the Court of Justice of the European Union (CJEU), such guidelines adopted by the Board by its authority to ensure the consistent application of the GDPR, cannot be ignored as a source of law.

The guidelines recommend that rather than providing a complex explanation of how algorithms or machine-learning work, the controller should consider using clear and comprehensive ways to deliver the information to the data subject [4, p. 31]). For example, the categories of data that have been or will be used in the profiling or decision-making process, the reason why these categories are considered pertinent, how a profile used in the process is constructed, including any statistics used in the analysis, and also how it is used for a decision concerning the data subject. The guidelines also recommend visualization and interactive techniques to aid algorithmic transparency. The controller should also, as part of the right to access, consider implementing a mechanism that allows data subjects to easily inspect their profile, including details of the information and sources used to develop it. The controller is, however, normally not required to disclose the full algorithm [4, p. 25]). When it adversely affects its rights, e.g. intellectual property or trade secrets, the controller can even refuse to give access to certain personal data [3, Article 15]. This can, however, never result in a complete denial of access to someone's personal data [3, Recital 63].

The principle of transparency and the right to information is not an end in itself, it is a means to ensure that the data subject can verify the lawfulness of the processing, and exercise control over his or her personal data by requesting rectification, erasure or object to further processing [3, Recital 63]. Hence, a correct implementation of the right to a meaningful explanation of the logic behind automated decision-making should primarily aid the data subject to determine whether the processing complies with the GDPR, especially whether the processing complies with the prohibition on automatic individual decision-making in Article 22 of the Regulation [3]. Unless the information given enables the data

subject to verify such compliance, which is designed to protect his or her fundamental rights, the information is insufficient and does not fully comply with the
GDPR.

4   Method

Following the inception of the idea, the first step was to phrase the request for
information. It was decided to keep it relatively short and to the point. The
request, translated from Swedish, is shown in Fig. 1.

```
Hi!

In accordance with article 15, section 1h, of the
General Data Protection Regulation 2016/679 I would like
information on how the premium of my home insurance is
determined. This article in the regulation should be
applicable if pricing (i) is automated and (ii) is based
on personal data (both collected from me and collected by
other means).

I would be pleased to receive this information in
suitable form (e.g., mathematical formulae or descriptive
text) that meets the requirements of the regulation
on meaningful information about the logic involved in
automated decision-making. Thanks a lot for your help!

Best regards etc.
```

Fig. 1. The request for pricing information made to the insurers (translation from
Swedish).

Home insurance was chosen for several reasons: (i) it is offered by several
different market actors so a reasonable number of separate answers could be
expected, (ii) it is a relatively straightforward form of insurance which is comparable across companies, (iii) it is a form of insurance that is nearly ubiquitous,
facilitating recruitment of volunteers, and (iv) it is not based on sensitive data
such as health conditions, again facilitating recruitment of volunteers willing to
share the answers.

The next step was to recruit volunteers, aside from the authors, to make
this request to insurance companies. In order to ascertain properly informed
consent, the volunteers approached were mostly colleagues (and in one case an
outside contact well versed in research methods), who could be expected to fully
understand the implications of participation in a research study. The recruitment of volunteers continued until a sufficient coverage of the Swedish home
insurance market in terms of market share was reached. Only a single customer

per insurance company was recruited. The reason for this was that the authors expected that the question posed would be fairly novel to each insurance company, and multiple identical questions to the same insurance company would perhaps arouse suspicion and less realistic responses.

The requests were made during the period from December 2018 to March 2019, meaning that the GDPR had been in effect for at least six months at the time of the request. While the question asked by the participants was standardized (Fig. 1), the means to contact each insurance company, naturally, were company-specific. Thus, questions were asked in online forms, by email to customer support, by email to DPOs, in chats or whatever else proved appropriate.

Once answers were obtained (via physical mail, e-mail, or chat), they were handed over to the authors for analysis.

In order to answer the question of whether the information provided constitute "meaningful explanation" and was provided in accordance with the GDPR, the empirical material has to be assessed using a legal standard. The relevant standard in this case is the Regulation as interpreted by other legal sources, such as the case law of the Court of Justice of the European Union and guidelines adopted by the Article 29 Working Party (now replaced by the European Data Protection Board).

5   Results

In the following, results are disclosed in three subsections, first giving some descriptive statistics, then characterizing the pricing information given, and lastly describing the procedural information offered by insurers as part of their answers.

5.1   Descriptive Statistics

Responses from 7 insurers with different sizes and profiles were received, covering a market share of some 90–95% of Swedish home insurance.[1] In the following, the 7 insurance companies are anonymously denoted C1–C7.

As illustrated in Fig. 2, there were relatively large variabilities in both the times elapsed from request to response (from 2 h to circa 2 months) and the length of the replies (from about 50 words to 600 words). Neither time nor

---

[1] These figures are based on the official market statistics of Q4 2018 from Insurance Sweden (https://www.svenskforsakring.se/globalassets/statistik/importerad-statistik/statbranch/branschstatistik/2018/branschstatistik-q4-2018.pdf).   Some uncertainty is introduced by the fact that only the 4 largest respondents are separately accounted for in the statistics, while the 3 smaller ones are lumped together in the 'Other' category. Furthermore, the statistics differentiate the markets for apartments (where the 4 large respondents had a 94.0% market share between them) and houses (where the 4 large respondents had a 90.3% market share between them).

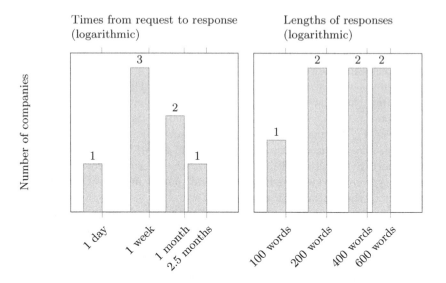

Fig. 2. Histograms with characteristics of responses received.

length, however, bear any obvious relation to the quality or contents of the reply.

The times depicted in the histogram are approximate. While exact times can be inferred for some answers, others are estimates as, e.g., the question was posed in a contact form on a website without acknowledged receipt, or the answer was delivered by physical mail. We have also not accounted for the difference between working days and holidays (including a Christmas break, in one case).

2 companies answered via physical mail, 4 via e-mail and 1 in a chat. Some linked to their websites for additional information, others copied information from the website into the response. In particular, two companies quoted text from such public information as a significant part of the answer. One (C4) is included in the word-count shown in Fig. 2, as it was written in an e-mail reply and was explicitly claimed to be curated by a selection of appropriate paragraphs. The other (C6) is not included in the word-count, as it was presented as a non-curated attachment to the main answer given.

In addition to the pricing information requested (detailed in Sect. 5.2), 4 companies also described their own process of answering the request (detailed in Sect. 5.3), including who was responsible and who was contacted.

One distinction between the cases is that C1, C3, and C7 cover insurance for apartments while C2, C4, C5, and C6 deal with house insurance.

5.2 Pricing Information

An overview of the pricing information obtained is given in Table 1.

As for the data directly related to pricing for home insurance, 6 included address, 5 included age of the policyholder, 4 included family status (which

Table 1. Overview of pricing information obtained, by company. X denotes that the type of data was mentioned; L that the type of data and the logic of its use was mentioned. Real estate data is only applicable to house insurance.

	C1	C2	C3	C4	C5	C6	C7
Living area (m^2)	X	X				X	
Family status (e.g., number of people)	X	X		X			X
Address	X	L	L	X	X		X
Real estate data		X		X		X	
Age	X	L	L		X		X
Deductible		X					
Indemnity limit		X					
Income and financial data		X		X			
Security measures (e.g., locks)		X		X			
Age of policy (loyalty)		L					X
Claims history		X		X			X

determines the number of people covered by the insurance), 3 companies included living area, 3 included real estate data such as general information about the building, 3 included claims history, 2 mentioned the age of the insurance policy (the time the policy-holder has been insured being a measure of loyalty), 2 mentioned income and other tax information, 2 mentioned security measures such as security doors and locks, and 1 mentioned deductible and indemnity limit. The latter in particular is quite noteworthy, as it is hard to imagine a premium for any insurance being calculated without taking deductibles and indemnity limits into account (for an introduction to insurance pricing, see, e.g., [23]).

Additionally, companies C2 and C3 made efforts to explain more in detail how a specific type of information might affect the price of the insurance. Such explanations of the logic behind data use are denoted by L in Table 1. This might be seen as a higher level of ambition in making the information meaningful (as required by the GDPR). An example is the following (translated): "We also use the insurance objects' address to see where it is located, since this affects your premium and we use the historic claims data for people in the same geographic area as you to set the price of the insurance" (from C3). While not disclosing any sensitive details, this response does contain an explanation of the logic behind using the specific type of data.

Overall, several different approaches to answering the request can be discerned. Some companies try to give an *exhaustive* list of all criteria that the pricing takes into account, while others give *a few examples* of the types of data. Some companies offer a *general explanation* of the logic behind either the algorithm or the insurance itself, some offer *specific examples* of how certain categories of data affect the algorithm, while others give *no information at all* about the logic behind the algorithm.

5.3   Procedural Information

An overview of the procedural information obtained is given in Table 2.

Table 2. Overview of procedural information obtained, by company.

	C1	C2	C3	C4	C5	C6	C7
Process description		X		X	X	X	
Fairness		X	X				X
Legal basis						X	
General logic						X	X
Contact details				X	X	X	X
Information on other customers		X					X
Business confidentiality						X	X
Visualization							
How a profile is created		X				X	

4 companies mentioned their internal process of answering the request—who was responsible, who was contacted and how the answer was written. 4 explicitly mentioned how to contact them again in case of further questions. 2 companies referred to business confidentiality but still described the logic in general terms. 2 included references to fair practices, 2 described how risk profiles are created, and 2 mentioned information about other customers, 1 mentioned what legal basis they have for processing that information. No company included any visualization or illustration in order to increase understanding.

A single company (C1) offered no procedural information what so ever. Only 3 provided more than two pieces of procedural information.

Aside from the logic applied to specific types of data, two companies explained the logic behind insurance in general. For instance; "Not all people get into accidents, but if an accident occurs it can be costly if one pays for everything oneself. When a collective carries the risk, the cost for each individual in the collective gets lowered." (from C7) is an example of such an explanation.

It is also noteworthy that whereas some companies offer a legal explanation for why they do not disclose all information, others simply do not disclose certain information. Contrary to intuition, the companies citing business confidentiality as a reason for not disclosing certain information were not the least forthcoming overall. Instead, the least forthcoming did not offer any (legal) explanations at all for their non-disclosures.

6   Discussion

6.1   Validity and Reliability

Overall, the validity of the study is very good: Real insurers were approached by real customers with real requests for information as mandated by the GDPR.

(It is instructive to contrast this with less valid hypotheticals, such as (i) researchers approaching insurers *qua* researchers, asking how requests would be answered if made by customers, (ii) researchers approaching an industry group such as Insurance Sweden asking how requests would be answered if made by customers, or (iii) researchers with access to pricing algorithms making a legal assessment of how an answer would probably look). In short, precisely the object of study was studied.

Reliability is strengthened by the careful selection of volunteers who were customers of insurance companies with a large market share between themselves. If additional requests were to be made, drawn at random from the population of Swedish home insurance policies written, there is a chance of some 90–95% that the corresponding companies are already included in the study. From this perspective, it is reasonable to believe that overall conclusions from a replicated study would not turn out significantly different. It is also probable that several identically worded queries to any company within a short time-frame would arouse suspicion from the person assigned to answer the request, and skew the responses in some way.

However, this logic is to some extent challenged by a discovery made only in the data analysis phase: Two requests made, to two different companies (C2 and C7), were answered by the same insurance clerk, but the answers were quite different (as can be summarily seen in Tables 1 and 2). As it turned out, one of the companies was a subsidiary of the other, and they shared certain functions, such as customer complaints handling. Now, the differences observed can have several possible explanations, e.g., (i) *systematic actual differences* in the products offered under the two different brands, (ii) *systematic marketing differences* that somewhat exaggerate the differences of products offered under the two brands, or (iii) *random* differences between the answers. Whereas explanations (i) and (ii) do not particularly threaten reliability, explanation (iii), if true, would call the study design into question, as several requests per company would be needed to fully appreciate and distinguish the variability *within* companies from the variability *between* companies. As stated above, such an approach would entail validity and reliability risks of its own; specifically the observer effect caused by companies identifying numerous identically worded requests and adapting their behavior accordingly.

There is also a temporal aspect of reliability: that there is a learning curve in answering requests from consumers, so that answers might improve over time. Despite the relatively short time between the data collection and writing this article, several of the companies have updated the information on websites and might give different answers today. The study still has high reliability in that the data collection shows a snapshot of the companies at the time of investigation, but a longitudinal study could probably map an evolution over time.

6.2 Alignment with GDPR

Do the answers fulfill the rights granted to customers under GDPR?

The requirements on transparency in the GDPR are that, among other things, the information given to the consumer ought to be meaningful regarding the logic involved in an automated decision. Reaching the requirement "meaningful" ought to mean that there should be some effort to present the information pedagogically, and to provide some information about how or why information is used, rather than simply stating what categories of data exist. However, judging whether the legal requirements of "meaningful information" are fulfilled requires a lot more information about the contracts signed and the real functionality of the pricing algorithms used by the insurance companies. As such, what we present here is only an analysis of the information contained in the answers and a rough estimate of whether the information is indeed meaningful.

Among the answers received in the study, three out of seven have not provided any information about the logic involved regarding the type of insurance (although one copied information from their website where some motivation was given for insurance in general). Out of the other four, C7 describes the logic of insurance in general, after having stated what information is processed in the specific insurance. They have not explained what the logic of the specific algorithm for home insurance is, although it could be said that it is implied. C6 gives an explanation of the logic of building risk categories, but it is also just implied that this is (also) the logic of the home insurance algorithm to be explained. C2 and C3 both provide explanations of how data is used in the algorithm and how that might affect its outcome.

The GDPR does not only regulate the content of the answer to a request for access to personal data. It also specifies some of the modalities for the exercise of the rights of the data subject. These procedural rules specify some time limits on the processing of such requests. The right of access in Article 15 of the Regulation [3], unlike the provisions on some other rights, does not stipulate any specific time limit. Hence, such requests fall under the Regulation's general provisions on time limits in Article 12(3) [3], which stipulates that information on action taken on a request shall be provided to the data subject without undue delay and in any event within one month of receipt of the request. That period may be extended by two further months where necessary, taking into account the complexity and number of the requests. The controller shall then also inform the data subject about the extension within one month of receipt of the request, together with the reasons for the delay. It is clear that none of the replies included in the study exceeded this outer time limit of three months, but given the content of the answers it is doubtful whether the 3 requests that took more than one week were handled without "undue delay". Routine requests should usually be handled within one or two days to comply with this legal standard.

6.3 Generalization to Other Contexts

It is natural to reflect on whether the results presented can be generalized to other contexts, such as other countries or other industries. Clearly, any such generalization should proceed with caution. Still, at least some hypotheses could be formulated:

1. First, comparing industries, answers from the insurance industry are probably among the more forthcoming and legally vetted. One reason for this hypothesis is that insurance is a relatively old industry that has been subject to regulation for a long time, so companies have compliance departments staffed with lawyers since well before the GDPR came into effect. Another reason for this hypothesis is that though the details of insurance pricing are confidential, it is well known that personal data is used to set premiums. Thus, there is less incentive to obscure data processing in insurance compared to industries where public understanding and acceptance of such data processing are smaller.

2. Second, comparing countries, Swedish answers are possibly more forthcoming than answers from other EU countries. One reason for this hypothesis is that Sweden has a long tradition of government transparency including the world's oldest freedom of information law [13,14]. It is not unreasonable to interpret this as a sign of an openness culture permeating not only the public sector, but also companies in the private sector. At least, the stark difference between the Swedish culture of open government and the comparably much less forthcoming government cultures of most other EU countries [15] should be taken into account in any attempt at generalization.

Of course, these hypotheses are only starting points which need further empirical investigation before they can be considered confirmed findings.

7   Conclusion and Future Work

While the cases studied in this article are relevant and we believe the validity is high, it only covers a small section of the consumer market, and a small section of the European insurance market. The results show that there are considerable differences between answers given in respect to both pricing data and procedural data.

The results shows that no company exceeded the upper three month time limit required by the GDPR, but since the nature of the requested information as well as the content of the replies gives no indication that for example the complexity of the request could justify an extension pursuant to Article 12(3) of the GDPR, at least one request did not live up to the Regulation in this respect. Since, in this particular case, the company also failed to notify the data subject about the reasons for the delay within the one-month period stipulated by the GDPR, the handling of this request clearly does not comply with data protection law. However, even though all other requests were handled within the one-month time limit, it is unlikely that two of those cases, taking up to a month, complies with the requirement to reply "without undue delay". Although its meaning has yet to be interpreted by the CJEU, its usual meaning in law indicates that the matter should be dealt with urgently and that any delay that exceeds a few working days must be justified. Since there is no indication that the nature of the request or other circumstances justified a one-month delay, it is likely that at least those two replies also did not live up to the GDPR.

For future work we invite other researchers to conduct similar experiments in their respective markets (preferably in insurance, for the sake of comparability). Once such data has been collected, we are interested in following up this study to obtain a more mature picture of what the GDPR right to meaningful information means in practice.

In order to judge whether the information presented was indeed meaningful, one option would be to conduct more through legal analysis of the products involved. Another option would be to do user studies on how much they comprehend from the answers, whether the answers increase trust in the products and if they find the information plausible. Such a study does not necessarily have to be done on the volunteers that sent in answers, but can instead be given to a randomly recruited group of people, seeing as how home insurances are a ubiquitous product.

Other potential future work includes following up the answers received in this study by eliciting further comments from the respondents—to be able to get a fuller picture of what data is used in the algorithms and why. The study could also be expanded longitudinally. A third option is to explore other industries.

References

1. Commission of the European Communities Communication on the protection of individuals in relation to the processing of personal data in the Community and information security. COM(90) p. 314 final
2. Directive 95/46/EC of the European Parliament and of the Council of 24 October 1995 on the protection of individuals with regard to the processing of personal data and on the free movement of such data. Official J. Eur. Communities (OJ), L 281, 23.11.1995, pp. 31–50 (1995)
3. Regulation (EU) 2016/679 of the European Parliament and of the Council of 27 April 2016 on the protection of natural persons with regard to the processing of personal data and on the free movement of such data, and repealing Directive 95/46/EC (General Data Protection Regulation). Official J. Eur. Union (OJ) L 119, 4.5. pp. 1–88. (2016). http://data.europa.eu/eli/reg/2016/679/oj
4. Article 29 data protection working party: guidelines on automated individual decision-making and Profiling for the purposes of Regulation 2016/679. WP251, adopted on 6 February 2018
5. Awad, N.F., Krishnan, M.S.: The personalization privacy paradox: an empirical evaluation of information transparency and the willingness to be profiled online for personalization. MIS Q. **30**(1), 13–28 (2006). https://doi.org/10.2307/25148715
6. Delade meningar 2018 [Shared opinions 2018]. Technical report insight intelligence (2018). https://www.insightintelligence.se/delade-meningar/delade-meningar-2018
7. Edwards, L., Veale, M.: Enslaving the algorithm: from a "right to an explanation" to a "right to better decisions" ? IEEE Secur. Priv. **16**(3), 46–54 (2018)
8. European Commission: The Digital Economy & Society Index (DESI) (2019). https://ec.europa.eu/digital-single-market/en/desi. Accessed 14 Jan 2019

 9. European Data Protection Board: Endorsement 1/2018 on the Article 29 Working Party guidelines on the GDPR. adopted 25 May 2018
10. Fischer-Hübner, S., Angulo, J., Karegar, F., Pulls, T.: Transparency, privacy and trust - technology for tracking and controlling my data disclosures: does this work? In: Habib, S.M., Vassileva, J., Mauw, S., Mühlhäuser, M. (eds.) Trust Manage. X, pp. 3–14. Springer International Publishing, Cham (2016). https://doi.org/10. 1007/978-3-319-41354-9_1
11. Kaminski, M.E.: The right to explanation, explained. Berkeley Technol. Law J. **34**, 189 (2019)
12. Karegar, F.: Towards improving transparency, intervenability, and consent in HCI (2018), the 3. article was in manuscript form at the time of the licentiate defense: Karegar, F. /User Evaluations of an App Interface for Cloud-based Identity Management // Manuskript (preprint)
13. Kassen, M.: Understanding transparency of government from a Nordic perspective: open government and open data movement as a multidimensional collaborative phenomenon in Sweden. J. Global Inf. Technol. Manage. **20**(4), 236–275 (2017). https://doi.org/10.1080/1097198X.2017.1388696
14. Nord, L.W.: Investigative journalism in Sweden: a not so noticeable noble art. Journalism **8**(5), 517–521 (2007). https://doi.org/10.1177/1464884907081045
15. Öberg, U.: EU citizens' right to know: the improbable adoption of a European freedom of information act. Cambridge Yearb. Eur. Legal Stud. **2**, 303–328 (1999). https://doi.org/10.5235/152888712802815897
16. OECD: OECD reviews of digital transformation: going digital in Sweden (2018). https://doi.org/10.1787/9789264302259-en
17. Rossi, A., Palmirani, M.: A visualization approach for adaptive consent in the european data protection framework. In: 2017 Conference for E-Democracy and Open Government (CeDEM), pp. 159–170, May 2017. https://doi.org/10.1109/ CeDEM.2017.23
18. Selbst, A.D., Powles, J.: Meaningful information and the right to explanation. Int. Data Priv. Law **7**(4), 233–242 (2017)
19. Temme, M.: Algorithms and transparency in view of the new general data protection regulation. Eur. Data Prot. Law. Rev. **3**, 473 (2017)
20. Turilli, M., Floridi, L.: The ethics of information transparency. Ethics Inf. Technol. **11**(2), 105–112 (2009)
21. Wachter, S., Mittelstadt, B., Floridi, L.: Why a right to explanation of automated decision-making does not exist in the general data protection regulation. Int. Data Priv. Law **7**(2), 76–99 (2017)
22. Wauters, E., Donoso, V., Lievens, E.: Optimizing transparency for users in social networking sites. Info **16**(6), 8–23 (2014). https://doi.org/10.1108/info-06-2014-0026
23. Zweifel, P., Eisen, R.: Insurance Economics. Springer, Heidelberg (2012). https:// doi.org/10.1007/978-3-642-20548-4

Measuring Users' Socio-contextual Attributes for Self-adaptive Privacy Within Cloud-Computing Environments

Angeliki Kitsiou[1]([⊠]), Eleni Tzortzaki[2], Christos Kalloniatis[1], and Stefanos Gritzalis[3]

[1] Privacy Engineering and Social Informatics Laboratory, Department of Cultural Technology and Communication, University of the Aegean, 81100 Lesvos, GR, Greece
{a.kitsiou,chkallon}@aegean.gr
[2] Information and Communication Systems Security Laboratory, Department of Information and Communication Systems Engineering, University of the Aegean, 83200 Samos, GR, Greece
etzortzaki@aegean.gr
[3] Laboratory of Systems Security, Department of Digital Systems, University of Piraeus, 18532 Piraeus, GR, Greece
sgritz@unipi.gr

Abstract. The examination of users' socio-contextual attributes and their impact on their privacy management is of great importance in order for self-adaptive privacy preserving schemes to be effectively designed within cloud computing environments. However, several ambitious adaptive privacy schemes, presented in previous literature, seem to fail to examine those attributes in depth. To address that, this paper proposes the development of an interdisciplinary measurement scale, embodying validated metrics from both privacy and sociological literature. The scale provides the thoroughly identification of users' social landscape interrelated with their privacy behaviours and its utilization is expected to lay the ground for the developers to meet efficiently both users' social requirements and systems' technical ones, before performing adaptive privacy mechanisms in cloud.

Keywords: Self-adaptive privacy · Social identity · Social capital · Measurement scale · Privacy metrics · Privacy management

1 Introduction

The dominant utilization of cloud computing poses new challenges for both providers and consumers, especially as far as privacy protection is concerned [1]. Despite the fact that several privacy models and data encryption technologies have been used to preserve privacy in the cloud, these - regardless of the selected deployment model - do not support perplexed computing [1, 2]. Due to the several stakeholders' involvement and interactions [3], the personal information gathered, analyzed and distributed is rapidly increasing, making privacy protection hard to be achieved [4]. Furthermore, although cloud providers specify and provide a variety of privacy policies, there is no guarantee that they employ these policies efficiently, while in many cases, it is difficult for users to

© Springer Nature Switzerland AG 2020
S. Gritzalis et al. (Eds.): TrustBus 2020, LNCS 12395, pp. 140–155, 2020.
https://doi.org/10.1007/978-3-030-58986-8_10

implement them by themselves. Either they often do not realize the implications of their privacy settings choices, e.g. within Facebook, or sometimes they voluntarily disclose personal information, since they value more the perceived benefits than the risks deriving from this procedure [5]. Up to this point, it had been acknowledged that privacy policies and technical measures cannot safeguard privacy, when ignoring users' social norms, since privacy is a normative concept, reflecting not only technical, but also social, legal and political notions [6]. Consequently, in parallel with cloud computing evolvement, privacy concept and respective frameworks are also shifting, outlined by several different terms and methodologies, e.g. networked privacy, on line privacy, intellectual privacy, informational privacy, decisional privacy, social privacy, institutional privacy, privacy in context, social network privacy [7–10]. Thus, besides their differences, it is important to note that a large body among them acknowledges that users' socio-technical context, characteristics and relationships are important for privacy examination and protection [11], indicating that privacy is defined multi-dimensionally, both individually and collectively [7]. This contextualized nature of privacy brings it to the forefront the need for a new customized design of privacy preservation schemes within cloud, in a more adaptive way, so as for the respective systems to be usable and to mitigate privacy risks [3, 4, 12]. Towards this, self-adaptive privacy schemes and mechanisms are introduced, aiming to provide integrated user-centric models, based on users' social and technological context [13]. Since cloud providers offer more personalized and context-aware services, there is a growing need to further understand users' socio-contextual factors that influence their privacy management and to redefine the interaction among them and the privacy aware systems [4]. Despite the fact that several ambitious adaptive privacy schemes presented in previous literature *(see Sect. 2)* consider users social attributes and context, these seem to fail to examine them in depth. However, in order for the self-adaptive privacy aware systems to be optimally developed, it is essential to take into account empirical data related to users' socio-contextual attributes within their interacting frameworks in and out of information systems [14]. Gaining more input from users [15] is critical for the provided services, so as to face the question of how they will be protected in an adaptive way, when using personal and context-aware services [4], and how to meet efficiently both users' social requirements [16] and systems' technical ones before performing adaptive privacy mechanisms. Consequently, the manner of adequately capturing these attributes is of major importance.

In order to address that, this paper proposes the development of an interdisciplinary measurement scale, embodying constructs and validated metrics from both privacy and sociological literature, aiming to identify in depth and to categorize users' socio-contextual attributes in order that they are introduced into self-adaptive privacy behavioural research models within cloud. The rest of the paper is organized as follows. Section 2 presents self-adaptive privacy preserving schemes, introduced in previous literature. Section 3 analyzes the need to focus on users' socio-contextual attributes, based on social identity and capital constructs, since these have been indicated to impact on users' privacy management and reflect efficiently users' social landscape. Section 4, after analyzing previous privacy validated measures, presents the constructs and metrics that our scale includes. Finally, Sect. 5 concludes our work.

2 Self-adaptive Privacy Preserving Schemes

Users' privacy safeguards within several applications are not adequately underpinned due to static privacy settings that do not fulfill their complex privacy needs in different situations and contexts [6]. Up to this, the necessity for the deployment of dynamic self-adaptation privacy processes is indicated, as a more proper way to support users' needs during their interactions within the systems [17]. To achieve that, according to [14], classified interaction strategies should be applied, which facilitate the connection among users and systems during three stages: a) privacy awareness, b) justification & privacy decision, c) control capabilities. In these stages, the inclusion of users' cognitive processes is crucial, so that preferences can be expressed and privacy settings employed in an adjusting way. Additionally, [18] supports that systems should enable users to select the information disclosure level, by providing the context and the control level over this information, indicating four operations to be performed. These concern monitoring, analysis, design and implementation, which should utilize not only frameworks that identify user's roles and interconnections, but also research behavioral models that indicate privacy threats and calculate users' benefits contrary to information disclosure cost. Thereby, an effective adaptive privacy scheme should provide the proper privacy features [12], capturing users' specific elements based on indicative behavioral models for their privacy management.

Towards this, adaptive solutions under the differential privacy scheme have been suggested from both theoretical and application perspectives [12, 19]. However, they are subsequent to many limitations, satisfying only specific criteria, such as: anonymity [20, 21], systems' access control architecture [22], noise insertion [19], sensitive ratings based on social recommendation [23] or streams data aggregation in real time [2]. So, several challenges cannot be addressed, since only static data were considered and the metrics used were proper only for static data as well. Most of them did not consider real-time aggregated data with high accuracy. The proposed algorithms were only optimally accurate, as it was difficult to have them applied to non-linear queries. Anonymity could not be applied in cases where users willingly disclosed information. Others solutions focused particularly on context-adaptive privacy schemes and mechanisms in order to provide the proper privacy-preserving recommendation and automatization [17]. Previous works put emphasis on users' perceived privacy within smart environments, exploring the grade of their awareness [24], investigate users' personal privacy risks contrary to their disclosure benefits within pervasive scenarios [25], examine the interrelation between privacy and context [26]. In [12] authors explored the interactions among users and their environments, based on users' requests for providing a balanced privacy protection scheme. However, these works rather focused on a specific element than the context as whole, while they ignored the interrelated users' contextual information in depth. In cases that interrelations were deeper considered, the solutions were based mainly on anonymity, while once again users' social attributes were statically analyzed. Efforts for these challenges to be addressed are described in following. [27] present a calendar for providing users with context-adaptive privacy by detecting present persons and giving schedule visibility according to their privacy preferences. In [28] authors proposed an Adaptive Privacy Policy framework to protect users' pictures within cloud, considering users' social settings, pictures' content and metadata. However, these works, focusing more on users' control, may provoke information and choice overload, making them more doubtful for their privacy decisions [5]. Furthermore, many works focused on context while exploring the location parameter [29–31]. Thus, despite the fact that location provides context information, it practically concerns only one attribute of a user's specific context [32]. In [33], authors, based on users' (un)awareness during information disclosure, aimed to determine their expected privacy utility deriving from the design of specified privacy objectives. However, the relationship among end-users and software designers is considered only from the designers' viewpoint. Other works examine context in social networks based only on users' friends' history ratings in order to provide recommendations, failing thus to distinguish the sensitive information ratings [23]. The contextual integrity framework in [10], considered to be a promising approach for implementing adaptive privacy mechanisms, supported that different stakeholders should comply with certain privacy principles in sensitive information transfer in each context. Although this has set the ground and put added value on the examination of users' socio-contextual attributes, it stands only for users' unique contexts in order to define their daily privacy experiences [8]. Authors in [5, 34] argued that by using recommender system algorithms, users' privacy preferences could be predicted based on their known characteristics. Consequently the systems may provide automatic smart settings according to users' disclosure behavior. Posing, thus, the question of how users' social characteristics could be measured efficiently, they propose the user-tailored privacy framework to address it. Based on this concept, authors in [35] found in their study on Facebook, that the optimal recommended adaptive privacy methods are different for each specific privacy setting, depending on users' awareness and familiarity with the privacy features. Despite the innovativeness of these last works, it should be noted that they ignore that recommendations themselves maybe untrustworthy, since current literature has shown that privacy leaks may occur, based on users' influence from systems' provisions [23]. Additionally, they do not consider users' off line attributes that may affect their privacy behaviors. In general, previous works examine fragmentally users' socio-contextual attributes. They focalize separately either on space or time, or on static social information, provided only within the systems, overlooking users' attributes beyond them, which may also be important for implanting privacy settings. Additionally, they are not flexible enough to execute proper privacy analysis that considers both users' social interactions and users and systems' interactions as well. Therefore, the main question posed is how to capture efficiently users' social attributes in and out of informational systems that affect their privacy management, in order to develop the proper behavioral models, which will enable an optimal design for self-adaptive privacy preserving schemes.

3 Exploring Users' Socio-contextual Attributes

Since cloud services are provided in a more personalized and context-aware way, the need to further understand users' differences in privacy management is indicated [4]. Within context-privacy approaches, and in our opinion beyond them, the definition of privacy is grounded on users' relationships, actors' actions, information and context, while this definition may vary across contexts [11]. Users' privacy notions and decisions are determined by specific actions in specific contexts, such as, the sensitivity in which decisions are made, the input from other users' decisions, the default privacy settings and the available options among them [34]. Despite these acknowledgements, the limited understanding on users' socio-contextual attributes that should be analyzed at runtime for self-adaptive privacy schemes has also been highlighted [3, 15].

Most of the current approaches do not consider users' semantic context information [29] and therefore in order to move beyond a fragment exploration of users' social attributes, a more user-distinct approach is needed. This should reflect both users' social contexts (e.g. family, employment, hobbies) and technological contexts (e.g. services, platforms, settings) [8], as well as their contextual changes [3], which impact on their social and technical privacy norms. As [34] support a critical step, in order to provide adequate self-adaptive privacy, is to determine its privacy calculus. The examination of how information disclosure is across users and how context-dependent it is will provide a deeper insight on the privacy risks and the social benefits that users consider during information disclosure, on the ways they value these and on how they are affected by systems' settings and provisions. In this regard, in order to determine users' social and privacy needs, previous literature has highlighted the importance of social capital theory [36, 37] and the identity theories (e.g. digital identity, personal identity) [38, 39]. With reference to social networks sites (SNS), as the most widespread cloud-computing environment, it has been shown that self-disclosure is a prerequisite, so as users to access information resources and gain social capital benefits within these, which are determined by shared values, common codes of communication and common decision criteria [40]. Thus, this exchanging procedure between social capital benefits and information disclosure leads to many privacy circumventions [37]. Although this is a recognized finding among researchers, still the perplexed relation between social capital and privacy management has not been examined efficiently [7, 37], due to piecemeal users' social capital investigation, which is taking place without considering users' specific context both online and offline. Networks' shared values and common practices, indicating users' social capital also reflect their social context and identity [41]. Up to this, previous literature has shown that, even though privacy management varies substantially among users, specific subgroups with similar privacy behaviours can be identified when their demographics or other shared attributes are mapped [5]. In this regard, some interesting works that explore users' social attributes in order to achieve self-adaptive privacy deployment within SNS have been elaborated [42, 43]. However, these works ignore that users are defined by multiple social identities, as social identity theory supports [44], which respectively differentiate their behaviours in each specific context, while users' attributes were narrowed to these that were presented within SNS. Consequently, in order to address the question of how to capture efficiently users' socio-contextual attributes in and out of informational systems that affect their privacy management, we argue that we should take input from both sociological and privacy literature, providing an interdisciplinary approach based on metrics from both disciplines. The first step for this exploration is to focus on the measurement of users' social identity and social capital in combination, since they are reinforced concepts and they are both indicated by previous privacy literature as significant parameters that affect privacy management,. Social identity refers to individuals' categorization in social groups, such as nations or organizations, indicating a category prototype. This prototype is defined by a set of attributes, which are intertwined, showing both similarities within the group and differences between the group and other groups. Prototypes also highlight the ways individuals are supposed to express their attitudes and to behave as category members. Additionally, they are typically not distinctive and tend to be shared, in and out of the groups, describing groups and identities, leading respectively to the determination of different groups' attitudes and group memberships [45]. However, individuals may belong to more than one category prototype and therefore they formulate multiple identities, resulting in several conflicts. In order to further understand their behaviours under this multiplicity, a social identity taxonomy is suggested in [44], as follows: a) *person-based social identities*, indicating individual's incorporation of the group attributes as a part of their self-concept figuration, b) *relational social identities*, reflecting individual's self under interactions with other group members within a specific context, c) *group-based social identities*, indicating the categories in which an individual belongs and d) *collective identities*, reflecting individual's self, based on group membership that differentiates them from the others.

Thereby, we support that the measurement of users' social identity based on this taxonomy and the interpretation of their social identity individual and collective processes will specify the attributes (e.g. the groups they belong, their leisure activities) that eventually define their privacy norms and influence their privacy management within a specific context. Previous literature has already shown that many privacy leaks derive from users' inadequate management of their multiple identities [38]. Additionally, as we pointed out before, this exploration should come along with users' social capital measurement simultaneously. Through this interrelated measurement, we will be able not only to define users' social norms, but also to capture the advantages that users consider they will gain by disclosing information, since social capital has been shown to be one of the major factors that affects the balance among users' social interactions and privacy needs [37]. Finally, we consider that the second step, for this interdisciplinary exploration to be achieved, should be the utilization of privacy metrics indicated by previous literature. In this regard, in the next section, the development of our interdisciplinary measurement scale is presented, aiming to provide a more holistic interpretation of users' privacy management, which may be useful in the developing of self-adaptive privacy aware systems.

4 An Interdisciplinary Scale for Self-adaptive Privacy

4.1 Previous Privacy Management Metrics

Privacy, as a multifaceted concept, has very often descriptive and measurable interactive functions within a society [9]. Hence, several measurement scales have been developed to examine users' privacy management issues [46, 47]. Thus, plenty of them do not include different socio-technical parameters that impact on users' privacy management, meeting privacy as one-bivariate construct. Additionally, they are usually not appropriately validated [4, 48]. In this regard, we moved on the examination among the existed validated privacy measurement scales, those of which consider even loosely users' personal and socio-contextual factors on privacy management.

One of the most used validated privacy scale in previous literature, was the Concern for Information Privacy scale, developed by [49], which focuses on users' privacy concerns in more detail. This identified four dimensions of privacy concerns, namely the collection, errors, secondary use, and unauthorized access to information. Emphasizing also on privacy concerns construct, authors in [50] introduced a scale to examine control, awareness and collection of users' personal information, while they adopted measures from other previous works, such as, unauthorized secondary use, improper access, global information privacy concerns and intention to give information. Users' social and contextual attributes that were examined, concerned sex, age, education, internet experience, misrepresentation of identification and privacy victim, while most of them were adapted from [49]. In [51] authors developed a scale, based on the construct of privacy concerns as well, presenting metrics for internet privacy concerns and social awareness. However, this scale does not focus on users' individual social attributes, but mostly on users' awareness regarding social reality. In [52] authors intended to predict users' on line privacy concerns by developing metrics for users' needs for privacy, their self-efficacy, their beliefs in privacy rights and their concerns about general online privacy and organizational privacy, as well their internet fluency and use diversity. However, these metrics ignored users' other significant socio-contextual attributes, besides gender. [48] introduced a new scale, validated on a group of students, which, beyond attitudinal and behavioral privacy concerns items and privacy caution metrics, included technical privacy protection ones as well. Thus, the users' attributes that were considered concerned only gender, age and educational status regarding their technology-based courses or not. In [53], focusing on Internet Privacy Concerns, authors adopted items from [49] and [50] and they provided metrics for the collection, secondary usage, errors, improper access, control and awareness constructs. [47] developed metrics for users' privacy concerns, privacy risks, privacy control, privacy awareness and users' previous privacy experience. In both [47, 53], users' social attributes were equally fragmentary explored, focusing only on demographics such as gender, age and internet usage frequency. An interesting scale was developed by [46], which considered not only users' demographics but also their roles, their common bonds and identity within an organization, presenting metrics for both individual and group privacy management. However, this scale does not consider the peculiarities of each users' context besides the examined organization. More recent works [54] introduced scales regarding collective privacy management within social network sites, focusing thus only on users' groups within social media. Finally, in [4] work, a scale, considering how users' personal data ecosystem, prior experiences and demographic characteristics may impact on their beliefs regarding the benefits and consequences of their adaptive cyber security behavior, was developed. Despite the novelty of this work, including several privacy-related metrics and considering users' individual differences and context, it should be mentioned that it focuses on users' online contexts, while it ignores their groups' privacy norms, studying only individual differences. In general, most of previous works tend to focus on informational privacy concept, while their metrics usually spotlight specific privacy constructs, such as privacy concerns, risks, trust, data collection [48], neglecting users' socio-contextual attributes. Therefore, they do not provide a more socio-technical perspective that would enable a further understanding of the relations among users' practices and technical data [5]. To our best knowledge, a measurement scale meeting these issues and focusing on self-adaptive privacy management in particular has not been developed in previous literature. Thereby, our aim is to develop systematic metrics for quantifying users' socio-contextual attributes that could be introduced into self-adaptive privacy behavioural research models within cloud. To address that, taking into consideration that existing privacy scales could benefit from expansion manifold [48], while the combination of the advantages of previous privacy metrics may improve the level of privacy within cloud [2], we present in the following subsection the development of a measurement scale that not only leverages the advantages of previous ones, but also includes metrics from sociological literature, emphasizing on social identity and social capital constructs.

4.2 Scale Development

Social Identity Metrics
As [5] emphatically supports "because privacy behaviors are contextualized, users' actions are based on complex identities that include their culture, world view, life experience, personality, intent, and so on, and they may thus perceive different features as risky and safe". Therefore, in order to further understand users' privacy management, it is important to increase the range of the constructs to be measured, taking input from social identity constructs and metrics. To address that, apart from the user's extended demographic attributes, our scale introduces a number of constructs and metrics, used in [55], in which an online Social Identity Mapping (oSIM) tool was designed to assess the multidimensional and intertwined nature of individuals' social identities. Beyond previous sociological works, which fail to identify the full extent of individuals' social group memberships and to interpret the interrelated nature of their multiple identities, limiting the social identity related information that could be analyzed [56], the oSIM may enable not only the identification of individuals' self-definitional attributes, but also these of their networks, collecting information regarding their relationships within their groups [55]. Even though this issue has been explored in many domains (e.g. work, health services, substance abuse), privacy, and self-adaptive privacy in particular, it does not constitute one of the cases where users' only separate identities or social networks have been fragmentary examined. In this regard, oSIM, compatible with [44] social identity taxonomy, may offer a deep insight on users' identity categories in a range of different life contexts, since it is based on previous scales that could be used at the same time. Based on this, in our measurement scale, the following constructs and their respective metrics are included, in Table 1, using mostly a 5-Point Likert scale.

Social Capital Metrics
Literature suggests that the more groups within individuals belong to, the more likely they are to have access to resources [55]. Bonding and bridging are two of the basic types of social capital that provide informational resources within online social networks. Bonding social capital concerns the development of coherent ties among individuals within tight networks, experiencing similar situations and exchanging support and trust, such as family or close friends. Bridging social capital refers to the development of connective

Table 1. Social identity constructs and metrics

Constructs	Items
Belonging in groups	Listing users' groups both offline and online, indicating: *a) Demographic: (e.g. American), b) Broad opinion-based: (e.g., feminist), c) Leisure or social: (e.g., theatre group), d) Family or friendship, e) Community: (e.g., belief-based or volunteer), f) Sporting or well-being: (e.g., tennis club, yoga, g) Work or professional: (e.g., marketing team), h) Health related: (e.g. cancer support group), i) other users' indicative groups* [55]
High-contact groups	*Rating of how often individuals interact within each of their offline and online declared group* [55]
Positive groups	*Rating individuals' perceived positivity for each of their offline and online declared group* [55]
Representative groups	*Rating of how representative individuals feel for each of their offline and online declared group* [55]
Supportive groups	*Rating of how much support individuals receive from each of their offline and online declared group* [55]
Identity importance	*a) Overall, my group membership [group inserted] has very little to do with how I feel about myself, b) The group [insertion] I belong to is an important reflection of who I am, c) The group [insertion] I belong to is unimportant to my sense of what kind of a person I am, d) In general, belonging to this group [insertion] is an important part of my self-image* [57]
Identity harmony	3 pairwise items: **1.** *a) Membership in one group [group inserted] has a very harmful or conflictual effect on the other[group inserted] & b) Membership in one group [group inserted] has a very facilitative or helpful effect on the other[group inserted].* **2.** *a) Membership in one group [group inserted] always takes up so much time and energy that it makes it hard to fulfill the expectations of the other group [group inserted] & b) Membership in one group [group inserted] always frees up time and energy for me to fulfill the expectations of the other group [group inserted].* **3.** *a) This group [group inserted] always expect conflicting behaviors from me & b) This group [group inserted] always expect the same behaviors from me"* [57]

ties among individuals within vulnerable, heterogeneous and diverse networks, experiencing different situations, without a common sense of belonging [40]. These types also were indicated that influence users' privacy management [37]. As a result, these constructs are included in our scale, using a 5-Point Likert system, incorporating the metrics derived from [58], as the most used and validated scales in previous privacy research (Table 2).

Table 2. Social capital constructs and metrics

Constructs	Items
Bonding social capital	a) If I urgently needed 100€ someone from online social network (OSN) could lend me, b) People from my OSN could provide good job references for me, c) I do not know anyone well enough to get him/her to do anything important, d) When I feel lonely there are several people on my OSN I could talk to, e) There are several people on my OSN I trust to solve my problems and f) I do not know anyone well enough from my OSN to get him/her to do anything important [58]
Bridging social capital	a) Interacting with people in my OSN makes me want to try new things, b) I am willing to spend time on supporting community activities, c) I meet new people very often, d) Interacting with people in my OSN makes me want to try new things, e) Interacting with people in my OSN makes me feel like a part of a larger community" and f) "Interacting with people in my OSN makes me realize that somehow we are all connected worldwide"[58]

Privacy Management Related Metrics

Based on previous privacy measurements, analyzed in Subsect. 4.1, the following privacy-related constructs and metrics will be included in our scale, using a 5-Point Likert scale *(strongly disagree-strongly agree)* (Table 3).

Our interdisciplinary measurement scale, while adopting constructs and their respective metrics from sociological and privacy literature, aims to provide multiple information about individuals' social landscape as they experience it, allowing a coherent interrelation both with their privacy norms and behaviours. All social media platforms and the majority of webservices nowadays are based on CCEs. Security and privacy issues in CCEs require specific attention since they bring new types of threats that designers should be aware of when designing respective services [59]. Additionally to the technical security and privacy aspects in CCEs the quantification of the types of users' social identities (e.g. parent, employee, husband), the types of their social groups (e.g. volunteer, feminist, tennis) and the types of their social capital benefits will provide researchers with a further understanding of users' privacy management within CCE, since users' belonging to several identities and groups influences their privacy attitudes and behaviours. Consequently, it will lay the ground for the identification of users' social privacy requirements in CCE, accordingly to their attributes, providing software developers with more concrete guidelines for designing self-adaptive privacy preserving schemes. Its utilization will also enable the developers to support GDPR enforcement, e.g. by providing users the ability to assess the options among their own privacy preferences and the systems' choices, in order for an effective decision-making procedure to be followed that respects subjects' data rights and satisfies their needs. Therefore, the development of an instrument such as the proposed scale, which is the first that promotes a self-adaptive privacy behavioural research model within CCE, has potential for both research and design practices in the field of self-adaptive privacy.

Table 3. Privacy management related Constructs and Metrics

Constructs	Items
Beliefs in privacy rights	*a) users' right to be left alone, b) users' right to use Internet anonymously, c) no gathering of disclosed personal information without users' consent and d) users' right control on their personal information* [53]
Privacy concerns	*a) I am concerned about my online information being linked to my publicly available offline one, b) I am concerned that the information I submit on Cloud Services (CS) could be misused, c) I'm concerned that too much personal information is collected by so many CS, d) It usually concerns me when I am asked to provide personal information on CS, e) I am concerned that others can find private information about me online, f) I am concerned about providing personal information on CS, because it could be used in a way I did not foresee.* [4, 47]
Information collection	*a) It usually bothers me when CS ask me for personal information, b) When CS ask me for personal information, I sometimes think twice before providing it and c) It bothers me to give personal information to so many CS* [49, 50]
Self-disclosure	*a) I frequently talk about myself online, b) I often discuss my feelings about myself online, c) I usually write about myself extensively online, d) I often express my personal beliefs and opinions online, e) I disclose my close relationships online and f) I often disclose my concerns and fears online* [54]
Trusting beliefs	*a) CS would be trustworthy in information handling, b) CS fulfill promises related to the information provided by me c) I trust that CS would keep my best interests in mind when dealing with my provided information* [50]
Privacy control	*a) I have control over who can get access to my personal information online, b) I always optimize my privacy settings when I create an online profile, c) I consider the privacy policy of CS where I give out personal information, d) I would opt out of a service due to privacy issues, e) I only upload information online that is suitable for everyone that can see* [4, 46, 47, 54]

(continued)

Table 3. (*continued*)

Constructs	Items
Privacy awareness	a) *Personal information is of value to CS providers, b) I am aware of the privacy issues and practices in CS, c) CS providers do not have the right to sell users personal information, d) I follow the developments about privacy issues and violations within cloud, e) I keep myself updated on privacy solutions that law and CS employ and f) I am aware of protecting my personal information from unauthorized access* [4, 47]
Collaborative privacy management	a) *Prior to disclosing content, my group members (group inserted) and I discuss the appropriate privacy settings, b) I ask for approval before disclosing content from those group members involved (group inserted), c) My group members (group insert-ed) ask for approval before uploading content concerning myself* [55]
Self-disclosure cost–benefit	a) *The risk posed to me if personal information is exposed outweighs the benefits of sharing it, b) In general, my need to obtain CS is greater than my concern about privacy, c) I am happy to provide personal information to support government policy and d) I value the personalized CS I received from providing such personal information* [4]

5 Conclusions

The emerge of Self-Adaptive Privacy schemes within CCE has been highlighted, aiming to protect users' privacy according to their social and privacy needs. Although ambitious self-adaptive privacy approaches have been introduced, these fail to capture efficiently users' socio-contextual attributes that influence their privacy management. To address that, we introduced the development of an interdisciplinary systematic metrics for quantifying users' socio-contextual attributes and privacy management, aiming to establish a research instrument, which focuses on the field self-adaptive privacy within cloud environments. Our scale takes input from constructs and metrics, derived from both sociological and privacy literature, enabling a wider exploration of the factors affecting self-adaptive privacy management. Specifically, it concludes seven constructs of social identity theory, namely, belonging in groups, high-contact groups, positive groups, representative groups, supportive groups, identity importance, identity harmony and two constructs of social capital theory, bonding and bridging social capital, since social identity and social capital have been indicated to affect users' privacy management. Contrary to previous privacy literature, the constructs of the two major concepts (social identity-social capital) are not only considered separately but in combination, since they reinforce one another. As far as the included privacy constructs is concerned, while previous privacy literature tends to focus on constructs such as collection, control, authorized use and awareness, our own provides more extensive ones, such beliefs in privacy rights, self-disclosure, trusting beliefs, collaborative privacy management, self-disclosure cost–benefit, aiming to address all the emerged issues regarding self-adaptive privacy within cloud. In this regard, our scale provides the thoroughly identification of users' social landscape interrelated with their privacy behaviours and its utilization is expected to lay the ground for the developers to meet efficiently both users' social requirements and systems' technical ones, before performing adaptive privacy mechanisms in cloud. Thus, this work as a first step to establish solid empirical structures among the social and technical aspects of privacy. Despite its novelty, since our presented approach is part of our ongoing project on the identification of socio-technical requirements in self adaptive privacy, the validation of the proposed measurement scale is critical towards leveraging knowledge about the respective issues, so that the adequate design of these systems is achieved.

Acknowledgments. This research is co-financed by Greece and the European Union *(European Social Fund- ESF)* through the Operational Programme "Human Resources Development, Education and Lifelong Learning 2014-2020" in the context of the project "Adaptive Privacy-aware Cloud-based Systems: Socio-technical requirements" (MIS:5047231)".

References

1. Cook, A., et al.: Internet of cloud: security and privacy issues. In: Mishra, B.S.P., Das, H, Dehuri, S., Jagadev, A.K. (eds.) Cloud Computing for Optimization: Foundations, Applications, and Challenges, SBD, vol. 39, pp. 271–301. Springer, Cham (2018). https://doi.org/10.1007/978-3-319-73676-1_11

2. Huo, Y., Yong, C., Lu, Y.: Re-ADP: real-time data aggregation with adaptive-event differential privacy for fog computing. Wirel. Commun. Mob. Comput. **2018**(6285719), 1–13 (2018)

3. Salehie, M., Pasquale, L., Omoronyia, I., Nuseibeh, B.: Adaptive security and privacy in smart grids. In: Proceedings of the 1st International Workshop on Software Engineering Challenges for the Smart Grid, Zurich, pp. 46–49. IEEE (2012)

4. Addae, J.H., Brown, M., Sun, X., Radenkovic, M.: Measuring attitude towards personal data for adaptive cybersecurity. Inf. Comput. Secur. **25**(5), 560–579 (2017)

5. Knijnenburg, Bart P.: Privacy in social information access. In: Brusilovsky, Peter, He, Daqing (eds.) Social Information Access. LNCS, vol. 10100, pp. 19–74. Springer, Cham (2018). https://doi.org/10.1007/978-3-319-90092-6_2

6. Nissim, K., Wood, A.: Is privacy? Philos. Trans. R. Soc. A Math. Phys. Eng. Sci. **376**(2128) 20170358 (2018)

7. Kitsiou, A., Tzortzaki, E., Kalloniatis, C., Gritzalis, S.: Towards an integrated socio-technical approach for designing adaptive privacy aware services in cloud computing. In: Benson, V. (ed) Cyber Influence and Cognitive Threats, pp.9–32. Elsevier, Amsterdam (2020)

8. Sujon, Z.: The triumph of social privacy: understanding the privacy logics of sharing behaviors across social media. Int. J. Commun. **12**, 3751–3771 (2018)

9. Chang, C.H.: New technology, new information privacy: social-value-oriented information privacy theory. NTU Law Rev. **10**(1), 127–175 (2015)

10. Nissenbaum, H.: Privacy in Context: Technology, Policy and the Integrity of Social Life. Stanford University Press, California (2009)

11. Martin, K.: Understanding privacy online: development of a social contract approach to privacy. J. Bus. Ethics **137**(3), 551–569 (2016)

12. Pallapa, G., Das, S.K., Di Francesco, M., Aura, T.: Adaptive and context-aware privacy preservation exploiting user interactions in smart environments. Pervasive Mob. Comput. **12**, 232–243 (2014)

13. Belk, M., Fidas, C., Athanasopoulos, E., Pitsillides, A.: Adaptive & personalized privacy & security workshop chairs' welcome and organization. In: Proceedings of 27th Conference on User Modeling, Adaptation and Personalization, Cyprus, pp. 191–192. ACM (2019)

14. Schaub, F., Könings, B., Weber, M.: Context-adaptive privacy: leveraging context awareness to support privacy decision making. IEEE Pervasive Comput. **14**(1), 34–43 (2015)

15. Weyns, D.: Software engineering of self-adaptive systems: an organised tour and future challenges. In: Cha, S., Taylor, R.N., Kang, K. (eds.) Handbook of Software Engineering, pp. 339–443. Springer, Cham (2019)

16. De Wolf, R., Pierson, J.: Researching social privacy on SNS through developing and evaluating alternative privacy technologies. In: Proceedings of the Conference on Computer-Supported Cooperative Work and Social Computing, Texas. ACM (2013)

17. Schaub, F.: Context-adaptive privacy mechanisms. In: Gkoulalas-Divanis, A., Bettini, C. (eds.) Handbook of Mobile Data Privacy, pp. 337–372. Springer, Cham (2018). https://doi.org/10.1007/978-3-319-98161-1_13

18. Omoronyia, I.: Reasoning with imprecise privacy preferences. In: Proceedings of the 24th International Symposium on Foundations of Software Engineering, Seattle, USA, pp. 920–923. ACM (2016)

19. Phan, N., Wu, X., Hu, H., Dou, D.: Adaptive laplace mechanism: differential privacy preservation in deep learning. In: Proceedings of the International Conference on Data Mining, New Orleans, pp. 385–394. IEEE USA (2017)

20. Dwork, C.: Differential privacy: a survey of results. In: Agrawal, M., Du, D., Duan, Z., Li, A. (eds.) TAMC 2008. LNCS, vol. 4978, pp. 1–19. Springer, Heidelberg (2008). https://doi.org/10.1007/978-3-540-79228-4_1

21. Hong, J.I., Ng, J.D., Lederer, S., Landay, J.A.: Privacy risk models for designing privacy-sensitive ubiquitous computing systems In: Proceedings of the 5th Conference on Designing Interactive Systems, Cambridge MA, USA, pp. 91–100 2004)

22. Li, C., Miklau, G.: An adaptive mechanism for accurate query answering under differential privacy (2012). arXiv:1202.3807. Accessed 01 Mar 2020

23. Meng, X., et al.: Personalized privacy-preserving social recommendation. In: Proceedings of 32nd AAAI Conference on Artificial Intelligence, Louisiana USA, pp. 3796–3803. AAAI (2018)

24. Beckwith, R.: Designing for ubiquity: the perception of privacy. IEEE Pervasive Comput. **2**(2), 40–46 (2003)

25. Lederer, S., Hong, J.I., Dey, A., Landay, J.: Personal privacy through understanding and action: five pitfalls for designers. Pers. Ubiquit. Comput. **8**(6), 440–454 (2004)

26. Heiber, T., Marrn, P.: Exploring the relationship between context and privacy. In: Robinson, P., Vogt, H., Wagealla, W. (eds.) Privacy, Security and Trust within the Context of Pervasive Computing, pp. 35–48. Springer, USA (2005). https://doi.org/10.1007/0-387-23462-4_4

27. Schaub, F., Könings, B., Lang, P., Wiedersheim, B., Winkler, C., Weber, M.: PriCal: context-adaptive privacy in ambient calendar displays. In: Proceedings of the International Joint Conference on Pervasive and Ubiquitous Computing, USA, pp. 499–510. ACM (2014)

28. Kumar, R., Naik, M.V.: Adaptive privacy policy prediction system for user-uploaded images on content sharing sites. Int. Res. J. Eng. Technol. **5**(7), 148–154 (2018)

29. Gu, Q., Ni, Q., Meng, X., Yang, Z.: Dynamic social privacy protection based on graph mode partition in complex social network. Pers. Ubiquit. Comput. **23**(3–4), 511–519 (2019)

30. Zhu, J., Kim, K.H., Mohapatra, P., Congdon, P.: An adaptive privacy-preserving scheme for location tracking of a mobile user. In: Proceedings of the International Conference on Sensing, Communications and Networking, USA, pp. 140–148. IEEE (2013)

31. Agir, B., Papaioannou, T.G., Narendula, R., Aberer, K., Hubaux, J.-P.: User-side adaptive protection of location privacy in participatory sensing. GeoInformatica **18**(1), 165–191 (2013). https://doi.org/10.1007/s10707-013-0193-z
32. Vgena, K., Kitsiou, A., Kalloniatis, C., Kavroudakis, D., Gritzalis, S.: Toward addressing location privacy issues: new affiliations with social and location attributes. Future Internet **11**(11), 234 (2019)
33. Omoronyia, I., Etuk, U., Inglis, P.: A privacy awareness system for software design. Int. J. Softw. Eng. Knowl. Eng. **29**(10), 1557–1604 (2019)
34. Knijnenburg, B., Raybourn, E., Cherry, D., Wilkinson, D., Sivakumar, S., Sloan, H.: Death to the Privacy Calculus? (2017). Available at SSRN 2923806. Accessed 05 Mar 2020
35. Namara, M., Sloan, H., Jaiswal, P., Knijnenburg, B.: The potential for user-tailored privacy on Facebook. In: Proceedings of the Symposium on Privacy-Aware Computing, USA, pp. 31–42. IEEE (2018)
36. Taddicken, M.: The privacy paradox in the social web: the impact of privacy concerns, individual characteristics, and the perceived social relevance on different forms of self disclosure. J. Comput. Med. Commun. **19**(2), 248–273 (2014)
37. Stutzman, F., Vitak, J., Ellison, N.B., Gray, R., Lampe, C.: Privacy in interaction: exploring disclosure and social capital in Facebook. In: Proceedings of 6th Annual International Conference on Weblogs and Social Media, Ireland, pp. 330–337. AAAI Publ. (2012)
38. Marwick, A.E., Boyd, D.: Networked privacy: how teenagers negotiate context in social media. New Med. Soc. **16**(7), 1051–1067 (2014)
39. Wessels, B.: Identification and the practices of identity and privacy in everyday digital communication. New Med. Soc. **14**(8), 1251–1268 (2012)
40. Tzortzaki, E., Kitsiou, A., Sideri, M., Gritzalis, S.: Self-disclosure, privacy concerns and Social Capital benefits interaction in FB: a case study. In: Proceedings of the 20th Pan-Hellenic Conference on Informatics, Greece, pp. 1–6. ACM (2016)
41. Kramer, R.M.: Social identity and social capital: the collective self at work. Int. Pub. Manag. J. **9**(1), 25–45 (2006)
42. Hoang, L.N., Jung, J.J.: Privacy-aware framework for matching online social identities in multiple social networking services. Cybern. Syst. **46**(1–2), 69–83 (2015)
43. Calikli, G., et al.: Privacy dynamics: learning privacy norms for social software. In: Proceedings of 11th International Symposium on Software Engineering for Adaptive and Self-Managing Systems, Texas, pp. 47–56. ACM (2016)
44. Hogg, M., Abrams, D., Brewer, M.: Social identity: the role of self in group processes and intergroup relations. Group Process. Intergroup Relat. **20**(5), 570–581 (2017)
45. Hogg, M., Smith, J.: Attitudes in social context: a social identity perspective. Eur. Rev. Soc. Psychol. **18**(1), 89–131 (2007)
46. De Wolf, R., Willaert, K., Pierson, J.: Managing privacy boundaries together: exploring individual and group privacy management strategies in Facebook. Comput. Hum. Behav. **35**, 444–454 (2014)
47. Xu, H., Dinev, T., Smith, I., Hart, P.: Information privacy concerns: linking individual perceptions with institutional privacy assurances. J. Assoc. Inf. Syst. **12**(2), 798–824 (2011)
48. Buchanan, T., Paine, C., Joinson, A.N., Reips, U.: Development of measures of online privacy concern and protection for use on the Internet. J. Am. Soc. Inform. Sci. Technol. **58**(2), 157–165 (2007)
49. Smith, J.H., Milberg, S.J., Burke, S.J.: Information privacy: measuring individuals concerns about organizational practices. MIS Q. **20**(2), 167–196 (1996)
50. Malhotra, N., Kim, S., Agarwal, J.: Internet users' information privacy concerns: the construct, the scale, and a causal model. Inf. Syst. Res. **15**(4), 336–355 (2004)
51. Dinev, T., Hart, P.: Internet privacy concerns and social awareness as determinants of intention to transact. Int. J. Electron. Commer. **10**(2), 7–29 (2005)

52. Yao, M., Rice, R., Wallis, K.: Predicting user concerns about online privacy. J. Am. Soc. Inform. Sci. Technol. **58**(5), 710–722 (2007)
53. Hong, W., Thong, J.Y.: Internet privacy concerns: An integrated conceptualization and four empirical studies. MIS Q. **37**, 275–298 (2013)
54. Cho, H., Knijnenburg, B., Kobsa, A., Li, Y.: Collective privacy management in social media: a cross-cultural validation. ACM Trans. Comput. Hum. Interact. **25**(3), 1–33 (2018)
55. Bentley, S., Greenaway, K., Haslam, S., Cruwys, T., Haslam, C., Cull, B.: Social identity mapping online. J. Pers. Soc. Psychol. **118**(2), 213–241 (2020)
56. Postmes, T., Haslam, S.A., Jans, L.: A single-item measure of social identification: Reliability, validity, and utility. Br. J. Soc. Psychol. **52**(4), 597–617 (2013)
57. Brook, A.T., Garcia, J., Fleming, M.A.: The effects of multiple identities on psychological well-being. Pers. Soc. Psychol. Bull. **34**(12), 1588–1600 (2008)
58. Williams, D.: On and off the 'net: Scales for social capital in an online era. J. Comput. Med. Commun. **11**(2), 593–628 (2006)
59. Kalloniatis, C.: Incorporating privacy in the design of cloud-based systems: a conceptual metamodel. Inf. Comput. Secur. J. **25**(5), 614–633 (2017)

Empowering Users Through a Privacy Middleware Watchdog

Patrícia R. Sousa(✉) , Rolando Martins , and Luís Antunes

CRACS/INESC TEC, Porto, Portugal
{psousa,rmartins,lfa}@dcc.fc.up.pt

Abstract. The ever-increasing number of interconnected devices in smart environments, i.e., homes and cities, is bolstering the amount of data generated and exchanged. These devices can range from small embedded platforms, such as those included in home appliances, to critical operational systems, such as traffic lights. However, this increasing adoption is raising significant security and privacy concerns. Although some researchers have already solved some of these issues, data privacy still lacks a viable solution, especially when considering a flexible, decentralized approach to avoid a central overseer. One of the biggest challenges regarding privacy is the lack of transparency about how data flows are mediated and regulated as, often, these resources share data with external entities without the users' knowledge. We argue that a novel data-sharing control mechanism is required to properly control users' privacy and their respective Internet of Things (IoT) devices. This work focuses on a middleware layer solution for the IoT devices, which allows the control of the data generated by the device by its owner. The platform places the user as an active participant in the data market, behaving as its own data intermediary for potential consumers by monitoring, controlling, and negotiating the usage of their data.

1 Introduction

The IoT is growing continuously and, according to *National Public Radio & Edison Research* [25], homes in the United States have an average of 2.6 smart speakers, explaining why the number of smart speakers is much larger than the number of its owners. People are increasingly adopting the concept of smart homes by acquiring more smart devices, such as smart lamps or thermostats, helping to save money. Authenticated users can remotely control many devices via their smartphone, such as refrigerators or garage doors. Some examples include alerts from refrigerators when items are missing or a pot that can be programmed to irrigate plants. Along with the usability enhancements, it is also possible to make homes more secure with wireless security cameras, sensors, and smoke alarms. Besides, this can help older people be more independent because these types of smart homes may include audible warnings or voice-activated alert systems that can help automate some tasks.

© Springer Nature Switzerland AG 2020
S. Gritzalis et al. (Eds.): TrustBus 2020, LNCS 12395, pp. 156–170, 2020.
https://doi.org/10.1007/978-3-030-58986-8_11

However, what is the cost of having all smart devices connected to the Internet, regarding some fundamental human rights, such as privacy? Also, these devices can communicate with their owner and other devices while potentially harvesting data. In turn, this data can be monitored by routers/switches that can send it as telemetry to their manufactures.

Jingjing Ren et al. [24] conducted a study with 81 different smart devices to examine data sharing activities. The authors found that 72 of the 81 IoT devices share sensitive data, such as IP addresses, device specifications and settings, usage habits, and location data, with third parties that were utterly unrelated with the original manufacturer, such as advertisers. This type of sharing can violate the user's privacy because, for example, according to the GDPR, IP addresses must be considered personal data as it falls within the scope of "online identifiers" or, more precisely, "Personal Identifiable Information" which is data that can identify a user [12]. This lack of consumer awareness is rapidly raising concerns about data privacy [17] as, for example, people who buy a Smart TV have no idea if their data is being shared or sold with technology providers from third parties. Worse, the authors found that 30 out of 81 devices shared data as an unencrypted text file. These examples raise significant privacy concerns, as those who collect these data streams can infer sensitive information, such as users' identity, location, or behavior.

Recent literature [4,36,37] highlighted that privacy concerns could be a significant barrier to the growth of IoT, highlighting security and privacy as a significant IoT research challenge. Some of the identified missing features include: a) decentralized authentication and trust models; b) data protection technologies; c) data ownership; d) repository data management; e) access and use rights; f) integration or connection with privacy preservation structures; and g) management of privacy policies. Currently, managing identity and access control of "things" in an interconnected world remains an open issue.

This article proposes a middleware layer that allows users to control the data generated by their IoT devices. Depending on the manufacturer's firmware, users can store specific data offline and control data sharing while preserving their privacy.

2   Related Work

The development of middleware solutions for IoT is an active area of research. *Christoph Haar and Erik Buchmann* [14] introduced a firewall between the device and the network to generate and enforce traffic rules autonomously. It tries to block what is not essential for operations. The system uses firewall rules to drop all packets that are not allowed by the set of generated rules. *Daniel Amkær Sørensen et al.* [32] also propose a system that generates rules based on the real-time traffic analysis.

Pi-hole [22] acts as a DNS sinkhole, providing a fake IP address when there is an IP request for known ad-trackers. The difference between this system and DNS-based blacklist providers, such as *OpenDNS* [20], is that the DNS server runs locally on the RP3, which inherently gives greater control and therefore privacy.

Security and Privacy for In-home Networks (SPIN) [16] is an anomaly detection module implemented in SIDN Labs. The authors promise to do traffic inspection and make automatic and personalized blocks by the user. In their work, the authors promise to block Distributed Denial of Service (DDoS) derived from malicious devices on the network and allow the user to block traffic. Blocking is done based on patterns (unusual behavior), lists, e.g., *Snort* [26], or customized by the user.

More recently, *Olha Drozd and Sabrina Kirrane* [7] contribute with a Consent Request User Interface (UI), giving users the ability to make a complete customization to control their consent specifically to their wishes. This system offers users the possibility to grant permission to process only specific data categories for chosen purposes, for example. Users can grant permission to process their heart rate and store it on their device without sharing it with anyone else. However, this paper only purposes the UI for the idea. *Abduljaleel Al-Hasnawi and Leszek Lilien* [2] provide a solution that enforces privacy policies anywhere in the IoT, so it is more related to the data itself and the identification of privacy threats, such as linkability, re-identification, non-repudiation, traceability, information disclosure, content unawareness and non-compliance. This solution can be a complement to our solution, helping to detect sensitive information to be blocked.

Vijay Sivaraman et al. [31] propose an architecture with three components: Internet Service Provider (ISP), Security Management Provider (SMP) and Home Network. The SMP component is responsible for the security management of access controls. The authors build a prototype evaluation with some devices, including a Nest smoke alarm; in this case, when privacy protection is enabled, the system requests the SMP to make an API call to prevent the device from accessing the log servers (where it sends 250 KB per day). Compared to our approach, the concept is different and can be integrated, because there is a limitation in the choice of permissions, as only developers can define what to block for each category (security or privacy), with no options for the regular user.

3   Conceptual Design

Secure and privacy-oriented data sharing remains an unsolved problem in IoT, especially for users' data. Users are generally unaware of how their data is being handled in the IoT environment, as they assume that the manufacturer has implemented the appropriate privacy and security mechanisms. However, this is not the case, mainly from the examples described in Sect. 1.

In our approach, users can decide the data and traffic exchanged according to their preferences. Users have the option to block all traffic by default and to make exceptions for some specific domains. Therefore, for example, users can block marketing/advertising sites and only communicate with the manufacturer's domains. Note that if users choose to block all communications from their devices to the Internet, some of the features may stop working, as some of these devices will not work in offline mode. Finally, users will have to choose between usability and privacy.

On existing routers, users can change the set of rules and block specific traffic, without the need for a middleware. However, there are no configurable privacy platforms that show connections made by default by the device (configured by the manufacturer), and that allow blocking those connections "on the fly". The middleware allows users to monitor incoming and outgoing connections so that users can verify that the device is running an untrusted program and block or disable updates to specific resources.

Along with this network traffic monitoring and, depending on the manufacturer's device firmware, users can store data offline on their home router for future reference. As users can connect with multiple routers (at home or work, for example), they can choose different permissions for their data depending on the device context, managing the data's life cycle. Users can also monetize data by selling them to external entities.

4   Architecture

The middleware consists of a secure data sharing model. From an architectural point of view, the system consists of IoT devices, the owner's smartphone that acts as *Permissions Controller*, and a router that acts as a manager and controls data sharing for external entities.

Figure 1 shows the different components of each device, as well as the interconnections between them and the Internet.

There are two types of IoT devices: white-box devices and black-box devices. White-box devices represent devices on which it is possible to install software, modify and access the firmware. On the other hand, black-box devices represent devices on which developers can not control the stack and do not have access to the software/firmware, so it is impossible to install applications with the level of granularity necessary to install and run the middleware.

4.1   White-Box Devices

This type of device has two main components: a *Middleware* and a *Sensor API*.

Sensor API has the necessary interface for IoT devices. Some manufacturers allow developers to interact with device data in their applications, products, and services. In such cases, the *Middleware* component integrates with the *Sensor API* to get access to the data. Then, the *Repository* receives the input from the API and can store the data locally (this component stores data for seven days maximum by default, but users can modify this configuration).

Sharing Decision Control consists of a firewall-based solution to control data sharing. The component uses context-aware access control and owner rules provided by the *Rules* component to control data sharing. The *Sharing Decision Control* must be deployed locally on the device to provide the owner with the security of their data under their control.

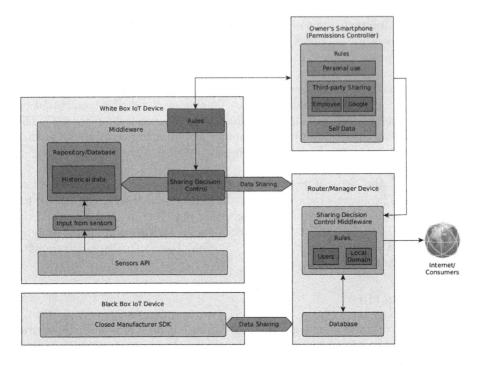

Fig. 1. Data sharing middleware

4.2   Black-Box Devices

When the manufacturer's firmware is closed/proprietary, it usually uses encrypted channels to support all communications, creating an opaque layer where it is impossible to distinguish between the transferred data. Thus, it is impossible to implement the middleware on the device, so the router has to perform all the traffic control (the router also has the middleware).

4.3   Permissions Controller

Our choice to use smartphones as a configuration controller to define rules and permissions aims to promote usability, as screens or keyboards are generally not used/available in IoT scenarios.

For black-box devices, the smartphone sends rules to the router, as it is impossible to control data sharing locally. For this reason, the only option available is third-party sharing for external sharing. *External Sharing* is related to the traffic that the device generates by default, which may include communications with the manufacturer and with entities unrelated to the manufacturer. In case of black-box devices, the traffic is encrypted and most of the times, devices communicate directly with an external server, and so, transferred data are not distinguished, but with this option, users can select the entities they want to share with (for example, *Google* is allowed, but *Facebook Ads* is not allowed).

Users can choose between two modes: primary or advanced mode. The primary mode has traffic data aggregated by the entity. In a use case based on *Google Assistant*, device connections include multiple subdomains of *googleapis.com*, but only the *Google* entity appears to users in primary mode. In this way, all connections to or from *Google* are blocked or allowed, according to the users' preferences. This mode is more accessible for *non-technical* users to control the entities with which devices communicate. Thus, users can also know which connections are related to the device manufacturer.

In advanced mode, all traffic is shown by Server Name Indication (SNI) [9]. According to the same use case, instead of showing only the *Google* entity with aggregated traffic, it shows detailed traffic in real-time (e.g. *192.168.1.6:38578 - 172.217.17.10:[443] 21:oauth2.googleapis.com, 192.168.1.6:36366 - 216.58.201.234:[443] 32:embeddedassistant.googleapis.com*), and users can block or allow specific connections.

As mentioned in Sect. 3, devices that do not work offline and depend on communication with the manufacturer, may not work after some traffic block. If only a few features stop working, users can choose between usability and privacy. In summary, in this component, the smartphone can display all traffic in real-time, and it is possible to choose the entities to share the data and specify the expiry time of these permissions.

For white-box devices, each owner has three main permissions to control the data sharing: *Personal Use*, *Third-party sharing* and *Sell Data*. In this case, both the IoT devices and the router implement all the rules defined on the smartphone.

Personal Use

Personal Use has two options: *yes* or *no*. When users set the permission to *yes*, the router's database can store the data produced by the device. This option allows owners to control their data locally, without an Internet connection.

Third-party Sharing

Third-party Sharing has two different components: *Internal Sharing* and *External Sharing*. *Internal Sharing* represents the data transmission that exists between the IoT device and the router to which it is connected. Owners can set different permissions according to the context of the IoT device, for example, if the device is in the *home* context, owners may want to store all data on their router but deny this permission on other contexts blocking the transmission of some confidential data. The owner's smartphone shows all sensors available for data sharing and allows users to set permissions for their data according to their preferences. *External Sharing* is explained in Sect. 4.3 and is also available for these white-box devices. In summary, *External Sharing* is related to the traffic that the device generates by default (communications configured by the manufacturer) so that users can manage these communication permissions. With this option, users can manage (allow or block) those connections made during normal device operation, but cannot choose other entities to share data.

Sell Data

Unlike *External Sharing*, which controls only standard device communications, the sell data option allows users to sell specific data to interested third parties. The sensors can gather additional data that may be of interest to marketers to reinforce marketing strategies in a region, creating accurate and personalized ads contextualized to the interests of a person or region. Our structure allows users to choose a set of data collected by the IoT sensors and stored in the router's database to be shared with external entities (also selected by the data owner) in exchange for monetary compensation, offering users the possibility to monetize their data. For example, users can choose to sell data about temperature, but not about lighting and air conditioning, because they know that a machine learning algorithm can combine data to determine the presence in a given household. Note that this sell data option is valid for white-box devices or devices with data APIs.

4.4 Router

The router has two different components: a *Sharing Decision Control* and a *Database*. The *Sharing Decision Control* component acts as a firewall between external entities on the Internet and local devices. This component receives the rules provided by the mobile application and controls data sharing.

When the device's *Personal Use* and the data's permission on the *Internal Sharing* component are synchronized with *yes*, these data can be transmitted to the *Database*, allowing data owners to query them offline. In the router, it is possible to make the interconnection between the mobile application and the *Database*, allowing users to query their data on the smartphone. For devices that continue to operate offline without connections to the manufacturer, this can be a way for users to view their data without interacting with the manufacturer's online application that stores the data in their proprietary database. In addition to this, the router also has a web interface that shows the data available for sale.

We choose to place data sharing control on both devices (IoT devices and router) to ensure that users have their data under control, regardless of the type of device. As we have black-box devices where we do not control the encrypted data between the two endpoints of the communication channel, we need to ensure that users are also in control of their data. The only way to do this is to have the middleware on the router so that users can allow or deny communications. Besides, this control allows router owners to have their internal permission policies. For example, when a new device connects to a router and does not block any traffic, the router owner can have internal default permissions to block specific traffic.

5 Evaluation

In this section, we present the setup and details about the implementation of the prototype, a use case, and results regarding performance and energy consumption.

5.1 Setup

We used two Raspberry PI 3 Model B+ (RP3): one representing a router and another to represent an IoT device. The IoT device has five sensor modules: Temperature and Humidity (DHT11), Luminosity (KY-018), LED (KY-016), a Heart-Rate sensor (SEN-11574) and a GPS (Adafruit Ultimate GPS Breakout).

These devices can simulate some personal assistants, such as Google Home or Amazon Alexa, as well as smart devices that connect to them, such as LEDs or thermostats. In this environment, we built a Google Assistant using the Google Assistant SDK to control by voice the LED connected to the RP3 GPIO pins. For this setup, we also plug a USB microphone and a set of speakers to the RP3.

We use power to connect the RP3s instead of extra batteries (for example, power banks). To measure energy consumption, we used a direct plug-in energy meter [10].

5.2 Implementation

This section presents details of the implementation of the proposed system. We describe the technical details about the sharing decision control component, including internal sharing with context-aware and authentication mechanisms, as well as the integration between the sell data component and marketplaces.

Sharing Decision Control

Most firewalls have blocking rules that deal primarily with IP addresses. The relationship between a domain and its IP addresses is slightly loose, because a domain can have multiple IP addresses that can change frequently. For example, in the *iptables* tool, even if the users specify a domain name as part of a rule, the DNS lookup will be done once, and the tool will create a new rule for the resulting IP address. Therefore, it is impossible to block any connection from a full domain name, including all subdomains. Besides, the tool creates a rule with the first IP address, and if the address changes, the *iptables* rules will be out of date.

Another problem is that an IP address can host many domains and, if users block or allow one of these IP addresses, all domains hosted on it will also be allowed/denied. Likewise, when we allow an IP that hosts many domains, we allow multiple services and create a security problem due to exposure to other types of services. An example is *Cloudflare* [23], which provides a large number of services to websites and sits between the public Internet and a server. *Cloudflare* users do not point their DNS to their server; instead, the users point their DNS to *Cloudflare* and then point *Cloudflare* to their server. Therefore, the same IP address is associated with millions of servers (*Cloudflare*'s IP addresses). Therefore, when one of these IP addresses is blocked/allowed, all sites pointed to them are also blocked/allowed.

Proxy servers are another widely used method of blocking access to websites. However, without an SSL introspection mechanism, a proxy generally can not decrypt HyperText Transfer Protocol Secure (HTTPS) and, therefore, can not know the IP address and content. To drop the connection, we would need at least information about the IP address/URL. For this setup, we tested Squid [27], which has an option to decrypt requests transmitted using the HTTPS protocol called SSL Bump. However, as HTTPS provides security and privacy, decrypting these HTTPS tunnels without consent may violate ethical standards and be illegal, depending on the jurisdiction [28]. From a practical point of view, in this scenario, we have data similar to an ISP; if we use the proxy, no communication will be secret, making the system incompatible with the General Data Protection Regulation (GDPR) with all messages exchanged in *WhatsApp* or *Google*, for example, exposed on the local and remote machine.

For these reasons, we choose a firewall solution based on the SNI. By default, Transport Layer Security (TLS) [6] connections do not provide a mechanism for a client to tell a server the name of the server it is contacting. The header containing the Fully Qualified Domain Name (FQDN) [35] is encrypted, so we are unable to access that name. To overcome this problem, we choose the SNI extension for TLS, where a client indicates which hostname it is attempting to connect to at the beginning of the handshaking process. This field is part of the ClientHello message of the TLS negotiation (before encrypted communications), so that we can access the unencrypted hostname.

The main advantage of choosing a firewall solution based on the SNI is that we can allow/block a specific hostname connection by solving the problems mentioned by the other solutions we tested.

For the implementation of this concept, we use an extension for *iptables* to filter TLS traffic based on the SNI [34]. In addition, we use a combination of *SNIdump* (similar to TCPdump) and *whois*, to provide the user with real-time information.

Context-Aware Internal Sharing

Context-aware systems can dynamically and automatically adapt to changes in the environment and users' current needs without requiring their attention. There are several definitions of context, such as ambiance, attitude, circumstance, dependence, environment, location, occasion, perspective, phase, place, position, posture, situation, status, standing, surroundings, and terms. There is much research on context-aware computing over the years [21,29,33], especially related to self-learning techniques in IoT and decision making.

In this work, we combine some concepts already introduced in other related works to achieve the goal of defining different identities and access control policies for a device. The initial goal is to understand the context of the device and what types of context we want to address. As an example, users can set different permissions for their smartwatches, depending on the context (for example, location: at *home* or *work*). In this example, users can decide not to share their heart rate in the *work* context, but do not mind sharing the number of steps per day; on the other hand, in the *home* context, users can decide to allow the storage of all data. In summary, context-based techniques are essential to automate some privacy settings in decision making.

However, there is a drawback to this approach, as it can be attractive for attackers, trying to set the user location to *home* when the user is actually at *work* or *mall*, to get their benefits (for example, opening the user's home window) [18]. To mitigate some of these risks associated only with the context, in addition to the authentication process, we use a set of sensors with some extra information, namely WiFi, Bluetooth, and GPS, instead of using only one sensor.

In addition to these conditions, it is essential to detect some possible abnormal patterns autonomously. For this, the middleware creates a database with a history of usage patterns on each device. Thus, if the middleware receives a request for permission to open a window due to the user's presence at home, at a time when the user is never at home according to historical usage patterns, the middleware should notify and request the user intervention manually to decide whether the window will open or not. In this example, this feature is vital to ensure that we are not facing a geolocation attack or other types of attacks based on changes to sensor data that influence context-based decisions. Therefore, if any of the predefined conditions fail (in terms of sensor data and usage patterns), the user will need to intervene and grant specific permissions for those specific cases manually.

Authentication

For security and testing purposes, the system uses certificates (public and private keys) where the router's owner is responsible for creating the Certificate Authority (CA) and distribute the certificates.

The system uses Elliptic Curve Digital Signature Algorithm (ECDSA) 256-bit to generate the CA and an Elliptic Curve Integrated Encryption Scheme (ECIES) 256-bit key pair to generate a shared key without the need for the Diffie-Hellman exchange. Elliptic Curve Cryptography (ECC) [15] can provide the security level relatively equal to the RSA with a smaller key [13].

We developed a Python implementation, requiring the *pycrypto* library. The *Crypto.PublicKey.ECC* module provides facilities for generating new ECC keys, allowing them to be rebuilt from known components, exported and imported. We use the Elliptic Curve Diffie Hellman Ephemeral (ECDHE) [19] algorithm for client authentication and the implementation is based on two existing implementations of ECC and ECIES [3,5].

Sell Data

This concept focuses on the control of data sharing on the user side, not necessarily on the market itself. The idea focuses on linking the middleware to an external third-party marketplace that does all sales management. For demonstration purposes, we integrate with the implementation of a market created by *Xiangchen Zhao et al.* [38]. With this implementation, user registration is manual, and users need to provide the data to the market for sale. For this, the middleware is ready and provides users with a well-defined API with the data they choose to sell.

5.3   Results

Regarding performance, we measure the latency that a request/response takes to reach our device if it has to go through a certain number of *iptables* rules. For that, we use *iPerf* [8], an open-source program that generates traffic to allow performance tests on networks to measure bandwidth and link quality between two points. Besides, it measures delay jitter. We generate *iptables* rules with random IPs that do not match the tested client's IP (therefore, the client's request needs to test all the rules).

We tested with 0, 50, 500, 5000 and 50000 rules, and we present the results of UDP jitter (in milliseconds (ms) with standard deviation (sd)) and TCP bandwidth (in Mbits per second with sd) on the Table 1.

Table 1. *iPerf* measures

Num. rules	0	50	500	5000	50000
TCP bandwidth (Mbits/sec $\pm$ sd)	26.7 ± 1.45	26.4 ± 1.84	25.9 ± 2.65	16.5 ± 0.78	3.35 ± 0.48
UDP jitter (ms $\pm$ sd)	0.43 ± 0.29	0.38 ± 0.42	0.46 ± 0.29	0.43 ± 0.41	4.98 ± 1.29

There is no significant difference in jitter and bandwidth using 0 or 5000 rules. These results show that the *iptables* tool is efficient, and that, despite the increased jitter and decreased bandwidth, when the number of rules is much higher (50000 rules), the solution remains viable and, therefore, the proposed solution can handle a large number of rules.

In terms of energy consumed, the RP3 spends 3.8 W without services running on the system. With middleware and a database, the energy consumption remains the same. When the middleware performs encryption and decryption, the energy spent is not significantly different, varying only 0.6 W up and down.

6   Security Analysis

This section overviews a threat model and some attack scenarios to perform a security analysis of our proposal.

6.1   Threat Model

The owner distributes the certificates to trusted devices; therefore, the owner is responsible for the safety of that component. Assuming that the CA is trusted, all keys signed by the CA will be implicitly trusted. The role of CAs is to ensure that a key belongs to a trusted device after authentication between them.

When the IoT device communicates with the router, it knows that it is the real router (as it belongs to the same certification authority) and not an attacker who impersonates it. All communications use HTTPS, and, therefore, all content transmitted between devices is encrypted.

Regarding context-aware access control, if an attacker successfully attacks the system, the user-defined assumptions will take action, and a new HTTPS server that behaves as a router will not be accepted. In brief, a traditional Man-in-the-Middle (MitM) will not work as HTTPS certificates will not match. Besides, as already described in Sect. 5.2, the user has to manually intervene when there is a coordination failure in the ambient sensors or based on historical usage patterns.

6.2   Attack Scenarios

In this section, we present and evaluate some attack scenarios regarding the system implementation. We used some set of theorems adapting those used by *Afifi et al.* [1] and we added more that we find essential for this approach.

Claim 1. Security against tag impersonation attacks.
As already mentioned, the owner is responsible for distributing certificates to trusted devices, making that security anchored on the owner.

For filtering traffic and prevent MitM attacks, we chose the *iptables* firewall solution. First, contrarily to the proxy solution, we do not need to do MitM on HTTPS communication to decrypt it, which would make us susceptible to MitM, as SSL bump already does this type of attack on its own.

SNI also constitutes some impersonation problems [30]. However, a device will not accept the connection with itself if the certificate does not match the desired one, so it is not a problem. Also, with *iptables*, the user can define a permission that takes effect only during a specific time window so that there are no unwanted communications outside the period defined by the user. For an attacker, it would be challenging to impersonate the certificate precisely during the period in which the user allows communication, in addition to needing to know which devices the user has.

Claim 2. Security against replay attacks.
HTTPS has a server-chosen random number, which is the server's first response in the handshake sequence [11]. If an attacker captures and tries to resend a message, the server must never allow it due to duplicate nonce. As nonce ensures that the server cannot reuse old communications, this method protects the replay attacks.

Claim 3. Resistance to Single Point of Failure.
On white-box devices, users can choose the data to be saved on the router or each of their devices, using a distributed model, rather than stored in a central database or cloud. The advantage of this model, unlike a central database, is that a central database server represents a single point of failure, in which, once compromised, it compromises the security of all users.

We know that we also have a single point of failure on the router, but we have reduced the attack surface because, in the event of an attack, it only compromises one user. Besides, users can choose not to save data on the router, leaving it only on each of their devices (for a limited time, also defined by the user). With that, we have a distributed model, even inside the user's homes.

7   Conclusions and Future Work

We offer a novel middleware to improve the privacy of users' data on the IoT, with implementation and evaluation. Middleware gives users the ability to control the privacy of their data. Also, users can store data to be controlled offline and to analyze current connections, discarding them according to the user's preferences, without delay, extensible to network communications.

Unlike previous work, the developed middleware is independent of the device's SDK, as control is placed at the device and router layers, allowing users to fully control the shared data.

We have a real implementation with an RP3 emulating a Google Home with a Google Assistant and sensors attached to it, with the middleware integrated.

Based on our evaluation, we can state that *iptables* are viable in the implementation, presenting only differences in performance for 50000 rules.

As future work, we will create a real environment with a router with *Open-WRT* running the middleware that we created and with black-box devices together with the Raspberry PI's. It is also essential to enhance the current marketplace implementations with aggregated data and anonymization selected by each user, maintaining privacy properties and compliance with GDPR.

Acknowledgements. This work is financed by National Funds through the Portuguese funding agency, FCT - Fundação para a Ciência e a Tecnologia, within project UIDB/50014/2020. Patrícia R. Sousa's work was supported by a scholarship from the Fundação para a Ciência e Tecnologia (FCT), Portugal (scholarships number SFRH/BD/135696/2018). This work has also been supported by the EU H2020-SU-ICT-03-2018 Project No. 830929 CyberSec4Europe (cybersec4europe.eu) and by National Funds through the Agência para a Modernização Administrativa, program POCI - Programa Operacional Competitividade e Internacionalização, within project POCI-05-5762-FSE-000229.1

References

1. Afifi, M.H., Zhou, L., Chakrabartty, S., Ren, J.: Dynamic authentication protocol using self-powered timers for passive internet of things. IEEE Internet Things J. 5(4), 2927–2935 (2017)
2. Al-Hasnawi, A., Lilien, L.: Pushing data privacy control to the edge in IoT using policy enforcement fog module. In: Companion Proceedings of the 10th International Conference on Utility and Cloud Computing, pp. 145–150 (2017)
3. Buchanan, B.: Elliptic curve integrated encryption scheme (ECIES) with rabbit (2019). https://asecuritysite.com/encryption/ecc2

4. Conti, M., Dehghantanha, A., Franke, K., Watson, S.: Internet of things security and forensics: challenges and opportunities (2018)
5. Corbellini, A.: Elliptic curve cryptography: a gentle introduction (2015). https://github.com/andreacorbellini/ecc
6. Dierks, T., Rescorla, E.: The transport layer security (TLS) protocol version 1.2. RFC 5246, August 2008
7. Drozd, O., Kirrane, S.: I agree: customize your personal data processing with the CoRe user interface. In: Gritzalis, S., Weippl, E.R., Katsikas, S.K., Anderst-Kotsis, G., Tjoa, A.M., Khalil, I. (eds.) TrustBus 2019. LNCS, vol. 11711, pp. 17–32. Springer, Cham (2019). https://doi.org/10.1007/978-3-030-27813-7_2
8. Dugan, J.: Iperf tutorial. Columbus: Summer JointTechs, pp. 1–4 (2010)
9. Eastlake, D.E.: Transport layer security (TLS) extensions: extension definitions. RFC 6066, pp. 1–25 (2011)
10. Efergy: Efergy home energy monitors: electricity usage power monitor (2006). https://efergy.com/about-efergy/
11. Forouzan, B.A.: Cryptography & Network Security. McGraw-Hill Inc., New York (2007)
12. Goddard, M.: The EU general data protection regulation (GDPR): European regulation that has a global impact. Int. J. Market Res. **59**(6), 703–705 (2017)
13. Gueron, S., Krasnov, V.: Fast prime field elliptic-curve cryptography with 256-bit primes. J. Cryptogr. Eng. **5**(2), 141–151 (2014). https://doi.org/10.1007/s13389-014-0090-x
14. Haar, C., Buchmann, E.: Fane: a firewall appliance for the smart home. In: 2019 Federated Conference on Computer Science and Information Systems (FedCSIS), pp. 449–458. IEEE (2019)
15. Koblitz, N.: Elliptic curve cryptosystems. Math. Comput. **48**(177), 203–209 (1987)
16. Lastdrager, E., Hesselman, C., Jansen, J., Davids, M.: Protecting home networks from insecure IoT devices. In: NOMS 2020–2020 IEEE/IFIP Network Operations and Management Symposium, pp. 1–6. IEEE (2020)
17. Lopez, J., Rios, R., Bao, F., Wang, G.: Evolving privacy: from sensors to the internet of things. Future Gener. Comput. Syst. **75**, 46–57 (2017)
18. de Matos, E., Tiburski, R.T., Amaral, L.A., Hessel, F.: Providing context-aware security for IoT environments through context sharing feature. In: 2018 17th IEEE International Conference on Trust, Security And Privacy in Computing and Communications/12th IEEE International Conference on Big Data Science and Engineering (TrustCom/BigDataSE), pp. 1711–1715. IEEE (2018)
19. Nir, Y., Josefsson, S., Pegourie-Gonnard, M.: Elliptic curve cryptography (ECC) cipher suites for transport layer security (TLS) versions 1.2 and earlier. Internet Requests for Comments, RFC Editor, RFC 8422 (2018)
20. OpenDNS: Phishtank: An anti-phishing site (2016). https://www.phishtank.com
21. Perera, C., Zaslavsky, A., Christen, P., Georgakopoulos, D.: Context aware computing for the internet of things: a survey. IEEE Commun. Surv. Tutor. **16**(1), 414–454 (2013)
22. Pihole: Pi-hole® network-wide ad blocking (2015). https://pi-hole.net/
23. Prince, M.: Technical details behind a 400Gbps NTP amplification DDoS attack. Cloudflare, Inc (2014)
24. Ren, J., Dubois, D.J., Choffnes, D., Mandalari, A.M., Kolcun, R., Haddadi, H.: Information exposure from consumer IoT devices: a multidimensional, network-informed measurement approach. In: Proceedings of the Internet Measurement Conference, pp. 267–279 (2019)

25. NPR and Edison Research: The smart audio report (2017). https://n.pr/2zEk4UE
26. Roesch, M.: Snort - lightweight intrusion detection for networks. In: Proceedings of the 13th USENIX Conference on System Administration, LISA 1999, pp. 229–238. USENIX Association, USA (1999)
27. Rousskov, A.: Squid: Optimising web delivery (2013). http://www.squid-cache.org/
28. Rousskov, A., Tsantilas, C.: Squid-in-the-middle SSL bump (2019). https://wiki.squid-cache.org/Features/SslBump
29. Sezer, O.B., Dogdu, E., Ozbayoglu, A.M.: Context-aware computing, learning, and big data in internet of things: a survey. IEEE Internet Things J. 5(1), 1–27 (2017)
30. Shbair, W.M., Cholez, T., Goichot, A., Chrisment, I.: Efficiently bypassing SNI-based https filtering. In: 2015 IFIP/IEEE International Symposium on Integrated Network Management (IM), pp. 990–995. IEEE (2015)
31. Sivaraman, V., Gharakheili, H.H., Vishwanath, A., Boreli, R., Mehani, O.: Network-level security and privacy control for smart-home IoT devices. In: 2015 IEEE 11th International Conference on Wireless and Mobile Computing, Networking and Communications (WiMob), pp. 163–167. IEEE (2015)
32. Sørensen, D.A., Vanggaard, N., Pedersen, J.M.: Automatic profile-based firewall for IoT devices (2017). https://bit.ly/3fjjCdA
33. Sukode, S., Gite, S., Agrawal, H.: Context aware framework in IoT: a survey. Int. J. 4(1) (2015)
34. Svee, N.A.: Filter TLS traffic with iptables (2016). https://github.com/Lochnair/xt_tls
35. Volz, B.: The dynamic host configuration protocol for IPv6 (DHCPv6) client fully qualified domain name (FQDN) option. RFC 4704, pp. 1–15 (2006)
36. Wang, H., Zhang, Z., Taleb, T.: Special issue on security and privacy of IoT. World Wide Web 21(1), 1–6 (2018). https://doi.org/10.1007/s11280-017-0490-9
37. Yang, C., Huang, Q., Li, Z., Liu, K., Hu, F.: Big data and cloud computing: innovation opportunities and challenges. Int. J. Digit. Earth 10(1), 13–53 (2017)
38. Zhao, X., Sajan, K.K., Ramachandran, G.S., Krishnamachari, B.: Demo abstract: the intelligent IoT integrator data marketplace-version 1. In: 2020 IEEE/ACM Fifth International Conference on Internet-of-Things Design and Implementation (IoTDI), pp. 270–271. IEEE (2020)

Utility Requirement Description for Utility-Preserving and Privacy-Respecting Data Pseudonymization

Saffija Kasem-Madani[1(✉)] and Michael Meier[1,2]

[1] University of Bonn, 53115 Bonn, Germany
{kasem,mm}@cs.uni-bonn.de
[2] Fraunhofer FKIE, 53177 Bonn, Germany

Abstract. Many of the existing pseudonymization techniques aim at preserving the use-case specific utility of the data. However, retracing under which condition a utility is present in pseudonymized data is hard. Therefore, specifying and applying pseudonymization techniques adequately becomes challenging to non-experts. There is the need for a solution that enables non-experts to generate pseudonymizations that can be utilized in their specific use case without deep understanding of pseudonymization techniques. To address this, we introduce a methodology for describing the utility that should be kept after pseudonymizing data together with privacy restrictions that must be respected while processing the pseudonymized data. We present Util, a description language for defining utility policies, i.e. policies that document utility requirements together with privacy requirements. Using Util does not require deeper knowledge of pseudonymization function and their parametrization. We sketch rules that can be used to translate from a utility policy to an appropriate data pseudonymization. For that, we introduce pseudonymization with utility tags.

Keywords: Privacy · Pseudonymization · Policy language · Utility · GDPR

1 Introduction

Analysing personal data is a common research task. A researcher who collects personal (survey) data for conducting a research study must consider legal and privacy requirements. Survey participants have concerns about their privacy and potential illegal leakage of their private information. Data protection rules, e.g. the General Data Protection Regulations (GDPR) [3], demand for at least pseudonymizing personal data. Many use cases, e.g. study questions demand that at least some individuals can be linked to their data under priorly defined strict conditions. An example is linking data belonging to exactly one

© Springer Nature Switzerland AG 2020
S. Gritzalis et al. (Eds.): TrustBus 2020, LNCS 12395, pp. 171–185, 2020.
https://doi.org/10.1007/978-3-030-58986-8_12

individual to each other without explicitly re-identifying the concerned individual or even to re-identify an individual. Linking data to each other is required when, for example, two data attribute values of an individual should be compared to each other, or when the identity of an individual must be disclosed for billing. Applying anonymization techniques on such data would destroy the desired utility, while providing privacy guarantees. In practice, data is therefore often "pseudonymized" by removing direct identifiers and keeping the remaining data in plaintext, allowing to be combined to quasi-identifiers and hence possibly revealing identities. Pseudonymizing plaintext data with techniques that hide most possible information of the plaintexts while keeping the desired utility is a compromise: Utility is guaranteed, while obtaining the whole information of the plaintext is made comparably hard. The GDPR [3] states in Article 4(5) that data is pseudonymized if, after transformation, it cannot be attributed to a specific data subject without the use of separately kept "additional information". This includes keyed encryption of personal data. Pseudonymization techniques transform personal data into utilizable representations that at least reduce the risk of disclosing their information and hence to their privacy. However, configuring and making use of pseudonymization techniques is nontrivial. This includes choosing and correctly parametrizing appropriate pseudonymization techniques that keep the desired utility while preserving privacy. Experts in other fields, e.g. researcher who analyse personal survey data have the burden to apply pseudonymization techniques correctly. They need to identify which data should be transformed using which pseudonymization techniques, how it should be parametrized and which implementation should be chosen. For example, whether to use a probabilistic or deterministic encryption mechanism, or to choose seeds or keys for cryptographic hashing. Finally, they need to know which seeds and keys should be kept under restricted access. This *data transformation process* requires a deeper understanding of PET than should typically be expected from non-experts.

In this work, we introduce an additional layer of abstraction to the data transformation process. Utility and privacy requirements are defined in a so-called utility policy written in a policy language named Util. A researcher could express the utility she needs for conducting analysis of personal (survey) data using Util policies. Following the translation rules we define, a Util policy can also be used to automatically configure pseudonymization functions. For that, we introduce a so-called utility-tag based pseudonym construction which allows for automatically producing a pseudonymization that keeps the data utility. By choosing strong security mechanisms, the risk to privacy is at least lowered. Making use of our mechanism does not require deep expertise in pseudonymization techniques. This would ease the use for a researcher.

Our contribution is as follows:

– We describe common utility and privacy requirements a data pseudonymization should fulfill.

– We define Util, a policy language that allows non-experts to define utility and privacy requirements that must be fulfilled by a dataset after being pseudonymized.
– We describe translation rules that can be used to automatically derive the functions and their parametrization for a pseudonymization which matches the utility requirements stated in a utility policy.
– We define a utility-tag based pseudonym construction that allows for a flexible construction of pseudonyms in the presented approach.

The rest of this paper is organized as follows: In Sect. 2, background knowledge is listed. In Sect. 3, Related Work is discussed. In Sect. 4, Utility and privacy requirements are explained. In Sect. 5, the utility policy language Util is introduced. In Sect. 6, the utility-tag based pseudonym construction and a translation from utility and privacy requirements from a utility policy into pseudonyms are explained. Finally, the work is concluded and future work is outlined in Sect. 7.

2   Background

In this section, relevant notions and techniques are basically introduced. We consider use cases in which semi-structured personal data are collected for analysis purposes. We assume that the planned analyses are already known, e.g. like in many medical and sociological studies. For legal and privacy reasons, the data ist protected by applying privacy enhancing technologies (PET) [10]. PET include anonymization and pseudonymization techniques. Anonymization techniques transform personal data to representations which do not allow to re-identify subjects using them [19]. Pseudonymization techniques transform personal data in such a way that it is not possible to re-identify subjects using that data unless dedicated additional data is combined with it. The GDPR [3] define data protection principles that should be followed when processing personal data. These include processing the data *lawfully* and in a way that is *fair* and *transparent* to the concerned individual. Processing personal data should be limited to a well-defined purpose *(purpose limitation)*, only be processed when absolutely necessary for fulfilling the desired purpose *(data minimization)*, and it should be accurate and up-to date. Personal data should not be stored longer that absolutely necessary for fulfilling the purpose of data processing *(storage limitation)*, and must be secured using organizational and technical means that ensure *integrity and confidentiality*, which imply accountability. In Sects. 4.2 and 6, we get back to these principles to build corresponding structures in Util.

As pseudonymization techniques, we especially consider building blocks of cryptographic hashing [15], symmetric and asymmetric encryption [18], and homomorphic encryption (HE) [1]. HE allows to perform homomorphic operations on the encrypted data. Data that is encrypted using $*$-HE allows for performing a set of operations that are homomorphic to $*$ on the encrypted data, i.e. yielding the result of performing $*$ on the underlying plaintexts and then encrypting them. Examples are additively (e.g. Paillier [14]), multiplicatively (e.g. ElGamal [4]), and fully homomorphic HE (e.g. Gentry [5]). For security reasons, only asymmetric HE is used.

For the rest of this work, we consider semi-structured datasets D of attribute values d_i or d alternatively. $P(D)$ is a pseudonymization of D.

3   Related Work

For this work, we identify three main categories of relevant related work: Policy-based data sanitization tools, privacy policy languages for the sake of comparing Util to them, and existing definitions of utility requirements for examining their suitability for the use within Util.

Policy-Based Data Pseudonymization. In LiDSec [11], a policy language is used to define which sanitization the presented pseudonymization framework should apply to textual semi-structured data for sharing purposes. Each data attribute value can either be kept in plaintext in the pseudonymization, or removed or suppressed, i.e. replaced with a pseudonym. It is also possible to specify entire rows of the data. In contrast to our work, the required utility cannot be explicitly formulated. It is only possible to state rules that sanitizes the data in an implicitly utility-preserving manner, i.e. expert knowledge of PET is required. FLAIM [20] follows a similar approach: a sanitization tool for log data uses sanitization rules of a so-called anonymization policy language. In contrast to LiDSec, an addressed data attribute value can be replaced by outputs of different rules, which imply the desired utility. None of the presented tools includes policy rules that allow for restrictions on the usage of utility.

Privacy Policy Languages. There exist several policy languages for defining privacy-relevant constraints on data usage and access [13,21]. Mostly, they do not provide structure that can be used for defining utility on the level of attribute values. Rather, they carry information on who is allowed to access already pseudonymized data for which purpose and duration in certain use cases. Gerl et al. define a pseudonymization language that allows for GDPR-friendly definition of pseudonyms in health data [6]. Similar to others, the specifications of the pseudonyms are described in terms of pseudonymization functions. To the best of our knowledge, none of the present policy languages allows for fine-grained description of utility requirements without the need of deep expertise in PET or remarkable extensions of the policy language.

Utility Definition. The known definitions of utility mostly rely on a holistic view on the utilizability of data [9,12,16,17]. Often, they are defined as optimization problems on the whole dataset. As a result, this kind of definitions enables for estimating the privacy risk and quality of analysis that result from the utility of a data collection and from applying a number of data analysis techniques. However, it does neither allow to define access restrictions and constraints nor to define explicit property preservation on selected attribute values. As a result, utility-preserving pseudonymization techniques cannot be easily addressed with these definitions of utility. Moreover, non-privacy experts would not be able to easily use these functions for a description of utility requirements.

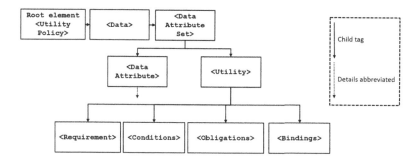

Fig. 1. Basic `Util` policy structure

4   Utility and Privacy Requirements

We describe the requirements a pseudonymization produced using the utility policy language `Util` should fulfill. This includes utility requirements which are originated in the use case, and privacy requirements which are originated in GDPR data protection principles.

4.1   Utility Requirements

For generating and processing meaningful pseudonymizations, we firstly address the requirements it should fulfill. In the following, we introduce utility requirements that can be addressed by pseudonymization functions to generate pseudonymizations appropriately. Note that the requirements are neither exhaustive nor necessarily disjunct. Rather, they enable users to easily describe the utility of various common use cases. Therefore, it is also meant to be extensible. Summarizing, `Util` offers an intuitional layer of abstract describability which can further be built upon.

Linkability demands to link attribute values of D to each other, i.e. use the corresponding pseudonyms to determine whether they belong to an l-dimensional relation r or not, with $l \geq 2$. We call pseudonyms that are linkable w.r.t. a relation r r-linkable. On $P(D)$, we distinguish between pseudonym-pseudonym and plaintext-pseudonym linkability. Examples are equality-linkability and less-equal-linkability. Pseudonyms $p_1, \cdots, p_l$ of plaintexts $d_1, \cdots, d_l$ respectively, are *r-pseudonym-pseudonym linkable*, if the underlying plaintexts $d_1, \cdots, d_l$ fulfill $(d_1, \cdots, d_l) \in r$ and if this condition can be tested using the pseudonyms $p_1, \cdots, p_l$ and without accessing $d_1, \cdots, d_l$. A pseudonym p of a plaintext d is *r-plaintext-pseudonym* linkable w.r.t. a set of plaintexts A if for each $a \in A$ it is possible to determine whether $(a, d) \in r$ using p without accessing d.

Disclosability allows for disclosure of the plaintext data d of a pseudonym p. Obviously, making use of disclosability leaks the entire underlying plaintext. Therefore, making use of disclosability should be restricted. Its criticality in the

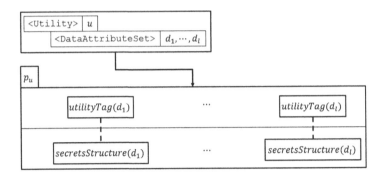

Fig. 2. Structure of a pseudonym of a utility u for attribute values $d_1, \cdots, d_l$.

sense of privacy depends on the sensitivity of the information and how likely it can be used to re-identify subjects with high probability.

Operation. $\star$ allows for effectively performing an operation $\star$ on plaintexts. This is achieved by producing pseudonyms that, when an operation $\ast$ is performed on it, the result is a representation from which one can acquire the result of performing $\star$ on the underlying plaintexts. One example is acquiring the sum of plaintexts by homomorphically adding the corresponding pseudonyms (operation addition). Note that making use of this utility may disclose the whole plaintexts and therefore must be specially secured, e.g. by monitoring and limiting the number and combination of accessed pseudonyms.

Algorithm. $\mathcal{A}$ allows for performing an implementation of an algorithm $\tilde{\mathcal{A}}$ on pseudonyms, $\tilde{\mathcal{A}}$ is a privacy-preserving variant of $\mathcal{A}$. The output of executing the implementation $\tilde{\mathcal{I}}$ of $\tilde{\mathcal{A}}$ should be at least close to the output of executing an implementation $\mathcal{I}$ of $\mathcal{A}$ on the underlying plaintexts, with respect to appropriate metrics. As for the Operation utility, (intermediate) computation results may allow for plaintext disclosure, and securing mechanisms must therefore be considered similarly. An example for the `Algorithm` utility is obtaining the result of a classification mechanism in an appropriate implementation using only the pseudonyms. Note that for security reasons, many privacy-preserving variants of algorithms are designed as multiparty protocols. Examples can be found in [8].

Obligations are auxiliary conditions that are defined together with a main utility requirement. Examples are following a certain data format, checking for feasibility of timestamps, postal codes and ages, and so on.

4.2 Privacy Requirements

Pseudonymized data should leak less information than plaintexts and hence, incorporate a reduced risk of re-identifiability of concerned individuals. However, for the reason of utilizability the remaining information does not vanish the risk of re-identifiability. Therefore, the GDPR demands pseudonymized data to be treated as careful as plaintext personal data, i.e., the pseudonymized data underlies some restrictions which we refer to as *privacy requirements*. In the following, we describe the data protection goals on pseudonymized data that are given special attention in Util.

Restriction of Re-identification of Data Subjects. Re-identification of data subjects should only be possible in case and in the duration that is necessary for fulfilling the purpose of processing. This implies that disclosure of plaintext data should be avoided whenever unnecessary, especially when the underlying plaintexts are sensitive or (quasi)-identifier. However, the GDPR allows for balancing utility and privacy. This is because, depending on the defined use case, is necessary to use less stronger privacy mechanisms to achieve appropriate practicability.

Storage Limitation. The data should not be stored longer than required for fulfilling the purpose of data processing and must be safeguarded by technical and organizational means. For that, one may define the durability of data whenever possible.

Data Minimization. Pseudonymizing data is an information-reducing and hence a data minimizing technique. Pseudonymized data should leak least personal information possible for fulfilling the desired purpose. Moreover, only purpose-necessary data should be represented in the data pseudonymization.

Sensitive Information and Implications of Processing. Sensitive personal data ease the re-identification or reveal very intimate information about an individual. The data processing and the underlying purposes are following the restrictions stated in article 9 of the GDPR. Among others, these restrictions include that the consent to processing for one or more specified purposes is explicitly given by the data subject.

Mitigation and Risk Minimization. State-of the art means of minimizing the risk of information disclosure must be implemented.

Retention Separation. Pseudonymized data should be stored secured and separated from additional information that is required to disclose plaintext data.

Purpose and Role Binding. Personal data should only be collected and further processed for a dedicated purpose. Thus, we bind the use of utility to a certain, well-defined initial purpose and to users who hold a role defined in the processing system.

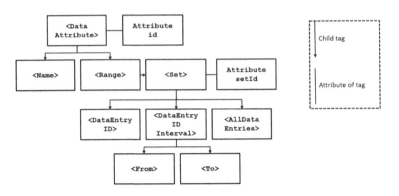

Fig. 3. Structure of the data attribute tag.

5   Utility Policy Language `Util`

`Util` is a machine-readable XML-based utility policy language. A utility policy U for data D written in `Util` is formulated to persist and document the utility requirements with privacy constraints that should be fulfilled by the pseudonymization P of data D. In the following, we describe `Util`: the structure of a policy, the data addressing and how utility and privacy requirements are combined in a single utility policy.

Each attribute value of the data under consideration has been priorly tagged with attribute names for addressing those that should be represented in the pseudonymization. We assume that only data that is referred to in the policy is represented in the pseudonymization (confidentiality by default).

Basic Policy Structure. The policy is of a data-attribute centric structure. The root tag `<UtilityPolicy>` denotes the beginning of a single policy for a single dataset D. For each utility requirement, a tag `<Utility>` is introduced. There, all involved data attributes that should fulfill that utility are declared together using the child tag `<DataAttributeSet>`. Note that the attribute values referred to in `<DataAttributeSet>` must be contained in `<Data>`. The utility requirement is specified using the child tag `<Requirement>`. The `<Conditions>` and `<Bindings>` children tags are used to specify explicit privacy requirements, i.e. bind the availability of the utility to dedicated conditions, roles or purposes. Additional utility requirements, e.g. following a certain data format, can be specified using the `<Obligations>`. Note that it is obligatory to specify at least one of the `<Conditions>` and `<Bindings>` tags. Figure 1 shows an overview of the basic structure of a utility policy.

Data Addressing. The tag `<Data>` is used with the tag attribute `type` to define whether the data is of the `type` of statically fixed dataset or a continuously extending data stream. This is because a privacy-enhancing technology that pseudonymizes the data according to a defined utility policy may significantly

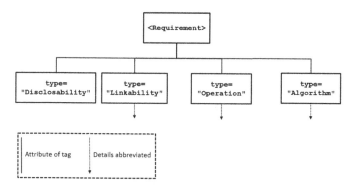

Fig. 4. The utility requirements.

differ based on the data type. To address data attribute values used for a utility, a `<DataAttributeSet>` contains one `<DataAttribute>` child tag for each different attribute. There, the attribute values are enumerated based on their order in D. Sensitive data attributes have the `sensitive` attribute of the corresponding `<DataAttribute>` tag set to the value `yes`. A single `<DataAttribute>` tag may define a single attribute value by its `id` (e.g. a row number or timestamp) using the `<DataEntryID>` tag, or all involved attribute values (`<AllDataEntries>`), or all attribute values within an interval (`<DataEntryIDInterval>`). This is to ease the exclusion of certain data attribute values. Each set of attribute values of a single data attribute is included in a `<Set>` tag and referred to with a unique `setId`, which is then used to address the involved subsets of the attribute values to specify the utility in the `<Requirement>` tag. Figure 3 shows the structure of `<DataAttributeSet>`.

Utility Requirements. Each utility requirement is represented as a child tag of the `<Requirement>` tag as shown in Fig. 4. The structure of the children tags for each of the utility requirements are sketched in Figs. 5 and 7. For obligations, bindings and conditions, the structure is sketched in Fig. 6.

6   Pseudonym Construction and Transformation Rules

For D, we consider a pseudonymization $P(D)$ of D as a collection of utility-wise transformations of the attribute values into pseudonyms. I.e., we consider a pseudonym $p_u(D')$ as a transformation of all attribute values of a subset $D' \subseteq D$ that are involved in fulfilling a utility requirement u. In order to construct a pseudonymization of D, the utility and privacy requirements are extracted from the utility policy U. The pseudonym $p_u(D')$ of a utility requirement u of U is a data structure of several utility tags which link to a so-called secrets structure. Each attribute value which is formulated in a utility requirement's `<DataAttributeSet>` is mapped to a single utility tag and a corresponding object variable in the secrets structure. The content of the utility tag and the

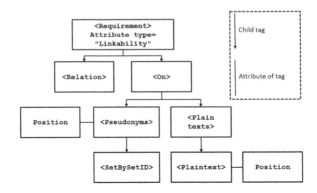

Fig. 5. The structure of the utility requirement linkability.

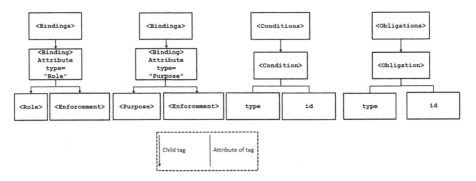

Fig. 6. The structure of the privacy requirements bindings and conditions, and the obligations utility requirement.

corresponding object variable depends on the desired utility and the privacy requirements that are defined for it. As a result, each pseudonym consists of a set of utility tags and a set of accompanying secrets object variables. Each utility tag is the result of applying a utility-preserving peudonymization function on a plaintext. Parameters of the pseudonymization function are separately stored in the accompanying object variable of the secrets structure. When making use of the utility tags, a monitoring mechanism of the processing system is assumed to manage the access to the required elements of the secrets structure, which should be outsourced to an especially secured separated system.

In the following, we describe possible translations from utility and privacy requirements of a Util policy into matching pseudonym constructions for a range of utilities. For each of the listed utility requirements, we describe the content of the utility tag and the object variable of the secrets structure. We show how privacy requirements influence the structure of the pseudonym. Remembering the definitions of the utility requirements in Sect. 4.1, a pseudonym fulfills a utility requirement u if it contains a utility tag which fulfills that requirement.

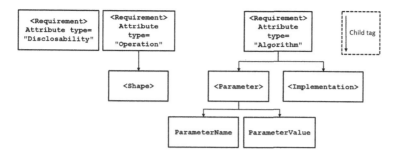

Fig. 7. The structure of the utility requirements disclosability, operation and algorithm.

Note that the listed utility requirements is neither exhaustive, nor are the translation rules exclusively possible PET transformation solutions. In Fig. 2, the basic structure of a pseudonym is sketched.

Utility Requirements

Linkability. For a `<Requirement>` tag attributed with ''Linkability'' with child tag `<Relation>` with the value r, a pseudonymization function is used that produces pseudonyms which can be linked according to r. Both pseudonym-pseudonym linkability and pseudonym-plaintext linkability can be specified and then produced by an appropriate pseudonymization function. The pseudonyms and the corresponding object variable of the secrets structure are tagged with the `setID` of the `<DataAttributeSet>`. An example is the equality relation. Firstly, a salt s is generated. Then, each attribute value d of the `<DataAttributeSet>` is hashed using a cryptographic hashing function together with s, e.g. $SHA3(d|s)$ [2] and the resulting value is stored in the utility tag. The optional attribute `Position` of the `<Pseudonym>` child tag in the linkability structure denotes the number of the position the declared pseudonyms should hold in the linkability relation r. For a `<DataAttributeSet>` $\{d_1, \cdots, d_n\}$ and pseudonym-pseudonym linkability, the resulting structure is

$$\{SHA3(d_1|s)\text{---}\{\}, \cdots, SHA3(d_n|s)\text{---}\{\}\}.$$

$\{\}$ refers to an empty object variable in the secrets structure, because the pseudonyms produced can be now checked for equality, and hence equality of the underlying plaintext without knowing s. For pseudonym-plaintext linkability, the plaintexts of the set A that are supposed to be linkable w.r.t. equality to the pseudonyms must be transformed into a similar representation. The resulting structure is

$$\{SHA3(d_1|s)\text{---}SHA3(A|s), \cdots, SHA3(d_n|s)\text{---}SHA3(A|s)\},$$

where $SHA3(A|s)$ is an refers to the set $\{SHA3(a|s)|a \in A\}$. Note that the latter structure is only practically feasible and meaningful in sense of information reduction if A is of small size. The linkability requirement is sketched in Fig. 5.

Disclosability. For a `<Requirement>` tag attributed with ''`Disclosability`'', a pseudonymization function is used that produces pseudonyms which, using additional information, allow for disclosure of the underlying plaintexts. For d, this can be achieved by firstly generating a random symmetric key k and computing the AES encryption in the cipher-block chaining mode $CBC_{IV} - AES_k(d)$ using a new initialization vector IV for each d. Because k is required for disclosure, the resulting structure is

$$\{CBC_{IV} - AES_k(d)\text{—}\{IV, k\}\}.$$

Note that if the `<DataAttributeSet>` contains multiple plaintexts $\{d_1, \cdots, d_n\}$, then all utility tags must be transformed as presented using a fresh initialization vector IV and the same secret key k for each of the d_i. This is to achieve probabilistically encrypted values that can be disclosed under the same conditions.

Operation. When the `<Requirement>` tag is attributed with ''`Operation`'' and a child tag `<shape>`, a pseudonymization function is used that produces utility tags which firstly allow for performing the operation denoted in `<shape>`. If the result of the operation is encrypted, e.g. when using a homomorphic encryption as a pseudonymization function, the secrets structure carries the secret key for allowing to decrypt the result. An example is computing the sum of values of D, denoted with the `<shape>` value `sum`. A possible pseudonymization function is to use the *Paillier* encryption [14]. For that, one generates a key pair $K = (k_{pub}, k_{priv})$ used solely for D. The public key k_{pub} is used to generate the pseudonyms and to perform the homomorphic addition on them. k_{priv} is used to decrypt the sum. Therefore, the resulting structure for inputs in D is

$$\{Pailler(k_{pub}, d_1)\text{—}\{k_{pub}\}, \cdots, Pailler(k_{pub}, d_1)\text{—}\{k_{pub}\}, \{\}\text{—}\{k_{priv}\}\},$$

where $\{\}$—$\{k_{priv}\}$ is a placeholder for the encrypted sum and the private key for sum decryption.

Algorithm. For complex ordered operations on pseudonyms, the `<Requirement>` tag is attributed with ''`Algorithm`'' and children tags `<Implementation>` and `<Parameters>`, which allow to specify the implementation that should be applicable on the pseudonyms and additional input parameters for the algorithm.

Privacy Requirements. Without securing mechanisms, the pseudonym construction described in this section obviously may leak plaintexts easily. Moreover, making use of the utility may rise the probability of re-identification. This is due to inherent information leakage present in pseudonymization functions which are not semantically secure [7]. Therefore, the access to the additional information which is stored in the secrets structure as well as the utility tags must be restricted. We therefore assume that the processing system monitors the accesses to the pseudonyms and limits them according to privacy requirements declared in the utility policy. In the following, we describe our design along the data protection principles.

Restriction of Re-identification of Data Subjects. Compared to anonymized data, pseudonymized data inherently carry a higher risk of re-identification of data subjects. To the best of our knowledge, no specific measures for quantifying that risk are known. However, it is assumed that this risk is reduced compared to providing personal data in plaintext. To reduce the assumed risk, access restrictions on the pseudonyms including the secrets structure are formulated in the Util tag <Conditions> and <Bindings>. Conditions and bindings may include restrictions that are organizationally ensured, e.g. access to a decryption keys for disclosure only according to a court decision. Conditions also may include restrictions that are ensured by technical means, e.g. a monitoring system or using signed code or restricting the number of computations a pseudonym should be involved in. <Bindings> used for role or purpose binding restricts the access to a pseudonym unless the processing subject prove to hold a certain role or fulfills a certain purpose, respectively. For that, the corresponding utility tag is probabilistically encrypted using a so-called binding key for each role or purpose that has been defined in the policy. A trusted party manages the access to the binding key in a separate structure.

Storage Limitation. The `type` attribute of the <Condition> is set to `validUntil`, a UNIX timestamp in the future, which denotes the time after which the corresponding pseudonyms must be deleted.

Data Minimization is ensured by including the least possible amount of personal information possible in the utility policy, by choosing the smallest possible amount of personal data before being pseudonymized, and by choosing state-of the art pseudonymization functions. We assume that the user of Util chooses the least information required.

Sensitive Information and Implications of Processing. Whenever this special kind of information is pseudonymized, this fact is denoted in the utility policy by setting the <DataAttribute> tag `sensitive` to `yes`. The processing system can then consider this fact upon crucial decisions, e.g. disclosure of data while involving the data protection officer.

Mitigation and Risk Minimization. To reduce the risk of re-identification, we assume access restrictions especially on the secrets structure and define conditions and bindings in Util. However, there is a remaining risk inherently carried by most pseudonymizations. At access time, this is lawfully tolerated as inevitable. On storage time, an additional layer of encryption induced by an obligatory <Conditions> or <Bindings> statement in the utility policy ensures probabilistic encryption. A subject without access to the secrets structure is not able to make use of the pseudonymization, and hence, the risk is reduced against such kind of attackers.

Retention Separation is ensured by carrying a separated and secured secrets structure which is linked to the utility tag structure. Securing can be done using e.g. a trusted platform module.

Purpose and Role Binding. For purpose and role binding, the `<Bindings>` offers the attribute values `purpose` and `role`, respectively. There, the dedicated purpose of the data processing and role of the user can be included. For each binding, an additional layer of probabilistic encryption is applied to the utility tag under consideration and a dedicated key is preserved.

7 Conclusions and Future Work

In this work, we have listed common utility and privacy requirements based on the data protection principles of the GDPR [3]. We have presented `Util`, a policy language that eases formulating utility and privacy requirements for the automatic generation of utility-preserving pseudonymizations of semi-structured data. `Util` enables users without deeper knowledge of PET to apply pseudonymization techniques on their data and obtaining utility-preserving pseudonymizations. For some utility and privacy requirements, we have sketched transformation rules that allow to automatically generate pseudonymizations out of utility policies written in `Util`. We have presented a structure that defines pseudonymizations as a set of pseudonyms, where each pseudonym expresses the realisation of a utility requirement on a set of data in form of utility tags with separate secrets structure for additional information required to make use of the utility represented in the utility tags. This allows the secrets structure to be stored in a separated, secured system.

In Future work, we would like to extend the translation rules with more utility. We would like to optimize the size consumption of the utility tags and secrets structures. In the future, we aim at providing tools that utilize `Util` to automatically generate and manage pseudonymizations.

References

1. Acar, A., Aksu, H., Uluagac, A.S., Conti, M.: A survey on homomorphic encryption schemes: theory and implementation. ACM Comput. Surv. (CSUR) **51**(4), 1–35 (2018)
2. Dworkin, M.J.: SHA-3 standard: permutation-based hash and extendable-output functions. Technical report (2015)
3. Regulation (EU) 2016/679 of the European Parliament and of the Council of 27 April 2016 on the protection of natural persons with regard to the processing of personal data and on the free movement of such data, and repealing Directive 95/46/EC (General Data Protection Regulation). Official Journal of the European Union L119/59, May 2016
4. ElGamal, T.: A public key cryptosystem and a signature scheme based on discrete logarithms. In: Blakley, G.R., Chaum, D. (eds.) CRYPTO 1984. LNCS, vol. 196, pp. 10–18. Springer, Heidelberg (1985). https://doi.org/10.1007/3-540-39568-7_2
5. Gentry, C., et al.: Fully homomorphic encryption using ideal lattices. STOC **9**, 169–178 (2009)
6. Gerl, A., Bölz, F.: Layered privacy language pseudonymization extension for health care. Stud. Health Technol. Inform. **264**, 1189–1193 (2019)

7. Goldwasser, S., Micali, S.: Probabilistic encryption & how to play mental poker keeping secret all partial information. In: Providing Sound Foundations for Cryptography: On the Work of Shafi Goldwasser and Silvio Micali, pp. 173–201 (2019)

8. Graepel, T., Lauter, K., Naehrig, M.: ML confidential: machine learning on encrypted data. In: Kwon, T., Lee, M.-K., Kwon, D. (eds.) ICISC 2012. LNCS, vol. 7839, pp. 1–21. Springer, Heidelberg (2013). https://doi.org/10.1007/978-3-642-37682-5_1

9. He, X., Machanavajjhala, A., Ding, B.: Blowfish privacy: tuning privacy-utility trade-offs using policies. In: Proceedings of the 2014 ACM SIGMOD International Conference on Management of Data, pp. 1447–1458 (2014)

10. Hes, R., Borking, J.: Privacy Enhancing Technologies: The Path to Anonymity. Registratiekamer, The Hague (2000)

11. Heurix, J., Khosravipour, S., Tjoa, A.M., Rawassizadeh, R.: LiDSec - a lightweight pseudonymization approach for privacy-preserving publishing of textual personal information. In: 2012 Seventh International Conference on Availability, Reliability and Security, pp. 603–608 (2011)

12. Ji, S., Li, W., Mittal, P., Hu, X., Beyah, R.: SecGraph: a uniform and open-source evaluation system for graph data anonymization and de-anonymization. In: 24th {USENIX} Security Symposium (USENIX Security 2015), pp. 303–318 (2015)

13. Kasem-Madani, S., Meier, M.: Security and privacy policy languages: a survey, categorization and gap identification. arXiv preprint arXiv:1512.00201 (2015)

14. Paillier, P.: Public-key cryptosystems based on composite degree residuosity classes. In: Stern, J. (ed.) EUROCRYPT 1999. LNCS, vol. 1592, pp. 223–238. Springer, Heidelberg (1999). https://doi.org/10.1007/3-540-48910-X_16

15. FIPS Pub: Secure hash standard (SHS). FIPS Pub 180(4) (2012)

16. Sankar, L., Rajagopalan, S.R., Poor, H.V.: A theory of utility and privacy of data sources. In: 2010 IEEE International Symposium on Information Theory, pp. 2642–2646 (2010)

17. Sankar, L., Rajagopalan, S.R., Poor, H.V.: Utility-privacy tradeoffs in databases: an information-theoretic approach. IEEE Trans. Inf. Forensics Secur. 8(6), 838–852 (2013)

18. Schneier, B.: Applied cryptography: Protocols, Algorithms, and Source Code in C. Wiley, Hoboken (2007)

19. Schwartmann, R., Weiß, S. (eds.): White paper on pseudonymization drafted by the data protection focus group for the safety, protection, and trust platform for society and businesses. Technical report, Digital Summit's data protection focus group (2017)

20. Slagell, A., Lakkaraju, K., Luo, K.: LISA 2006: Proceedings of the 20th Conference on Large Installation System Administration, Berkeley, CA, USA (2006)

21. Zhao, J., Binns, R., Van Kleek, M., Shadbolt, N.: Privacy languages: are we there yet to enable user controls? In: Proceedings of the 25th International Conference Companion on World Wide Web, pp. 799–806. WWW 2016 Companion, International World Wide Web Conferences Steering Committee, Republic and Canton of Geneva, CHE (2016)

DEFeND DSM: A Data Scope Management Service for Model-Based Privacy by Design GDPR Compliance

Luca Piras[1]([✉]), Mohammed Ghazi Al-Obeidallah[1], Michalis Pavlidis[1], Haralambos Mouratidis[1], Aggeliki Tsohou[2], Emmanouil Magkos[2], Andrea Praitano[3], Annarita Iodice[3], and Beatriz Gallego-Nicasio Crespo[4]

[1] Centre for Secure, Intelligent and Usable Systems,
University of Brighton, Brighton, UK
{l.piras,m.al-obeidallah2,m.pavlidis,h.mouratidis}@brighton.ac.uk
[2] Ionian University, Corfu, Greece
{atsohou,emagos}@ionio.gr
[3] Maticmind SpA, Rome, Italy
{andrea.praitano,annarita.iodice}@maticmind.it
[4] Atos, Madrid, Spain
beatriz.gallego-nicasio@atos.net

Abstract. The introduction of the European General Data Protection Regulation (GDPR) has brought significant benefits to citizens, but it has also created challenges for organisations, which are facing with difficulties interpreting it and properly applying it. An important challenge is compliance with the Privacy by Design and by default (PbD) principles, which require that data protection is integrated into processing activities and business practices from the design stage. Recently, the European Data Protection Board (EDPB) released an official document with PbD guidelines, and there are various efforts to provide approaches to support these. However, organizations are still facing difficulties in identifying a flow for executing, in a coherent, linear and effective way, these activities, and a complete toolkit for supporting this. In this paper, we: (i) identify the most important PbD activities and strategies, (ii) design a coherent, linear and effective flow for them, and (iii) describe our comprehensive supporting toolkit, as part of the DEFeND EU Project platform. Specifically, within DEFeND, we identified candidate tools, fulfilling specific GDPR aspects, and integrated them in a comprehensive toolkit: the DEFeND Data Scope Management service (DSM). The aim of DSM is to support organizations for continuous GDPR compliance through Model-Based Privacy by Design analysis. Here, we present important PbD activities and strategies individuated, then describe DSM, its design, flow, and a preliminary case study and evaluation performed with pilots from the healthcare, banking, public administration and energy sectors.

Keywords: Privacy by Design · Privacy engineering · Security engineering · Data protection · GDPR · Data Scope Management · Privacy

© Springer Nature Switzerland AG 2020
S. Gritzalis et al. (Eds.): TrustBus 2020, LNCS 12395, pp. 186–201, 2020.
https://doi.org/10.1007/978-3-030-58986-8_13

1   Introduction

The European General Data Protection Regulation (GDPR) was introduced to enforce citizen data protection and privacy rights. Despite the clear benefits for citizens, GDPR is posing a major challenge for organisations, as they need to comply with a large number of areas including data classification, tracking of data processing activities with reporting and registers, data monitoring, breach detection, fast intervention and fast data deletion. Organisations failing to comply are liable to huge financial fines from relevant authorities [13]. A major problem is that GDPR is abstract and lacks detailed and clear information on how the various articles can be implemented in practice.

One of the most challenging and difficult principles to adhere with is Data Protection by Design and by Default; hereafter, for the sake of simplicity, we refer to these principles as Privacy by Design (PbD). Although GDPR defines PbD and makes it clear that it should be followed, it does not provide details on how it can be implemented. This is problematic because organisations do not have a structured way to ensure that PbD is followed when developing new systems and services. Recently, in order to try to cover this important lack of practical guidance, the European Data Protection Board (EDPB), released an official document for providing PbD guidelines[1]. However, those guidelines, even helping in reducing such gap, are still at high-level, and offer few practical indications. What is still missing is a clear structured approach that will enable organisations to implement PbD and a set of tools that would support the automation of such structured approach.

This paper provides a novel structured framework and a toolkit that fulfils this gap of the current state of the art. The Data Scope Management (DSM) solution presented is part of the DEFeND EU Project[2] platform [12], and builds on previous work presented at TrustBus-19 [12]. In particular, this paper addresses the following Research Questions (RQs):

RQ1: What are the analysis and implementation activities required by PbD and how these can be carried out in a structured and methodological way?
RQ2: Can PbD activities being automated and supported by software tools?

RQ1 is the main RQ that this paper tries to answer while RQ2 is a supportive question. To answer the first question we elicited information from Data Protection Officers (DPOs), experts and end-users [16,17] of organizations from different GDPR relevant sectors (e.g., banking, public administration, healthcare, energy). We analysed the outcome of these activities and derived a set of activities, strategies and factors that are important for the implementation of PbD. We then, based on those factors and activities developed a novel service, DSM, to support those. We also individuated a number of tools, and extended them, to make them to provide automated support to DSM.

---

[1] https://edpb.europa.eu/sites/edpb/files/consultation/
edpb_guidelines_201904_dataprotection_by_design_and_by_default.pdf.
[2] https://www.defendproject.eu/.

The rest of the paper is organized as follows. Section 2 summarizes the requirements we elicited in previous works [16,17], and answers to RQ1 providing the activities and strategies for PbD we derived for the DSM flow and toolkit. Section 3 addresses RQ2 and describes the DSM flow, toolkit, data models, our case study and preliminary evaluation within DEFeND. Section 4 compares our work with the industry and the literature. Section 5 concludes this paper.

2   PbD Activities and Strategies for GDPR Compliance

As indicated above, an important aspect of our work was to identify a set of analysis and implementation activities related to PbD. in doing so, we employed a Human-Centered Design (HCD) approach [8], where questionnaires and interviews were used as the basic tool to capture the main stakeholders' requirements with regards to PbD and also to understand the main characteristics that an automated toolkit should possess to support PbD [16,17]. Our approach consisted of 3 main stages [16,17] describe in the next.

Questionnaire Preparation. After an initial phase where the internal and external key stakeholders were identified, e.g., DPOs, IT managers, citizens etc., a questionnaire was prepared, for each user category, in a systematic way [17], aiming to capture the legal, functional, security, privacy and technology acceptance needs [11]. Specifically, we followed the approach of [1] for customer development, including steps such as Customer Segmentation, Problem Discovery and Validation, Product Discovery and Validation [17]. Two online questionnaires were prepared: 1 for end-users[3] and 1 for citizens[4];

Questionnaire Validation and Distribution. A validation phase were organized, where: **(i)** 10 DPOs from all project partners commentated on the questionnaires, and **(ii)** a focus group with internal stakeholders from the banking sector were set to revise and discuss final questionnaires. Questionnaires were then distributed to both end-users (i.e., organisations from 4 different sectors: banking, energy, health, public administration) and citizens from 7 European countries (i.e. Italy, Greece, Spain, Bulgaria, France, Portugal, UK), and were filled using semi-structured interviews and online surveys [17];

Data Analysis. During a data collection phase, we collected information from 10 DPOs via interviews and 31 DPOs via online survey, representing the energy, education, banking, health, public administration and information technology consultancy sectors. We also collected data from 174 citizens. The captured needs were analyzed, using qualitative data techniques and value analysis, and translated into software development requirements.

---

[3] https://ec.europa.eu/eusurvey/runner/DEFeNDEndUser.
[4] https://ec.europa.eu/eusurvey/runner/DEFeNDCitizens.

2.1   Identified Activities and Strategies for PbD

Our analysis of the above interviews, and questionnaires, identified Activities and Strategies (AS), which are important for PbD. We discuss them below.

AS1: *Organization Situation and Context.* It is fundamental to execute deep analyses and data collection on the organization, for having an important baseline on which to perform PbD activities identified in the next AS. Thus, from the very early stages of the analysis, for achieving GDPR compliance in a PbD way, it is needed to start the data collection by working on the GDPR self-assessment of the organization. This will help to produce, later, according to the other AS, a GDPR action plan identifying current gaps of compliance of an organization, on which to perform further PbD analyses.

AS2: *Organization and 3rd Parties Profiles.* On the basis of the high-level contextual information identified in AS1, it is needed to further analyse and collect more details for creating complete profiles of the organization and 3rd parties, including economic, financial and legal aspects.

AS3: *Data Processing Activities and Data Categories.* It is also needed to conduct a deep analysis on data processing activities performed by the organization itself, and in collaboration with 3rd parties. This should include also the identification of data categories and assets involved.

AS4: *GDPR Data Syntheses, Graphical Representations and Model-Based, Visual Support.* At support of all the AS, in particular for the analyses, it is beneficial to provide further support and guidance with graphical representations and synthesis of GDPR information analysed and collected. These should be provided to business analysts, privacy/security experts and other end-users involved, based on the completion of the GDPR Self-Assessment, and at support to other activities (e.g., Data Protection Impact Assessment, data minimization analysis, creation of GDPR action plans). While, privacy/security analysiss, threat analysis, continuous risk assessment configurations, and other critical activities and analyses, could be performed supported by visual model-based techniques enhanced and adapted for GDPR purposes.

AS5: *Data Protection Impact Assessment (DPIA), Preventive/Reacting Analyses and GDPR Action Plan.* On the basis of the elements identified by the other AS, it is important to analyse, in a preliminary way, GDPR lacks, vulnerabilities and assets that can be affected by data issues/breaches, and which preliminary mitigation mechanisms to adopt, and if preventive/reactive actions are in place (e.g., data breach plans). These analyses should be performed for producing a DPIA and a GDPR Action Plan, for identifying current gaps of compliance of an organization, on which to perform further PbD analysis.

AS6: *Privacy/Security Model-Based, and Pattern-Based, Analysis.* The GDPR Action Plan of AS5 identifies the gaps, but it is at high-level, thus, needs to be enacted by further critical analysis, performed by privacy/security analysts, supported by visual model-based techniques enhanced and adapted for GDPR (AS4). This concerns analysis of the organization context, data/assets/accountability mapping with also analysis of risks, threats and measures in place, privacy/security requirements constraints and conflict resolution, supported via libraries of patterns and modeling techniques specifically designed for GDPR.

AS7: *Continuous Model-Based GDPR Compliance.* On the basis of analyses performed for the previous AS, it is needed to support the organization to: **(i)** have software systems able to put in place GDPR compliance solutions individuated, **(ii)** receive automated support for configuring such systems, **(iii)** monitor continuously the compliance, according to the GDPR plan, for identifying new potential lacks with GDPR and data breaches, **(iv)** enable the organization to react to such problems, and **(v)** make this process iterative, for a continuous Model-Based GDPR compliance, by enabling the analysts to analyse in a visual, model-based way the new GDPR lacks, and to perform again AS analysis, in a continuous way, for updating/re-configuring the system for being again GDPR compliant.

3   DEFeND Data Scope Management (DSM) Service, Case Study and Evaluation

Based on the above set of Activities and Strategies (AS), we have designed a flow for such AS, and developed a novel service, the Data Scope Management service (DSM), for the DEFeND platform to support PbD. According to our AS, DSM supports organizations in performing GDPR self-assessments by collecting organizational information (AS1), also related to 3rd parties (AS1), data processing activities (AS3), and creating a profile of the organization regarding multiples perspectives such as legal, economic and financial aspects (AS2). Furthermore, it also enables organizations in executing DPIA (AS5) by collecting/revising and refining organizational assets (AS3), and elaborating the other information collected for supporting the organizations with data synthesis and graphical representations (AS4) through a set of DSM tools. Moreover, DSM helps organizations in performing threats analysis (AS4, AS6), data minimization analysis (AS4), privacy/security analysis and design with tool-supported modelling techniques (AS4, AS6), continuous risk assessment (AS4, AS6), and configuration for executing a continuous model-based GDPR compliance (AS7).

In the next subsections, we start giving an overview of DSM, its components, the tools we selected, extended and integrated for creating DSM, and the data models used by the tools for exchanging PbD information needed by our AS. Then, we outline our case study, performed by involving pilots from the healthcare, banking, public administration and energy sectors. Together with the case study, we describe the DSM PbD flow through a healthcare storyline. In the last subsection, we discuss our preliminary evaluation.

3.1   DSM Components, Integrated Tools and Data Models

In order to design and develop DSM, we individuated candidate tools, supporting specific features, and extended and integrated them, according to AS and the
DSM flow, for creating a service supporting the entire set of features required for
a PbD approach. Specifically, DSM involves the following tools: the MM-Assess
(MaticMind-Assess) tool, which supports the business analyst to conduct a self-
assessment for the organization; MM-REPA (MaticMind Record of Processing
Activities), which is a tool that creates a list of all data processing activities in
the organization based on a guided questionnaire; MM-PIA, a Risk Assessment
Management (RAM) tool, which provides a centralized system to identify risks,
evaluate their impact, probability, and the vulnerability they pose to organizational assets, linking them to mitigating controls and managing their resolution;
the SecTro tool, which is a CASE tool guiding and supporting analysts in the
construction of appropriate models, based on the Secure Tropos method [9,10];
the Risk Assessment Engine (RAE), which is an ATOS tool supporting organizations in the assessment of cyber-risks.

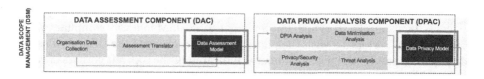

Fig. 1. DSM components, modules and DSM Data Models (green rectangles) [12,16,17]
(Color figure online)

Interactions of the DSM tools are made through the exchange of information stored in data models as shown in Fig. 1. Therefore, data models involved
in DSM are the Data Assessment Model (DAM) and the Data Privacy Model
(DPM). DAM is produced in the Data Assessment Component (DAC), then
read in the Data Privacy Analysis Component (DPAC) that in turn produces
the DPM model. The DPM model is then used by other services of the DEFeND
Platform, for instance from the GDPR Reporting Service [12]. Concerning DSM
components and modules (Fig. 1), DAC is constituted by the Organization Data
Collection (ODC) module and the Assessment Translator (ATr) module. While,
DPAC is composed of the DPIA Analysis module, Data Minimization Analysis
module, Privacy/Security Analysis module and the Threats Analysis module.

3.2   Case Study, Storyline and DSM PbD Flow

Our case study used a storyline, we devised, for touching the most important PbD
activities of DSM, and we used such storyline for demonstrating and discussing
DSM, and our approach, with pilots from the banking, healthcare, public administration and health sectors, within the DEFeND Project (see Footnote 2). In the

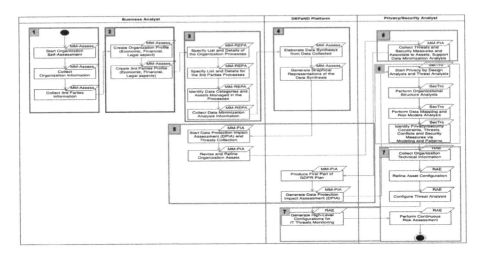

Fig. 2. Activity diagram of the DSM flow

following, we start introducing our storyline, then describe DSM and its flow, phase by phase, by using the storyline, for demonstrating DSM in a way compliant with the case study performed with the pilots. Figure 2 represents the DSM flow as an activity diagram: **(i)** the phase number is indicated in the top, left corners of rectangles; **(ii)** some phases include more than one rectangle; **(iii)** each activity has a label in the top, right corner indicating the name of the tool fulfilling it.

Storyline Introduction. A Hospital wants to improve its GDPR compliance by using the DEFeND DSM service. It is important to note that, even though for this example we are considering the healthcare sector, the DSM service has been designed and delivered to be as much flexible as possible to support organizations from heterogeneous sectors. One of the most critical aspects for a hospital is to manage the patient medical record and to have verifications, from a supervisor, for any changes happening to it (for instance adding a new medical exam result, etc.), and to establish retention periods for this data. Furthermore, this data has not to be stolen or to be compromised; for instance, in relation to potential threats and data breaches; therefore, the Hospital needs to analyse, design and put in place monitoring of those potential problems; in the organizational processes are involved also 3rd parties (external laboratories for medical exams), therefore it is needed to consider also this for improving GDPR compliance.

DSM Flow: Phase 1 (DAC: Initial Organization Data Collection). Phase 1 covers mainly AS1 and partially AS2. Its activities are represented in Fig. 2. Main objectives of this phase are to support the organization in: performing GDPR self-assessment (AS1), collecting high-level organization information (AS1) and 3rd parties information (AS2). This phase is associated to the MM-Assess tool (Fig. 2) within the DAC component and the ODC module (Fig. 1). The user of the organization for this phase is typically a business analyst (Fig. 2). Most of the activities performed during this phase are related to collection of information through questionnaires compilation. Information collected are saved in the DAM model. This phase is illustrated by the following part of the storyline:

> *"The Hospital starts using the DSM service and inputs in the system relevant Organizational and 3rd Parties information by compiling initial questionnaires for giving an overview of the organizational context."*

For instance, the business analyst of the hospital can collect, by using MM-Assess questionnaires, the laboratory information, i.e. the lab in charge of executing medical exams to patients for the hospital, and related information will be populated in the DAM data category called "3rd Parties".

DSM Flow: Phase 2 (DAC: Organization Data Collection for Profiles Creation). This phase covers AS2, and its activities are represented in Fig. 2. Here, the organization is able to create complete profiles, both for the organization and 3rd parties, concerning economic, financial and legal aspects (AS2). This phase is performed by a business analyst of the organization, in the context of the DAC component and the ODC module (Fig. 1), using the MM-Assess (Fig. 2) by being guided in compilation of questionnaires, which will populate the DAM model. This phase is illustrated by the following part of the storyline:

> *"Afterwards, the system proposes to the user to compile more detailed questionnaires able to create a complete organizational profile and 3rd parties profile regarding economic, financial and legal aspects."*

For example, the business analyst can input information on the organization business, legal and economic situation that could be related to organization debts of the hospital (data category "Organization General Information" of DAM).

DSM Flow: Phase 3 (DAC: Organization Data Collection of Data Processing Activities). This phase covers mainly AS3 and partially AS4. Its activities are represented in Fig. 2. The main objectives of this phase are to complete the self-assessment by identifying the data processing activities of the organization (AS3), including also the ones occurring with 3rd parties, the data categories and assets involved and managed (AS3), and to collect data minimization analysis information in relation to how it has been conducted so far by the organization (AS4). This phase is performed with the MM-REPA tool (Fig. 2) within the DAC component and the ODC module (Fig. 1). To execute these activities, a business analyst of the organization inputs this information via questionnaires compilation. Information collected are saved in the DAM model. This phase is illustrated by the following part of the storyline:

> *"Subsequently, categories of data managed within data processing activities are inserted in the system. Them are mainly related to medical exams results managed by the hospital. Also, the full list, and details, of data processing activities of the hospital, and 3rd parties, is collected."*

For instance, the business analyst of the hospital collects, by using MM-REPA, the processing activities related to the interaction of the lab and the hospital concerning performing medical exams and sending the results to the hospital; related information will be populated in the DAM data categories such as "Processing List" and "Processing Description, Scope, Purpose and Legal Basis".

DSM Flow: Phase 4 (DAC: Assessment Translation and Data Synthesis). This phase covers mainly AS4. Its activities are represented in Fig. 2. On the basis of all the data collected in the previous steps, in this phase the aim is to translate this data for creating data synthesis and data graphical representations of them, to facilitate the organization in understanding the current situation (self-assessment) both textually and graphically (AS4). This information will be also the baseline for important activities in the next phases. This phase is associated to the MM-Assess tool (Fig. 2) within the DAC component and the ATr module (Fig. 1). This phase does not require user intervention, it is completely automated by MM-Assess. However, business analysts will be able to see, and to use in the next steps, results produced here. This phase is illustrated by the following part of the storyline:

> "*Then, on the basis of the answers, the platform produces a self-assessment of the organization, data synthesis and graphical representations.*"

For example, data synthesis elaborated and saved are hospital percentage of readiness and index of complexity (DAM data category "GDPR Self-Assessment").

DSM Flow: Phase 5 (DPAC: Data Protection Impact Assessment, Preliminary Threat Analysis and Data Minimization Analysis). This phase covers AS5 and partially AS6 and AS4. Its activities are represented in Fig. 2. The main objectives of this phase are to support the organization in performing DPIA (AS5), generating the GDPR Plan (AS5), conducting a preliminary Threat Analysis by collecting threats, security measures and revising/refining assets (AS6) involved and collected previously. Finally, in this phase the organization is supported also concerning data minimization analysis, through visual data synthesis and graphical representations (AS4). This phase is fulfilled by the MM-PIA tool (Fig. 2) within the DPAC component and the DPIA Analysis, Threats Analysis, and Data Minimization Analysis modules (Fig. 1). The user of the organization for this phase is typically a privacy/security analyst (Fig. 2), which could collaborate with the business analysts that used the DEFeND platform in the previous steps. Most of the activities performed here, are related to collection of information through questionnaires compilation for collecting information related to the goals outlined above, and automated activities for producing related results. Some results are shown in visual/graphical ways. Baseline information, collected in previous phases, are read by MM-PIA from the DAM Model, and information collected and generated here saved in the DPM model. This phase is illustrated by the following part of the storyline:

> "*On the basis of data collected so far, and new data collected also in this step with further questionnaires, the system generates a DPIA and proposes a GDPR plan.*"

Regarding DAM and DPM models, for instance MM-PIA, reading from DAM, shows to hospital privacy/security analysts information regarding assets collected before (DAM data category "Processing Assets"), and asks to revise/refine them by adding also other relevant information (saved in DPM by MM-PIA), via questionnaires, for collecting GDPR risks and vulnerabilities (data category "Vulnerabilities" in DPM) related to assets, privacy/security requirements to guarantee (e.g., confidentiality, integrity and availability of patient medical records, data category "Privacy and Security Requirements" in DPM) and potential threats that could attack them (e.g., illegitimate access to patient medical records, and malwares that could perform attacks affecting hospital computers, data category "Threats" in DPM) and security measures to apply (e.g., antivirus and firewalls, data category "Security Mechanisms" in DPM).

DSM Flow: Phase 6 (DPAC: Privacy/Security and Threat Analysis Based on Modelling and Privacy Patterns). This phase covers mainly AS6 and partially AS4 and AS7. Its activities are represented in Fig. 2. High-level goals of this phase concern to support the organization in performing GDPR Privacy/Security Analysis and Threat Analysis (AS6) based on Modelling (AS6, AS4, AS7) and Privacy Patterns (AS6). In detail, in DSM, this is performed via Organizational Structure Analysis, Data Mapping and Risk Models Analysis, Privacy/Security Requirements Analysis, Requirements Conflicts Analysis and Resolution based on Patterns, Threat Analysis, Attacks Analysis and Security Measures Identification based on Patterns. This phase is associated to the Secure Tropos (SecTro) tool (Fig. 2), and its method, extended in DEFeND, within the DPAC component and the Privacy/Security and Threat Analysis modules (Fig. 1). Users of this phase are privacy/security analysts (Fig. 2). Activities performed during this phase concern modelling by using graphical editors showing models, where it is possible to add concepts and relationships from a palette to editors, according to semantic and syntactic constraints related to the modelling language and method behind, and being supported having the possibility to leverage on ready-to-use libraries of patterns. The SecTro method supports the analyst via modelling in different steps by focusing on different perspectives of the problem. Such perspectives are called views in SecTro, and are the: Organizational View, Data Mapping View, Privacy/Security View and Attack View. This phase is partially illustrated by the following extract of the storyline:

> *"The platform, on the basis of the info collected, the assessment and the GDPR plan elaborated, shows graphical models of the Organizational Structure of the Hospital, with the main actors and interactions."*

In fact, SecTro reads some of the information mentioned above by DAM and DPM models, and generates the organizational model in the Organizational View, where it is possible to perform organizational structure analysis. For instance, identifying main actors involved such as hospital departments, doctors, supervisors, the lab - as 3rd party -, high-level interactions among them, processing activities, organization assets, initial privacy/security requirements occurring in the interactions, etc. Also the next storyline extract illustrates part of this phase:

"On the basis of this, DEFeND users are able to identify the importance of fulfilling the confidentiality and integrity of patient medical record, through also validation processes, and to perform data mapping with organizational assets. Specifically, the hospital privacy/security analyst improves the graphical representation by modelling how a Doctor can change the patient medical record (for instance by adding exam results received by 3rd parties as external labs) and obtaining a validation for them from a Supervisor."

This means that initial privacy/security requirements occurring in the interactions can be refined (e.g., confidentiality and integrity) by modeling validation processes related to data processing activities, and mapping organizational data assets involved (e.g., patient medical record and medical result) in the Data Mapping View. Also next storyline extract illustrates part of this phase:

"Furthermore, the modelling helps also in identifying further important privacy/security requirements (e.g., accountability, anonymity, etc.) relevant also for performing threat analysis. Accordingly, the system helps a hospital privacy/security analyst in modelling potential threats that could affect confidentiality, integrity and availability of this important kind of data, and privacy and security measures that could mitigate/solve those potential problems. For instance, concerning threat analysis, a threat is modelled and considered regarding the possibility that the computer and web applications, used by the Doctor for changing the medical record, are affected by a malware, for example a Trojan."

Accordingly, in the Privacy/Security View the focus is deeply oriented on privacy/security requirements, potential requirements conflicts, threats and security mechanisms. In fact, the analyst can individuate vulnerabilities in the system, and by doing this deeper analysis, can identify even more privacy/security requirements to be satisfied. Here, the analyst can model at high-level potential threats affecting vulnerabilities, and use libraries of patterns, provided by SecTro, including security mechanisms for threats mitigation. Threats Analysis is done iteratively, at different levels of abstraction, by switching from the Privacy/Security View to the Attack View of each of the threats individuated.

Concerning DAM and DPM models, for example SecTro for generating the model of the organizational view can read from DAM the actors ("Organization Departments", "Employees, Roles and Responsibilities" and "3rd Parties" data categories in DAM), which in the storyline are the doctor, the supervisor and the lab. While, output of analysis activities regarding threats and attacks is saved in the DPM model. For instance, assets that could be involved in threats such as the computer, the patient medical record and the exam results are saved in DPM in the data category "Privacy related Resources and Assets".

DSM Flow: Phase 7 (DPAC: Threat Analysis for Continuous GDPR Risk Assessment and Compliance). This phase covers mainly AS7 and partially AS4 and AS6. Its activities are represented in Fig. 2. Goals of this phase are to support the organization in collecting organization technical information, refining IT assets configuration and configuring threats analysis (AS7, AS4, AS6), generating high-level configurations for IT threats monitoring (AS7, AS4), and creating the conditions for performing continuous GDPR risk assessment and compliance (AS7). This phase is satisfied by the RAE tool (Fig. 2) within the DPAC component and the Threat Analysis module (Fig. 1). Users of this phase are privacy/security analysts (Fig. 2). Activities performed regard collection of technical information via technical questionnaires compilation, automatic generation of high-level configurations for IT threats monitoring, verification and revision of them by analysts, and starting continuous GDPR risk assessment and compliance monitoring based on those configurations. Some information is read by DAM and DPM models, while information collected, generated and revised is saved in DPM. This phase is illustrated by the following storyline part:

> *"The system, on the basis of the GDPR Self-Assessment, DPIA, Risk Assessment, Processes modelled for changing data and validating changes, Threats modelled, and additional technical information asked through technical questionnaires, generates monitoring configurations. A hospital privacy/security analyst read such configurations, and optionally improve them by adding further specific information. After all these complex analyses, the system is able to perform monitoring of threats for Continuous Model-Based GDPR risk assessment and Compliance."*

Regarding DAM and DPM models, RAE can read from them some information. For instance, 3rd parties information such as the lab for the hospital (data category "3rd Parties" of DAM), and privacy/security requirements the hospital should fulfil such as confidentiality, integrity, availability, accountability and anonymity (DPM data category "Privacy and Security Requirements"). Such information is used by RAE, together with other technical information collected in this phase, for executing automated activities, and to support the manual activities of the privacy/security analyst of the hospital. For example, RAE collects, through IT technical questionnaires, IT monitoring configuration such as IT assets and their IP addresses. Thus, in this step the analyst is guided, and supported, in refining IT assets, and to configure threat analysis monitoring (DPM data categories "Risk Information" and "Risk Mapping"). RAE, on the basis of all this information, generates high-level configurations for IT threat monitoring, and asks the analyst to verify and potentially refine such configuration These steps create the conditions for performing Continuous Model-Based GDPR Compliance, by reiterating the previous phases in a systematic way.

3.3   Evaluation

Having described the DSM service in the previous sections, here we present our preliminary evaluation. First, we present our evaluation strategy towards the evaluation of the DSM service, and then the obtained results.

Evaluation Strategy. PbD activities and strategies presented in this paper are inherently human-centred activities. From collecting organisational and 3rd parties information, identifying assets and processing activities through data minimisation, DPIA, threat analysis, and continuous risk assessment, the inputs, processes, and outputs are primarily created, performed, and evaluated by humans. For this reason, we used humans for our preliminary evaluation of our research claims, and in particular members of the pilot organisations that participate in the DEFeND project. Therefore, we had users that work in the healthcare, banking, energy, and public administration sectors. Our user evaluation was descriptive, artificial, and qualitative. Descriptive, because it involved asking participants questions about their experiences, artificial because we created artefacts and context for the purposes of the user evaluation, and qualitative because it was aimed at establishing how well the methods and tools fit the needs and culture of organisations. In particular, we created a storyline that covered all the features of the methods, and the toolkit that were demonstrated, and created some artificial data for demonstration purposes. The user evaluation was carried out in three iterations. Three physical workshops were held, where the methods and tools were demonstrated, in order to receive feedback from the participating users, and incorporate the feedback in the subsequent versions of the method and toolkit.

Evaluation Results. Inline with our RQs, Participants in our evaluation were asked whether the method and toolkit, demonstrated to them, would likely be appropriate to support them concerning the execution of complex PbD activities for GDPR compliance. In the next, we summarize some of the descriptive questions made to participants: **(i)** To what extent do the proposed AS are the ones required and relevant for PbD GDPR compliance? **(ii)** To what extent do the proposed flow, demonstrated with the toolkit, offers a structured method for PbD GDPR compliance? **(iii)** To what extent do the automation and guidance, provided by the toolkit, is appropriate, clarify how to perform PbD GDPR compliance, and provide support for this? The three iterations of user evaluation, which we performed, enabled us to gain insights which we may not otherwise have had. In general, the results of the user evaluation exercises were favourable. In each physical workshop the participating users expressed their confidence that their needs are satisfied by the features of the method and of the toolkit. However, they expressed concerns and criticisms about the usability and look and feel of the toolkit. This can be explained as the service was not fully integrated to the whole DEFeND platform and was lacking the full final user interface.

4   Related Work

4.1   Industry Comparison

The EC-funded H2020 project cyberwatching.eu has launched the GDPR Temperature Tool, to help European SMEs understand just how at risk they are to sanctions or fines [4]. By answering a set of questions on data protection, the Tool provides an indication of a company's risk to sanctions. In addition, a free customised set of recommendations is provided. However, the provided recommendations are too generic and not specific to the company. According to the 2019 Privacy Tech Vendor Report from IAAP [13], the number of vendors providing privacy management tools is constantly increasing, although as the report highlights "there is no single vendor that will automatically make an organization GDPR compliant" [13]. The IAAP's report classifies the solutions into 2 key categories: Privacy Program Management and Enterprise Privacy Management. The first are grouped into 6 subcategories: assessment managers, consent managers, data mapping, incident response, privacy information managers and website scanning. The second are grouped in 4 subcategories: activity monitoring, data discovery, de-identification/pseudonymity and enterprise communications. None of the listed vendors is able to provide solutions that cover all sub-categories. Differently than the tools presented in the report, DEFeND and DSM cover a much wider set of subcategories. Forrester [3] released a report evaluating the 12 most significant providers in the market of EU GDPR compliance and privacy management. Platforms are evaluated with 10 criteria. One important conclusion of the report is that a functionality such as data discovery across systems, is a key feature to avoid bad consequences of doing such task manually (i.e. inaccuracies, guesswork), and increases assurance for accountability. DSM supports this functionality via the Organization Data Collection module, where organizational data is collected and transformed automatically in a Data Assessment Model.

4.2   Research Novelty

This section briefly discusses literature and research challenges in areas associated with the Data Scope Management, and describes how DSM addresses them.

Privacy by Design (PbD). PbD is an important principle of GDPR (Data Protection by Design and by Default), but only few efforts exist to support practical implementation of PbD [2,6,7,15]. The Data Scope Management service facilitates the implementation of PbD principles using methods and techniques from privacy requirements engineering, and privacy design.

Privacy Impact Assessment (PIA). Systematic assessment of privacy-related risks, in the form of PIA, is requested by GDPR (art. 35). PIA shall be embedded in the early phases of software design and development. PIA adoption in most industry sectors is considered at an early stage [14], while state of the art methodologies and tools to implement PIA are very few (e.g., [5]. The DEFeND DSM service advances the current state of the art in PIA by providing an in-depth processing analysis based on a recognized methodology and international standards. DSM integrates PbD approaches with PIA and threat analysis at planning level, to provide organisations with the abilities to check GDPR compliance, measure and review their privacy level, analyse safeguards and security measures for mitigating potential risks, but also with the capability to develop new services and systems in accordance with GDPR.

5   Conclusions

In this paper, we presented a set of Activities and Strategies (AS) for Privacy by Design (PbD), a flow and a toolkit, DSM (the Data Scope Management service of the DEFeND EU project platform), supporting them, for carrying out major activities for PbD GDPR compliance. The need to individuate the most relevant AS, and designing a PbD flow for them, derives from the fact that organizations are facing many difficulties regarding interpreting GDPR and properly understanding how to apply it. Our DSM flow, presented here, provides organizations with a clear, coherent, linear flow of activities, and method, for performing GDPR compliance in a PbD fashion. Furthermore, it is missing, from the literature and the industry, a complete toolkit supporting the organization in performing, in automated ways, such complex PbD activities. We individuated candidate tools, fulfilling isolated GDPR aspects, extended and integrated them for developing the DSM service, as a comprehensive toolkit, compliant with the DSM flow we designed, and able to automate PbD activities to support organizations for continuous model-based GDPR compliance. To evaluate our proposed method, toolkit, and flow, we organised 3 workshops and performed a qualitative user survey evaluation. During the workshops the DSM service was demonstrated to pilots from the healthcare, banking, public administration and energy sectors, and feedback was collected. The feedback was favourable, as the organisations' responses were that the features of the method, toolkit, and flow satisfy their needs and have the potential to support them for a systematic and structured PbD GDPR compliance. As future work, we plan to deploy the whole DEFeND platform at the pilots' infrastructures, and assess the effectiveness of DSM by carrying out quantitative and qualitative case study evaluations.

Acknowledgments. This work has received funding from the European Union's Horizon 2020 research and innovation programme under grant agreement No. 787068.

References

1. Blank, S.: The Four Steps to the Epiphany: Successful Strategies for Products that Win. Wiley, Hoboken (2007)
2. Deng, M., Wuyts, K., Scandariato, R., Preneel, B., Joosen, W.: A privacy threat analysis framework: supporting the elicitation and fulfilment of privacy requirements. Requirements Eng. J. **16**(1), 3–32 (2011)
3. The Forrester New Wave^{TM}. https://www.forrester.com/report/The%20Forrester%20New%20Wave%20GDPR%20And%20Privacy%20Management%20Software%20Q4%202018/-/E-RES142698
4. GDPR temperature tool. http://gdprtool.cyberwatching.eu/Pages/Home.aspx
5. Horák, M., Stupka, V., Husák, M.: GDPR compliance in cybersecurity software: a case study of DPIA in information sharing platform. In: 14th International Conference on Availability, Reliability and Security (2019)

6. Kalloniatis, C., Belsis, P., Gritzalis, S.: A soft computing approach for privacy requirements wngineering: the PriS framework. Appl. Soft Comput. **11**(7), 4341–4348 (2011)

7. Kurtz, C., Semmann, M., et al.: Privacy by design to comply with GDPR: a review on third-party data processors. In: Americas Conference on Information Systems (2018)

8. Maguire, M.: Methods to support human-centred design. Int. J. Hum.-Comput. Studies **55**(4), 587–634 (2001)

9. Mouratidis, H.: Secure software systems engineering: the secure Tropos approach. JSW **6**(3), 331–339 (2011)

10. Mouratidis, H., Argyropoulos, N., Shei, S.: Security requirements engineering for cloud computing: the secure Tropos approach. In: Karagiannis, D., Mayr, H., Mylopoulos, J. (eds.) Domain-Specific Conceptual Modeling, pp. 357–380. Springer, Cham (2016). https://doi.org/10.1007/978-3-319-39417-6_16

11. Piras, L., Dellagiacoma, D., Perini, A., Susi, A., Giorgini, P., Mylopoulos, J.: Design thinking and acceptance requirements for designing gamified software. In: 13th International Conference on Research Challenges in Information Science (RCIS). IEEE (2019)

12. Piras, L., et al.: DEFeND architecture: a privacy by design platform for GDPR compliance. In: Gritzalis, S., Weippl, E.R., Katsikas, S.K., Anderst-Kotsis, G., Tjoa, A.M., Khalil, I. (eds.) TrustBus 2019. LNCS, vol. 11711, pp. 78–93. Springer, Cham (2019). https://doi.org/10.1007/978-3-030-27813-7_6

13. Privacy Tech Vendor Report. https://iapp.org/resources/article/2019-privacy-tech-vendor-report/

14. Rantos, K., Drosatos, G., Demertzis, K., Ilioudis, C., Papanikolaou, A., Kritsas, A.: ADvoCATE: a consent management platform for personal data processing in the iot using blockchain technology. In: Lanet, J.-L., Toma, C. (eds.) SECITC 2018. LNCS, vol. 11359, pp. 300–313. Springer, Cham (2019). https://doi.org/10.1007/978-3-030-12942-2_23

15. Romanou, A.: The necessity of the implementation of privacy by design in sectors where data protection concerns arise. Comput. Law Secur. Rev. **34**(1), 99–110 (2018)

16. Tsohou, A., et al.: Privacy, security, legal and technology acceptance elicited and consolidated requirements for a GDPR compliance platform. Inf. Comput. Secur. J. (2020)

17. Tsohou, A., et al.: Privacy, security, legal and technology acceptance requirements for a GDPR compliance platform. In: Katsikas, S., et al. (eds.) Cyber-ICPS/SECPRE/SPOSE/ADIoT -2019. LNCS, vol. 11980, pp. 204–223. Springer, Cham (2020). https://doi.org/10.1007/978-3-030-42048-2_14

Privacy and Machine Learning

A Distributed Trust Framework for Privacy-Preserving Machine Learning

Will Abramson, Adam James Hall, Pavlos Papadopoulos$^{(\boxtimes)}$,
Nikolaos Pitropakis, and William J. Buchanan

Blockpass Identity Lab, Edinburgh Napier University, Edinburgh, UK
{will.abramson,adam.hall,pavlos.papadopoulos,n.pitropakis,
b.buchanan}@napier.ac.uk

Abstract. When training a machine learning model, it is standard procedure for the researcher to have full knowledge of both the data and model. However, this engenders a lack of trust between data owners and data scientists. Data owners are justifiably reluctant to relinquish control of private information to third parties. Privacy-preserving techniques distribute computation in order to ensure that data remains in the control of the owner while learning takes place. However, architectures distributed amongst multiple agents introduce an entirely new set of security and trust complications, including data poisoning and model theft. This paper outlines a distributed infrastructure which can be used to facilitate peer-to-peer trust between entities; collaboratively performing a privacy-preserving workflow. Our outlined prototype enables the initialisation of industry gatekeepers and governance bodies as credential issuers under a certain application domain. Before participating in the distributed learning workflow, malicious actors must first negotiate valid credentials from these gatekeepers. We detail a proof of concept using Hyperledger Aries, Decentralised Identifiers (DIDs) and Verifiable Credentials (VCs) to establish a distributed trust architecture during a privacy-preserving machine learning experiment. Specifically, we utilise secure and authenticated DID communication channels in order to facilitate a federated learning workflow related to mental health care data.

Keywords: Trust · Machine learning · Federated learning ·
Decentralised Identifiers · Verifiable credentials

1 Introduction

Machine learning (ML) is a powerful tool for extrapolating knowledge from complex data-sets. However, it can also represent several security risks concerning the data involved and how that model will be deployed [37]. An organisation providing ML capabilities needs data to train, test and validate their algorithm. However, data owners tend to be wary of sharing data with third-party processors [9]. This is due to the fact that once data is supplied, it is almost impossible to ensure that it will be used solely for the purposes which were originally

© Springer Nature Switzerland AG 2020
S. Gritzalis et al. (Eds.): TrustBus 2020, LNCS 12395, pp. 205–220, 2020.
https://doi.org/10.1007/978-3-030-58986-8_14

intended. This lack of trust between data owners and processors is currently an impediment to the advances which can be achieved through the utilisation of big data techniques. This is particularly evident with private medical data, where competent clinical decision support systems can augment clinician-to-patient time efficiencies [1, 21]. In order to overcome this obstacle, new distributed and privacy-preserving ML infrastructures have been developed where the data no longer needs to be shared or even known to the Researcher in order to be learned upon [43].

In a distributed environment of agents, establishing trust between these agents is crucial. Privacy-preserving methodologies are only successful if all parties participate in earnest. If we introduce a malicious Researcher, they may send a Trojan model which, instead of training, could store a carbon copy of the private data. Conversely, if we introduce a malicious actor in place of a data owner, they may be able to steal a copy of the model or poison it with bad data. In cases of model poisoning, malicious data is used to train a model in order to introduce a bias which supports some malicious motive. Once poisoned, maliciously trained models can be challenging to detect. The bias introduced by the malicious data has already been diffused into the model parameters. Once this has occurred, it is a non-trivial task to de-parrallelise this information.

If one cannot ensure trust between agents participating in a Federated Learning (FL) workflow, it opens the workflow up to malicious agents who may subvert its integrity through the exploitation of resources such as the data or the ML model used. In this work, we show how recent advances in digital identity technology can be utilised to define a trust framework for specific application domains. This is applied to FL in a healthcare scenario and reduces the risk of malicious agents subverting the FL ML workflow. Specifically, the paper leverages: Decentralized Identifiers (DIDs) [41]; Verifiable Credentials (VCs) [46]; and DID Communication, [24]. Together, these allow entities to establish a secure, asynchronous digital connection between themselves. Trust is established across these connections through the mutual authentication of digitally signed attestations from trusted entities. The authentication mechanisms in this paper can be applied to any data collection, data processing or regulatory workflow, and are not limited to solely the health care domain.

This paper contributes the following:

- We improve upon the current state-of-the-art with respect to the integration of authentication techniques in privacy-preserving workflows.
- We enable stakeholders in the learning process to define and enforce a trust model for their domain through the utilisation of DID mechanisms.
- We apply a novel use of DIDs and VCs in order to perform mutual authentication for FL.
- We specify a peer-to-peer architecture which can be used as an alternative to centralised trust architectures such as certificate authorities, and apply it within a health care trust infrastructure.

Section 2 provides the background knowledge and describes the related literature. Furthermore, Sect. 3 outlines our implementation overview, followed by

Sect. 4, where the threat model of our infrastructure is set, alongside with its scope. In Sect. 5, we provide an evaluation of our system, and conclude with Sect. 6 that draws the conclusions and outlines approaches for future work.

2 Background and Related Work

ML is revolutionising how we deal with data. This is catalysed by hallmark innovations such as AlphaGo [28]. Attention has turned to attractive domains, such as healthcare [51], self-driving cars and smart city planning [26]. Ernst and Young estimate that National Health Service (NHS) data is worth £9.6 Billion a year [45]. While this burgeoning application of data science has scope to benefit society, there are also emerging trust issues. The data-sets required to train these models are often highly sensitive, either containing personal data - such as data protected under the GDPR in the EU [48] - or include business-critical information. Additionally, developing and understanding ML models is often a highly specialised skill. This generally means that two or more separate parties must collaborate to train an ML model. One side might have the expertise to develop a useful model, and the other around the data which they want to train the model, to solve a business problem.

2.1 Trust and the Data Industry

Trust is a complicated concept that is both domain and context-specific. Trust is directional and asymmetric, reflecting that between two parties, the trust is independent for each party [54]. Generally, trust can be defined as the willingness for one party to give control over something to another party, based on the belief that they will act in the interest of the former party [27]. In economic terms, it is often thought of as a calculation of risk, with the understanding that risk can never be fully eliminated, just mitigated through mutual trust between parties [33]. The issue of trust is ever-present in the healthcare industry. Healthcare institutions collect vast amounts of personal medical information from patients in the process of their duties. This information can in turn be used to train an ML model. This could benefit society by enhancing the ability of clinicians to diagnose certain diseases.

DeepMind brought the debate around providing access to highly sensitive, and public, data-sets to private companies into the public sphere when they collaborated with the Royal Free London NHS Trust in 2015. This work outlined 'Streams', an application for the early detection of kidney failure [40]. However, the project raised concerns surrounding privacy and trust. DeepMind received patient records from the Trust under a legal contract dictating how this data could be used. Later this was criticised as being vague and found to be illegal by the Information Commissioner's Office [15]. Furthermore, DeepMind did not apply for regulatory approval through the research authorisation process to the Health Research Authority - a necessary step if they were to do any ML on the data. The team working on Streams has now joined Google, raising further concerns about the linkage of personal health data with Google's other records [29].

While there was significant push back against the DeepMind/Royal Free collaboration, this has not prevented other research collaborations. This includes the automated analysis of retinal images [13] and the segmentation of neck and head tumour volumes [10]. In both these scenarios, the appropriate authorisation from the Health Research Authority was obtained, and the usage of the data transferred was clearly defined and tightly constrained.

2.2   Decentralised Identifiers (DIDs)

DIDs are tools which can be used to manage trust in a distributed or privacy-preserving environment. DIDs represent a new type of digital identifier currently being standardised in a World Wide Web Consortium (W3C) working group [41]. A DID persistently identifies a single entity that can self-authenticate as being in control of the identifier. This is different from other identifiers which rely on a trusted third party to attest to their control of an identifier. DIDs are typically stored on a decentralised storage system such as a distributed ledger, so, unlike other identifiers such as an email address, DIDs are under the sole control of the identity owner.

Any specific DID scheme that implements the DID specification must be resolvable to its respective document using the DID method defined by the scheme. Many different implementations of the DID specification exist which utilise different storage solutions. These include Ethereum, Sovrin, Bitcoin and IPFS; each with their own DID method for resolving DIDs specific to their system [49].

The goal of the DID specification is thus to ensure *interoperability* across these different DID schemes such that, it is possible to understand how to resolve and interpret a DID no matter where the specific implementation originates from. However, not all DIDs need to be stored on a ledger; in fact, there are situations where doing so could compromise the privacy of an individual and breach data protection laws, such as with GDPR. Peer DIDs are one such implementation of the DID specification that does not require a storage system, and in this implementation DIDs and DID documents are generated by entities who then share them when establishing peer-to-peer connections. Each peer stores and maintains a record of the other peer's DID and DID Document [25].

2.3   DID Communication (DIDComm)

DIDComm [24] is an asynchronous encrypted communication protocol that has been developed as part of the Hyperledger Aries project [30]. The protocol uses information within the DID Document, particularly the parties' public key and their endpoint for receiving messages, to send information with verifiable authenticity and integrity. The DIDComm protocol has now moved into a standards-track run by the Decentralized Identity Foundation [47].

As defined in Algorithm 1, Alice first encrypts and signs a plaintext message for Bob. She then sends the signature and encrypted message to Bob's endpoint. Once the transaction has been received Bob can verify the integrity of the message, decrypt it and read the plaintext. All the information required for this interaction is contained within Bob and Alice's DID Documents. Examples of public-key encryption protocols include ElGamal [17], RSA [42] and elliptic curve based [52]. Using this protocol both Bob and Alice are able to communicate securely and privately, over independent channels and verify the authenticity and integrity of the messages they receive.

2.4 Verifiable Credentials (VCs)

The Verifiable Credential Data Model specification became a W3C recommended standard in November 2019 [46]. It defines a data model for a verifiable set of tamper-proof claims that is used by three roles; *Issuer*, *Holder* and *Verifier* as it can be seen in Fig. 1. A verifiable data registry, typically, a distributed ledger, is used to store the credential schemes, the DIDs, and DID documents of Issuers.

Algorithm 1. DID Communication Between Alice and Bob

1: Alice has a private key sk_a and a DID Document for Bob containing an endpoint ($endpoint_{bob}$) and a public key (pk_b).
2: Bob has a private key (sk_b) and a DID Document for Alice containing her public key (pk_a).
3: Alice encrypts plaintext message (m) using pk_b and creates an encrypted message (e_b).
4: Alice signs e_b using her private key (sk_a) and creates a signature (σ).
5: Alice sends (e_b, σ) to $endpoint_{bob}$.
6: Bob receives the message from Alice at $endpoint_{bob}$.
7: Bob verifies σ using Alice's public key pk_a
8: **if** Verify(σ, e_b, pk_a) = 1 **then**
9:    Bob decrypts e_b using sk_b.
10:    Bob reads the plaintext message (m) sent by Alice
11: **end if**

When issuing a credential, an Issuer creates a signature on a set of attributes for a given schema using a private key associated with their public DID through a DID document. The specification defines three signature schemes which are valid to use when issuing a credentials; JSON Web Signatures [32], Linked Data Signatures [36] and Camenisch-Lysyanskaya (CL) Signatures [7]. This paper focuses on the Hyperledger stack, which uses CL Signatures. In these signatures, a blinded link secret (a large private number contributed by the entity receiving the credential) is included in the attributes of the credential. This enables the credential to be tied to a particular entity without the Issuer needing to know the secret value.

When verifying the proof of a credential from a Holder, the Verifier needs to confirm a number of aspects:

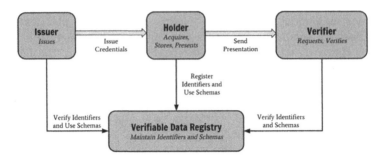

Fig. 1. Verifiable credential roles [46]

1. The DID of the Issuer can be resolved on the public ledger to a DID document. This document should contain a public key which can be used to verify the integrity of the credential.
2. The entity presenting the credential knows the secret that was blindly signed by the Issuer. The Holder creates a zero-knowledge proof attesting to this.
3. The issuing DID has the authority to issue this kind of credential. The signature alone only proves integrity, but if the Verifier accepts credentials from any Issuers, it would be easy to obtain fraudulent credentials. In a production system at-scale, this might be done through a registry, supported by a governance framework; a legal document outlining the operating parameters of the ecosystem [12].
4. The Issuer has not revoked the presented credential. This is done by checking that the hash of the credential is not present within a revocation registry (a cryptographic accumulator [2]) stored on the public ledger.
5. Finally, the Verifier needs to check that the attributes in the valid credential meet the criteria for authorisation in the system. An often used example is that the attribute in a valid passport credential is over a certain age.

All the communications between either the Issuer and the Holder, or the Holder and the Verifier are done peer-to-peer using DIDComm. It is important to note that the Issuer and the Verifier never need to communicate.

2.5   Federated Machine-Learning (FL)

In a centralised machine learning scenario, data is sent to the Researcher, instead in a FL setup the model is being sent to each data participant. The FL method has many variations, such as *Vanilla*, *Trusted Model Aggregator*, and *Secure Multi-party Aggregation* [6]. However, at a high level, the Researcher copies one atomic model and distributes it to multiple hosts who have the data. The hosts train their respective models and then send the trained models back to the Researcher. This technique facilitates training on a large corpus of federated data [5,14]. These hosts then train models and aggregate these model updates into the final model. In the case of Vanilla FL, this is the extent of the protocol. However, we can extend this with a secure aggregator, a middle man in between the Researcher and the hosts, which averages participant models before they reach the Researcher. To further improve security, this can be extended using Secure Multiparty Aggregation to average models whilst they have been encrypted into multiple shares [43]. The Researcher thus never sees the data directly, and only aggregates model gradients at the end [11]. However, this requires high network bandwidth and is vulnerable to invalidated input attacks [3], where an attacker might want to create a bias toward a particular classification type for a particular set of input data.

3   Implementation Overview

Our work performs a basic FL example between Hyperledger Aries agents to validate whether distributed ML could take place over the DIDComm transport protocol. A number of Docker containers representing entities in a health care trust model were developed; creating a simple ecosystem of learning participants and trust providers (Fig. 2). The technical specifications of the system are as follows: 2.0 GHZ dual-core Intel Core i5 CPU, with 8 GB RAM and 256 GB SSD. For each Docker container running a Hyperledger Aries agent, we used the open-source Python Aries Cloud Agent developed by the Government of British Columbia [31]. Hospital containers are initialised with the private data that is used to train the model.

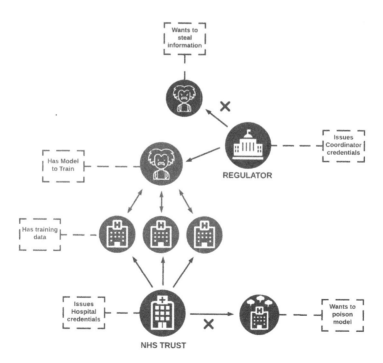

Fig. 2. ML healthcare trust model

3.1   Establishing Trust

We define a domain-specific trust architecture using verifiable credentials issued by trusted parties for a healthcare use case. This includes the following agent types: a) NHS Trust (Hospital Credential Issuer); b) Regulator (Researcher Credential Issuer); c) Hospital (Data Provider); and d) Researcher (ML Coordinator).

This is used to facilitate the authorisation of training participants (verifiable Hospitals) and a Researcher-Coordinator. A data scientist who would like to train a model is given credentials by an industry watchdog, who in a real-world scenario could audit the model and research purpose. In the United Kingdom, for example, the Health Research Authority is well placed to fulfil this role. Meanwhile, Hospitals in possession of private health data are issued with

---

Algorithm 2. Establishing Trusted Connections

1: *Researcher-Coordinator* agent exchanges DIDs with the *Regulator* agent to establish a DIDComm channel.
2: *Regulator* offers an *Audited Researcher-Coordinator* credential over this channel.
3: *Researcher-Coordinator* accepts and stores the credential in their wallet.
4: **for** each *Hospital* agent **do**
5:     Initiate DID Exchange with *NHS Trust* agent to establish DIDComm channel.
6:     *NHS Trust* offers *Verified Hospital* credentials over DIDComm.
7:     *Hospital* accepts and stores the credential.
8: **end for**
9: **for** each *Hospital* agent **do**
10:     *Hospital* initiates DID Exchange with *Researcher-Coordinator* to establish DIDComm channel.
11:     *Researcher-Coordinator* requests proof of *Verified Hospital* credential issued and signed by the *NHS Trust*.
12:     *Hospital* generates a valid proof from their *Verified Hospital* credential and responds to the *Researcher-Coordinator*.
13:     *Researcher-Coordinator* verifies the proof by first checking the DID against the known DID they have stored for the *NHS Trust*, then *resolving* the DID to locate the keys and verify the signature.
14:     **if** *Hospital* can prove they have a valid *Verified Hospital* credential **then**
15:         *Researcher-Coordinator* adds the connection identifier to their list of *Trusted Connections*.
16:     **end if**
17:     *Hospital* requests proof of *Audited Researcher-Coordinator* credential from the *Researcher-Coordinator*.
18:     *Researcher-Coordinator* uses *Audited Researcher-Coordinator* credential to generate a valid proof and responds.
19:     *Hospital* verifies the proof, by checking the signature and DID of the Issuer.
20:     **if** *Researcher-Coordinator* produces a valid proof of *Audited Researcher-Coordinator* **then**
21:         *Hospital* saves connection identifier as a trusted connection.
22:     **end if**
23: **end for**

---

credentials by an NHS authority enabling them to prove they are a real Hospital. The credential schema and the DIDs of credential Issuers are written to a public ledger – we used the development ledger provided by the government of British Columbia [20] for this work.

The system is established following the steps described in Algorithm 2. Once both the *Researcher-Coordinator* and the *Hospital* agents have been authenticated, the communication of the model parameters for FL can take place across this secure trusted channel.

3.2   Vanilla Federated Learning

This paper implements Federated Learning in its most basic form; where plaintext models are moved sequentially between agents. The Researcher-Coordinator entity begins with a model and a data-set to validate the initial performance. We train the model using sample public mental health data which is pre-processed into use-able training data. It is our intention to demonstrate that privacy-preserving ML workflows can be facilitated using this trust framework. Thus, the content of learning is not the focus of our work. We also provide performance results relating to the accuracy and resource-requirements of our system. We refer to our chosen workflow as Vanilla FL, and this is seen in Algorithm 3. In order to implement Vanilla FL, the original data-set was split into four partitions, three training-sets and one validation-set.

This amalgamation of Aries and FL allowed us to mitigate some of the existing limitations caused by a lack of trust among training participants. Specifically, these were: 1) Malicious data being provided by a false Hospital to spoil model accuracy on future cases, and 2) Malicious models being sent to Hospitals to later compromise them to leak information around training data values.

Algorithm 3. Vanilla Federated Learning

1: *Researcher-Coordinator* has validation data and a *model, Hospitals* have *training data.*

2: **while** *Hospitals* have unseen *training data* **do**

3:    *Researcher-Coordinator* benchmarks *model* performance against *validation data* and sends *model* to the next *Hospital.*

4:    This *Hospital* trains the *model* with their data and then sends the resulting *model* back to the *Researcher-Coordinator.*

5: **end while**

6: *Researcher-Coordinator* benchmarks the final *model* against *validation* data.

---

4   Threat Model

Since no data changes hands, FL is more private than traditional, centralised ML [38,53]. However, some issues still exist with this approach. Vanilla FL is vulnerable to model stealing by ML data contributors who can store a copy of the

Researcher's model after training it. In cases where the model represents private intellectual-property (IP), this setup is not ideal. On the other hand, with the knowledge of the model before and after training on each private data-set, the Researcher could infer the data used to train the model at each iteration [44]. Model inversion attacks [18,19] are also possible where, given carefully crafted input features and an infinite number of queries to the model, the Researcher could reverse engineer training values.

Vanilla FL is also potentially vulnerable to model poisoning and Trojan-backdoor attacks [3,4,35]. If data providers are malicious, it is possible to replace the original model with a malicious one and then send it to the Researcher. This malicious model could contain some backdoors, where the model will behave normally and react maliciously only to given trigger inputs. Unlike data poisoning attacks, model poisoning attacks remain hidden. They are more successful and easier to execute. Even if only one participant is malicious, the model's output will behave maliciously according to the injected poison. For the attacker to succeed, there is no need to access the training of the model; it is enough to retrain the original model with the new poisoned data.

For the mitigation of the attacks mentioned above, our system implements a domain-specific trust framework using verifiable credentials. In this way, only verified participants get issued with credentials which they use to prove they are a trusted member of the learning process to the other entity across a secure channel. This framework does not prevent the types of attacks discussed from occurring, but, by modelling trust, it does reduce the risk that they will happen. Malicious entities could thus be checked on registration, or are removed from the trust infrastructure on bad behaviour.

Another threat to consider is the possibility of the agent servers getting compromised. Either the trusted Issuers could get compromised and issue credentials to entities that are malicious, or entities with valid credentials within the system could become corrupted. Both scenarios lead to a malicious participant having control of a valid verifiable credential for the system. This type of attack is a threat; however, it is outside the scope of this work. Standard cybersecurity procedures should be in-place within these systems that make successful security breaches unlikely. OWASP provides guidelines and secure practices to mitigate these *traditional* cybersecurity threats [39]. The defensive mechanisms are not limited to these and can be expanded using Intrusion Detection and Prevention Systems (IDPS) [22].

5   Evaluation

To evaluate the prototype, malicious agents were created to attempt to take part in the ML process by connecting to one of the trusted Hyperledger Aries agents. Any agent without the appropriate credentials, either a Verified Hospital or Audited Researcher-Coordinator credential, was unable to form authenticated channels with the trusted parties (Fig. 2). These connections and requests to initiate learning or contribute to training the model were rejected. Unauthorised entities were able to create self-signed credentials, but these credentials were rejected. This is because they had not been signed by an authorised and trusted authority whose DID was known by the entity requesting the proof.

The mechanism of using credentials to form mutually verifiable connections proves useful for ensuring only trusted entities can participate in a distributed ML environment. We note that this method is generic and can be adapted to the needs of any domain and context. Verifiable credentials enable ecosystems to specify meaning in a way that digital agents participating within that ecosystem can understand. We expect to see them used increasingly to define flexible, domain-specific trust. The scenario we created was used to highlight the potential of this combination. For these trust architectures to fit their intended ecosystems equitably, it is imperative to involve all key stakeholders in their design.

Our work is focused on the application of a DID based infrastructure in a Federated Learning scenario. It is assumed that there is a pre-defined, governance-oriented trust model implemented such that key stakeholders have a DID written to an integrity assured ledger. The discovery of appropriate DIDs, and willing participants, either valid Researchers-Coordinators or Hospitals, related to a specific ecosystem is out-of-scope of our paper. This paper focuses on exploring how peer DID connections, once formed, facilitate participation in the established ecosystem. A further system can be developed for the secure distribution of the DIDs between the agents that are willing to participate.

Furthermore, performance metrics for each host were recorded during the running of our workflow. In Fig. 3a), we see the CPU usage of each agent involved in the learning workflow. The CPU usage of the Researcher-Coordinator raises each time it sends the model to the Hospitals, and CPU usage of the Hospitals raises when they train the model with their private data. This result is consistent with what is expected given Algorithm 3 runs successfully. The memory and network bandwidths follow a similar pattern, as it can be seen in Fig. 3b), Fig. 3c) and Fig. 3d). The main difference is that since the Researcher-Coordinator is averaging and validating each model against the training dataset every time, in turn, the memory and network bandwidth raises over time. From these results we can conclude that running federated learning in this way is compute heavy on the side of the Hospitals but more bandwidth and slightly more memory intensive on the side of the Researcher-Coordinator.

The aim of this research is to demonstrate that a decentralised trust framework could be used to perform a privacy-preserving workflow. The authors train a dummy model on some basic example data. The intention here is merely to demonstrate that this is possible using our trust framework. We give the confusion matrix of the model tested on the Researcher-Coordinator's validation data after each federated training batch. This demonstrates that our model was successfully adjusted at each stage of training upon our federated, mental health dataset. The model develops a bias toward false-positives and tends to get less TNs as each batch continues. However, this may be due to the distribution of each data batch. Other than this, the learning over each batch tends to maximise true-positives. This can be observed in Table 1.

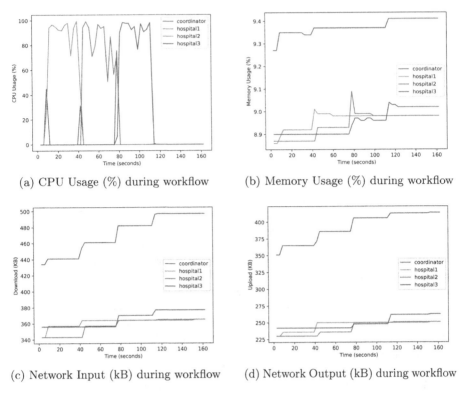

(a) CPU Usage (%) during workflow   (b) Memory Usage (%) during workflow

(c) Network Input (kB) during workflow   (d) Network Output (kB) during workflow

Fig. 3. CPU, Memory usage and network utilization of Docker container agents during workflow

Table 1. Classifier's accuracy over batches

Batch	0	1	2	3
True positives	0	109	120	134
False positives	0	30	37	41
True negatives	114	84	77	73
False negatives	144	35	24	10

6   Conclusion and Future Work

This paper combines two fields of research, privacy-preserving ML and decentralised identity. Both have similar visions for a more trusted citizen-focused and privacy-respecting society. In this research, we show how developing a trust framework based on Decentralised Identifiers and Verifiable Credentials for ML scenarios that involve sensitive data can enable an increased trust between parties, while also reducing the liability of organisations with data.

It is possible to use these secure channels to obtain a digitally signed contract for training, or to manage pointer communications on remote data. While Vanilla FL is vulnerable to attacks as described in Sect. 4, the purpose of this work was to develop a proof of concept showing that domain-specific trust can be achieved over the same communication channels used for distributed ML. Future work includes integrating the Aries communication protocols, which enables the trust model demonstrated here, into an existing framework for facilitating distributed learning, such as PyGrid, the networking component of OpenMined [43]. This will allow us and others to apply the trust framework to a far wider range of privacy-preserving workflows. Additionally, it will allow us to enforce trust, mitigating model inversion attacks using differentially private training mechanisms [16]. Multiple techniques can be implemented for training a differentially private model; such as PyVacy [50] and LATENT [8]. To minimise the threat of model stealing and training data inference, Secure Multiparty Computation (SMC) [34] can be leveraged to split data and model parameters into shares. SMC allows both gradients and parameters to be computed and updated in a decentralised fashion while encrypted. In this case, custody of each data item is split into shares to be held by relevant participating entities.

In our experiments, we utilised the Hyperledger Aries messaging functionality to convert the ML model into text and to be able to send it to the participating entities. In future work, we will going to focus on expanding the messaging functionality with a separate structure for ML communication. We also hope to evaluate the type of trust that can be placed in these messages, exploring the Message Trust Context object suggested in a Hyperledger Aries RFC [23].

In this work, we address the issue of trust within the data industry. This radically decentralised trust infrastructure allows individuals to organise themselves and collaboratively learn from one another without any central authority figure. This breaks new ground by combining privacy-preserving ML techniques with a decentralised trust architecture.

References

1. Ahmad, O.F., Stoyanov, D., Lovat, L.B.: Barriers and pitfalls for artificial intelligence in gastroenterology: ethical and regulatory issues. Tech. Gastrointest. Endosc. **22**, 150636 (2019)
2. Au, M.H., Tsang, P.P., Susilo, W., Mu, Y.: Dynamic universal accumulators for DDH groups and their application to attribute-based anonymous credential systems. In: Fischlin, M. (ed.) CT-RSA 2009. LNCS, vol. 5473, pp. 295–308. Springer, Heidelberg (2009). https://doi.org/10.1007/978-3-642-00862-7_20
3. Bagdasaryan, E., Veit, A., Hua, Y., Estrin, D., Shmatikov, V.: How to backdoor federated learning. arXiv preprint arXiv:1807.00459 (2018)
4. Bhagoji, A.N., Chakraborty, S., Mittal, P., Calo, S.: Analyzing federated learning through an adversarial lens. arXiv preprint arXiv:1811.12470 (2018)
5. Bonawitz, K., et al.: Towards federated learning at scale: system design (2019). http://arxiv.org/abs/1902.01046
6. Bonawitz, K., et al.: Practical secure aggregation for federated learning on user-held data. CoRR abs/1611.04482 (2016). http://arxiv.org/abs/1611.04482

7. Camenisch, J., Lysyanskaya, A.: A signature scheme with efficient protocols. In: Cimato, S., Persiano, G., Galdi, C. (eds.) SCN 2002. LNCS, vol. 2576, pp. 268–289. Springer, Heidelberg (2003). https://doi.org/10.1007/3-540-36413-7_20

8. Chamikara, M., Bertok, P., Khalil, I., Liu, D., Camtepe, S.: Local differential privacy for deep learning. arXiv preprint arXiv:1908.02997 (2019)

9. Chen, D., Zhao, H.: Data security and privacy protection issues in cloud computing. In: 2012 International Conference on Computer Science and Electronics Engineering, vol. 1, pp. 647–651. IEEE (2012)

10. Chu, C., et al.: Applying machine learning to automated segmentation of head and neck tumour volumes and organs at risk on radiotherapy planning CT and MRI scans. F1000Research 5, 1204 (2016)

11. Das, D., et al.: Distributed deep learning using synchronous stochastic gradient descent. arXiv preprint arXiv:1602.06709 (2016)

12. Davie, M., Gisolfi, D., Hardman, D., Jordan, J., O'Donnell, D., Reed, D.: The trust over IP stack. RFC 289, Hyperledger, October 2019. https://github.com/hyperledger/aries-rfcs/tree/master/concepts/0289-toip-stack

13. De Fauw, J., et al.: Automated analysis of retinal imaging using machine learning techniques for computer vision. F1000Research 5, 1573 (2016)

14. Dean, J., et al.: Large scale distributed deep networks. In: Advances in Neural Information Processing Systems, pp. 1223–1231 (2012)

15. Denham, E.: Royal free - google DeepMind trial failed to comply with data protection law. Technical report Information Commisioner Office (2017). https://ico.org.uk/about-the-ico/news-and-events/news-and-blogs/2017/07/royal-free-google-deepmind-trial-failed-to-comply-with-data-protection-law/

16. Dwork, C.: Differential privacy. In: van Tilborg, H.C.A., Jajodia, S. (eds.) Encyclopedia of Cryptography and Security, pp. 338–340. Springer, Boston (2011). https://doi.org/10.1007/978-1-4419-5906-5_752

17. ElGamal, T.: A public key cryptosystem and a signature scheme based on discrete logarithms. IEEE Trans. Inf. Theory 31(4), 469–472 (1985)

18. Fredrikson, M., Jha, S., Ristenpart, T.: Model inversion attacks that exploit confidence information and basic countermeasures. In: Proceedings of the 22nd ACM SIGSAC Conference on Computer and Communications Security, pp. 1322–1333. ACM (2015)

19. Fredrikson, M., Lantz, E., Jha, S., Lin, S., Page, D., Ristenpart, T.: Privacy in pharmacogenetics: an end-to-end case study of personalized warfarin dosing. In: 23rd USENIX Security Symposium USENIX Security 2014, pp. 17–32 (2014)

20. Government of British Columbia: British Columbia's verifiable organizations (2018). https://orgbook.gov.bc.ca/en/home

21. Hall, A.J., Hussain, A., Shaikh, M.G.: Predicting insulin resistance in children using a machine-learning-based clinical decision support system. In: Liu, C.-L., Hussain, A., Luo, B., Tan, K.C., Zeng, Y., Zhang, Z. (eds.) BICS 2016. LNCS (LNAI), vol. 10023, pp. 274–283. Springer, Cham (2016). https://doi.org/10.1007/978-3-319-49685-6_25

22. Hall, P.: Proposals for model vulnerability and security (2019). https://www.oreilly.com/ideas/proposals-for-model-vulnerability-and-security

23. Hardman, D.: Message trust contexts. RFC 29, Hyperledger, May 2019. https://github.com/hyperledger/aries-rfcs/tree/master/concepts/0029-message-trust-contexts

24. Hardman, D.: Did communication. Github Requests for Comments, January 2019. https://github.com/hyperledger/aries-rfcs/tree/master/concepts/0005-didcomm
25. Hardman, D.: Peer did method specification. Technical report (2019). https://openssi.github.io/peer-did-method-spec/index.html
26. Hashem, I.A.T., et al.: The role of big data in smart city. Int. J. Inf. Manage. **36**(5), 748–758 (2016)
27. Hoffman, A.M.: A conceptualization of trust in international relations. Eur. J. Int. Relat. **8**(3), 375–401 (2002)
28. Holcomb, S.D., Porter, W.K., Ault, S.V., Mao, G., Wang, J.: Overview on Deep-Mind and its alphago zero ai. In: Proceedings of the 2018 International Conference on Big Data and Education, pp. 67–71. ACM (2018)
29. Hughes, O.: Royal free: 'no changes to data-sharing' as google absorbs streams, November 2018. https://www.digitalhealth.net/2018/11/royal-free-data-sharing-google-deepmind-streams/
30. Hyperledger: Hyperledger aries. https://www.hyperledger.org/projects/aries
31. Hyperledger: Hyperledger aries cloud agent - python (2019). https://github.com/hyperledger/aries-cloudagent-python
32. Jones, M., Bradley, J., Sakimura, N.: JSON web signatures. RFC, May 2015. https://tools.ietf.org/html/rfc7515
33. Keymolen, E.: Trust on the line: a philosophycal exploration of trust in the networked era (2016)
34. Lindell, Y.: Secure multiparty computation for privacy preserving data mining. In: Wang, J. (ed.) Encyclopedia of Data Warehousing and Mining, pp. 1005–1009. IGI Global, Hershey (2005)
35. Liu, Y., et al.: Trojaning attack on neural networks. Purdue University Libraries e-Pubs (2017)
36. Longley, D., Sporny, M., Allen, C.: Linked data signatures 1.0. Technical report (2019). https://w3c-dvcg.github.io/ld-signatures/
37. Muñoz-González, L., et al.: Towards poisoning of deep learning algorithms with back-gradient optimization. In: Proceedings of the 10th ACM Workshop on Artificial Intelligence and Security, pp. 27–38. ACM (2017)
38. Nilsson, A., Smith, S., Ulm, G., Gustavsson, E., Jirstrand, M.: A performance evaluation of federated learning algorithms. In: Proceedings of the Second Workshop on Distributed Infrastructures for Deep Learning, pp. 1–8 (2018)
39. OWASP: Top 10 2017. The ten most critical web application security risks. Release Candidate 2 (2018)
40. Powles, J., Hodson, H.: Google DeepMind and healthcare in an age of algorithms. Health Technol. **7**(4), 351–367 (2017). https://doi.org/10.1007/s12553-017-0179-1
41. Reed, D., Sporny, M., Longely, D., Allen, C., Sabadello, M., Grant, R.: Decentralized identifiers (DIDs) v1.0, January 2020. https://w3c.github.io/did-core/
42. Rivest, R.L., Shamir, A., Adleman, L.: A method for obtaining digital signatures and public-key cryptosystems. Commun. ACM **21**(2), 120–126 (1978)
43. Ryffel, T., et al.: A generic framework for privacy preserving deep learning, pp. 1–5 (2018). arXiv:1811.04017v2. http://arxiv.org/abs/1811.04017
44. Shokri, R., Stronati, M., Song, C., Shmatikov, V.: Membership inference attacks against machine learning models. In: 2017 IEEE Symposium on Security and Privacy (SP), pp. 3–18. IEEE (2017)
45. Spence, P.: How we can place a value on health care data (2019). https://www.ey.com/en_gl/life-sciences/how-we-can-place-a-value-on-health-care-data
46. Sporny, M., Longely, D., Chadwick, D.: Verifiable credentials data model 1.0. Technical report W3C, November 2019. https://w3c.github.io/vc-data-model/

47. Terbu, O.: Dif starts didcomm working group (2020). https://medium.com/decentralized-identity/dif-starts-didcomm-working-group-9c114d9308dc

48. Voigt, P., von dem Bussche, A.: The EU General Data Protection Regulation (GDPR). A Practical Guide. Springer, Cham (2017). https://doi.org/10.1007/978-3-319-57959-7

49. W3C Credential Community Group: Did method registry. Technical report (2019). https://w3c-ccg.github.io/did-method-registry/

50. Waites, C.: Pyvacy: privacy algorithms for pytorch (2019). https://pypi.org/project/pyvacy/

51. Wiens, J., Shenoy, E.S.: Machine learning for healthcare: on the verge of a major shift in healthcare epidemiology. Clin. Infect. Dis. **66**(1), 149–153 (2017)

52. Wohlwend, J.: Elliptic curve cryptography: pre and post quantum. Technical report MIT (2016)

53. Yang, Q., Liu, Y., Chen, T., Tong, Y.: Federated machine learning: concept and applications. ACM Trans. Intell. Syst. Technol. (TIST) **10**(2), 1–19 (2019)

54. Young, K., Greenberg, S.: A field guide to internet trust (2014). https://identitywoman.net/wp-content/uploads/TrustModelFieldGuideFinal-1.pdf

Trust

A Fuzzy Trust Model for Autonomous Entities Acting in Pervasive Computing

Kostas Kolomvatsos$^{(\boxtimes)}$, Maria Kalouda, Panagiota Papadopoulou, and Stathes Hadjieftymiades

Department of Informatics and Telecommunications,
National and Kapodistrian University of Athens, Athens, Greece
{kostasks,std04014,peggy,shadj}@di.uoa.gr

Abstract. Pervasive computing applications involve the interaction between autonomous entities for performing complex tasks and producing knowledge. Autonomous entities can interact to exchange data and knowledge to fulfill applications requirements. Intelligent Agents (IAs) 'activated' in various devices offer a lot of advantages when representing such entities due to their autonomous nature that enables them to perform the desired tasks in a distributed way. However, in such open and dynamic environments, IAs should be based on an efficient mechanism for trusting unknown entities when exchanging data. The trust level of an entity should be automatically calculated based on an efficient methodology. Each entity is uncertain for the characteristics and the intentions of the others. Fuzzy Logic (FL) seems to be the appropriate tool for handling such kind of uncertainty. In this paper, we present a model for trust calculation under the principles of FL. Our scheme takes into consideration the social dimension of trust as well as personal experiences of entities before they decide interactions with an IA. The proposed model is a two-level system involving three FL sub-systems to calculate (a) the social trust (based on experiences retrieved by the community), (b) the individual trust (based on personal experiences) and (c) the final trust. We present our results by evaluating the proposed system compared to other models and reveal its significance.

Keywords: Pervasive computing · Autonomous entities · Trust · Reputation · Fuzzy Logic

1 Introduction

The rapid evolution of pervasive computing sets new challenges in the research community about the development of new services and applications. The combination of wireless technologies (e.g. Wireless Sensors Networks) and the Internet accompanied by the respective hardware allows for numerous nodes to be interconnected. Pervasive computing involves the adoption of numerous devices embedded into everyday objects for supporting intelligent applications. The transition from closed networks to interconnected autonomous nodes interacting with their environment and performing simple

© Springer Nature Switzerland AG 2020
S. Gritzalis et al. (Eds.): TrustBus 2020, LNCS 12395, pp. 223–233, 2020.
https://doi.org/10.1007/978-3-030-58986-8_15

processing tasks should be enhanced by intelligent applications increasing the quality of services that end users enjoy.

Pervasive computing applications usually involve the interaction between autonomous nodes to exchange data and knowledge, creating a complex architecture. Such architectures can assist in deriving knowledge necessary to support complex services and applications. The automated knowledge discovery and data exchange can be realized by *Intelligent Agents* (IAs) having the form of software or hardware components capable of acting autonomously to achieve goals defined by their owners. However, IAs should retrieve data and knowledge and rely upon trusted entities (i.e. other IAs) to ensure a reliable data exchange and efficiently support pervasive applications. Usually, IAs take into consideration the reputation and trust levels of other IAs to start and conclude an interaction. However, the calculation of the trust level of an external entity is a very difficult task.

Trust management has long been a significant domain in Computer Science and refers to various aspects of entities behaviour, in areas such as e-commerce. The meaning of the trust concept varies depending on the context [2]. Trust can be seen as the extent to which one entity intends to depend on somebody else in a given situation [16]. When focusing on interactions between autonomous entities, one can easily detect the uncertainty behind any decision for concluding these interactions. Such an uncertainty refers in the intended behaviour that an entity may possibly exhibit rendering it as suitable to be trusted or not. For handling this uncertainty, we propose a *Fuzzy Logic* (FL) based system for estimating the trust level of an IA.

We define an efficient modeling process that seeks to imitate human behavior. IAs aim is to interact only with those entities having a high trust value. The system is based on: a) the *social aspect of trust*, b) the *individual experiences* of each IA and c) their combination. The significance of the proposed model is that it combines both social and individual trust values in an efficient way. The proposed model employs a distributed approach as IAs can calculate the trust level in an autonomous manner. The proposed model extends previous research in two aspects: (i) We do not deal with binary ratings or specific values like in Ebay (−1, 0 or 1) [10, 21]. Binary ratings are considered insufficient to capture various degrees of judgment [1]; (ii) In previous models [10, 11, 13], trust is based only on one value, the final rate, i.e. the final trust value. In the proposed model, trust is defined and estimated by a number of parameters, thus every referrer rates the examinee for these parameters.

The remainder of this paper is organized as follows: Sect. 2 reports prior work while Sect. 3 gives the necessary description of our scenario. Section 4 is devoted to the description of our model analyzing its three sub-systems for calculating the social, the individual and the final trust. In Sect. 5, we discuss our results while Sect. 6 concludes our paper.

2 Related Work

The authors in [6] define the notion of trust and describe simple models for trust calculation. Trust can have a cognitive and a mathematical aspect, which involve the underlying beliefs concerning trust as well as equations for trust extraction. The Fire system is described in [9], a trust and reputation model integrating various information sources to calculate IA performance, based on interaction trust, role-based trust, witness reputation and certified reputation. In [12], the authors provide a detailed overview of reputation and trust models highlighting their importance to open environments. A categorization of trust is presented in [18]. Decentralized and centralized trust is reviewed in [21], presenting a model with Bayesian networks combining different trust aspects, applied for a file sharing peer-to-peer application.

In [1] a trust establishment model is described going beyond trust evaluation to outline actions to guide trusters. The model relies on a multicriteria approach for measuring and analysing trusters needs and evaluates the satisfaction level of trusters based on their values and expressed preferences. The authors of [2] propose a framework for trust calculation based on the assumption that the more values agents share, the more they should trust one another. The model relies on agents' past behavior to conclude the final trust taking into account if agents trust cautiously or boldly, and if they depend on others in carrying out a task. According to [23], IAs from the same system should be evaluated differently from agents in different multi-agent systems. The trust level is affected by the platform they are activated in. In [5] a model of trust that incorporates competence and integrity is proposed. The threshold for trustworthiness in a particular context is viewed as a function of agents' relationship with the truster and potential impacts of decisions. In [4], the human-agent collaboration is studied with current approaches to measure trust and how they can be inadequate in a real time setting, critical to know the user's trust in the agent.

FL has been widely used for evaluating trust. An FL based system for trust and reputation calculation is presented in [2], which is actually a Fuzzy extension of the Beta reputation model in [10]. Two fuzzy subsets are proposed, namely 'satisfied' and 'unsatisfied'. Based on the combination of the two fuzzy sets, the authors present mathematical formulations for calculating the agreement level between two partners. In [7], trust calculation between cooperative IAs is studied. FL is used for representing trust, allowing IAs to handle uncertainty. The authors present a mechanism for agents to make use of distrust. Distrust has not only a negative meaning, the opposite of trust, but represents the belief that an IA will act against the goals of another. Membership functions and the FL rule base are studied. In [8] a proposed model for trust calculation based on FL is presented, taking into consideration different trust sources aiming to minimize wrong evaluations. The final trust is based on a weighted fuzzy calculation. In [13], a comparison between fuzzy aggregation models and existing methods for trust evaluation is presented. FL is used to build the final trust level based on a number of values that should be aggregated. The results show superiority of the proposed FL algorithm. The adaptation of a bio-inspired trust model to deal with linguistic fuzzy labels seems to be more efficient and closer to the human way of thinking [15]. Linguistic fuzzy sets represent the satisfaction level of a client. The model calculates the final trust value in five steps.

In [17], the authors describe a model that attempts to identify the information customers expect to find on vendors websites in order to increase their trust and, thus, the likelihood of a successful transaction. Fuzzy reasoning can handle imprecise data and uncertainty when measuring the trust index of each vendor. Trust for mobile IAs is studied in [20]. Customers can collect feedback using IAs and, thus, build trust. Once a customer performs a transaction with a provider the feedback is received and, thus, can be taken into consideration in the trust calculation.

3 Preliminaries

3.1 Trust

Trust is a key concept in various contexts, including transactions between IAs. In order to interact with their peers, IAs should be able to rely on an efficient mechanism enabling the estimation of trust of other entities. Hence, trust can be seen as part of a directional relationship of unknown entities that try to interact in order to exchange data and services. This term is presented in [19], discerning *hard* and *soft* security mechanisms. Hard tools are authentication or cryptography while soft tools involve social control issues (i.e. trust and reputation). Based on [7] trust can be defined as:

Trust (T) represents an agent's individual assessment of the reliability of another to accomplish a task

Trust is a complex, dynamic and context-specific phenomenon, largely based on beliefs that an entity has for another [16]. Such beliefs are largely subjective and of unclear origin. This means that an IA may be reliable only for a set of IAs and not for all of them. The level of trust is also dependent on the context. For example, an IA may be trustworthy for providing information but not for selling products. Furthermore, trust is dynamic. An IA may consider another entity as reliable in a specific time point but its opinion may change by the behaviour of the target entity. In general, trust can be considered as a function of the following parameters: the beliefs of the examiner, the reputation of the examinee, previous trust values and the context.

3.2 Reputation

Reputation is a concept representing a belief which has a social aspect and has been the topic of study in various fields, including IA systems, in conjunction with trust. Mainly, reputation reflects the opinion that the society has for a specific entity. Based on [7] reputation can be defined as follows:

Reputation (R) is a social concept corresponding to a group assesment of the reliability of an entity to accomplish a task

The concepts of reputation and trust are closely related but different. The main differences between trust and reputation are: (a) Usually, trust is a score that reflects the subjective view of an entity for another entity whereas reputation is a score that reflects the view of the community for an entity; (b) In trust systems, the transitivity aspect is considered explicitly, while in reputation systems, it is seen implicitly [22].

In the proposed system, reputation may be derived from direct experiences of the truster with the target entity or from others' past experiences with the target entity. It may be positive or negative and mainly serves to moderate the weight of referrals and their contribution to trust calculation.

3.3 Referrals

Trust estimation can depend on referrals made by the society members for an entity based on their interactions with it. Based on [10], referral can be defined as:

Referral is the individual assessment of a third entity for the trust level of another

Apart from their own experience with an entity or in the lack of interaction history with it, IAs can be based on other IAs assessments to determine an entity's trust level. Usually, there is a central authority responsible for handling referrals. Every IA that wants to calculate the trust level of an entity relies on this authority and retrieves referrals for the entity, with which the IA can calculate the social trust value that reflects the society's opinion for the specific entity.

In our case, a key issue is trust's dynamic nature. Trust evolves over time as entities cooperate with others. Thus, it is critical to define a trust update process. Especially, in open environments like those in pervasive computing, where goals, beliefs and intentions of IAs continually change, there is a need for dynamic adaptation of trust. For this purpose, we use FL for handling this uncertainty. In FL models trust and reputation are described with linguistic fuzzy values. Fuzzy inference is adopted to determine trust. Personal experience typically has more weight than second-hand trust referrals or reputation, but in absence of personal experience, trust often has to be based on referrals from others [10].

4 The Fuzzy Trust Model

4.1 High Level Architecture

Trust can be calculated by multiple parameters depicting the behavior of an entity. Our model focuses on detecting if an entity can offer timely a specific service with a desirable quality. The reason is that we want to have IAs collaborating to support pervasive computing applications, thus, we want to have real time quality responses. We propose that the trust value is calculated based on two aspects (a) the quality of the offered data/service; (b) the time required for other IAs to produce a response to IA's requests. These parameters can be easily extended by many more. Referrals concern realizations of the aforementioned parameters and represent the experience of

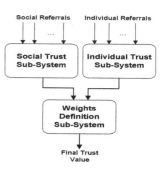

Fig. 1. The proposed system

IAs retrieved by interactions with the specific IA that offers the data/service. Simultaneously, IAs store information about the reputation of others and use each referral in combination with the reputation of the referrer. The aim is to be protected by entities that provide false referrals. For instance, if a referral is made by an IA with high reputation, it can affect the final social trust much more than a referral made by an entity with a low reputation. Every referral consists of two values in $[-1, 1]$, one for each attribute (quality, communication).

The proposed system has three sub-systems (Fig. 1) calculating respectively: (a) the social trust value, based on referrals by others; (b) the individual trust value, based on

IA's personal experiences and (c) the weights for the social and the individual trust values to have the final one.

4.2 The Social Trust Subsystem

We provide a FL scheme for the social aspect of trust. An IA completing an interaction with another grades it for the two major system parameters: quality and speed of interaction. Each parameter is graded with a real number in $[-1, 1]$. Each referral has a timestamp and is stored by a central authority so as to be available to all entities. The degree to which a referral contributes to social trust is inversely proportional to the age of the referral. The older the referral, the less it contributes to the final social trust. Each referral has an expiration point, over which it is no longer taken into account. Another factor that influences social trust is the referrer reputation. Every IA is characterized by a degree of reputation, represented by a real number in $[0, 1]$. The degree to which a referral contributes to social trust is proportional to the reputation of the referrer. Referrals coming from IAs with a high reputation (close to 1) affect social trust more. We propose an FL model with referrals as inputs and social trust as the output. If no referrals are available for an IA, social trust is set equal to 0 (a neutral value).

The social trust value is calculated by $ST_{s_i} = \frac{\sum_{j=1}^{n}(T_j \cdot R \cdot F)}{n}$, where ST_{s_i} is the social trust s_i, and n is the number of referrals made by community members for s_i. T_j is the weight of each referral according to its age, defined as $T_j = max\left(1 - e^{\frac{d_j - d\text{max}}{\text{sm}}}, 0\right)$, where d_j is the difference of days between the referral timestamp and the time that the IA calculates the trust, d_{max} is a maximum value (in days) and sm is a 'smoothing' factor. sm affects the strategy that the IA follows for realizing the weight of the referral. The higher the sm is, the more 'strict' the IA becomes. When sm is high, even for a low d_j (i.e., the referral is recent), T_j is very low (close to 0) and the referral has limited contribution to the final value. Moreover, over the d_{max}, a referral is characterized as obsolete and T_j is 0, i.e. it does not contribute to the calculation process. Parameter R refers to the reputation of the entity making the referral and is defined as $R = \left(a \cdot e_m + (1 - a) \cdot \frac{R_m}{\sum_{i=1}^{E} R_i}\right)$. The reputation of the referrer is calculated from the opinion of the IA about the referrer and the reputation of the other IAs making referrals about the referrer. We consider that there is a mechanism handling reputation values, which is beyond the scope of this paper. Parameter e_m is a number in $[0, 1]$ representing the personal experience of the IA with the entity making the referral (m is the index of the specific entity). The e_m is based on ratings that the IA gives to any entity having an interaction with. The closer to 1 the e_m is, the more the IA trusts the entity making the referral. Parameter a is constant (defined by the developer) and represents the weight of parameter e_m, i.e., the weight of the IA's opinion. The right part of the sum in the above equation refers to the reputation of the referrer as a percentage of the sum of the reputation values of all the entities that made referrals for the specific IA (E is the number of entities making referrals for the referrer). We involve in the calculation process the opinion of the IA community for the entity. The higher the number of entities, the lower this factor becomes, even for large reputation values. With parameter a, the IA increases or decreases the weight of her opinion or that of the community. If a $= 1$ the referrer reputation is based only on the IA's experience with it while if a $= 0$ the reputation is based only on the community opinion. Last, parameter F is the result of the FL sub-system, defined as $F = \frac{\sum_{k=1}^{N} \mu_m(u_k) \cdot u_k}{\sum_{k=1}^{N} \mu_m(u_k)}$. The fuzzification process involves triangular membership functions $(\mu_m(u_k))$ applied for the two input variables, i.e. the IA's individual opinion and the community's opinion about the referrer. Each membership variable takes values in $[-1, 1]$ for inputs and the output. Crisp input values are fuzzified through the proposed membership functions and transformed into values in $[0, 1]$. The output is the social trust value. The linguistic representation of the discussed parameters is *Low*, *Medium* and *High*. The final result is retrieved by the defuzzification process. The degrees of membership of inputs are combined to get the degree of membership of the output variable. For the defuzzification phase, we adopt the *Center of Gravity* (CoG) method [3]. Finally, it should be noted that fuzzy sets and membership functions are defined by experts.

4.3 The Individual Trust Sub-system

In the individual trust sub-system, we follow a similar approach. Every IA has past experiences with some other IAs. These experiences provide useful information about upcoming interactions. The individual trust is calculated as $IT_{s_i} = \frac{\sum_{j=1}^{n}(T_j \cdot F)}{n}$ where IT_{s_i} represents individual trust for IA s_i, T_j and F are the weight and the fuzzy value respectively of IA's opinion for s_i for each past interaction, as defined above. In fact, F is the result of the FL individual trust sub-system. Parameter n indicates the number of past transactions with the specific IA. If no past experiences are present, then the individual trust value is set to 0 (a neutral value). As in the social trust sub-system, we use triangular membership functions for inputs and output in the interval $[-1, 1]$. The linguistic values of them are *Low*, *Medium* and *High*. The fuzzification and defuzzification processes are as in the social trust sub-system while membership functions and fuzzy rules are defined by experts.

4.4 The Final Trust Calculation

The IA, after the calculation of social and individual trust, adopts a weighted sum for the final trust value, using a FL system for the extraction of the weight for social trust. Figure 2 shows the architecture of the system. In this rationale, the final trust is calculated as $T_{s_i} = w_s \cdot ST_{s_i} + (1 - w_s) \cdot IT_{s_i}$, where T_{s_i} is the final trust for s_i, ST_{s_i} represents the social trust of s_i, IT_{s_i} represents the individual trust and w_s is the weight for the social trust calculated by the proposed FL sub-system. The input variables for the third FL sub-system are (i) the total number of social referrals made for the specific entity (SR), (ii) the total number of individual past transactions with the specific entity (IR) and (iii) an error value (er). The error is calculated as $er = ST_{s_i} - IT_{s_i}$ and gets values in $[-2, 2]$. The output variable of the FL final trust sub-system is the social trust weight (w_s). In this FL sub-system, we also adopt triangular membership functions for inputs and output and the linguistic values for them are *Low*, *Medium* and *High*. Table 1 presents the FL rule base for the social weight definition. Membership functions and fuzzy rules are defined by experts while fuzzification and defuzzification are applied as in the previous sub-systems.

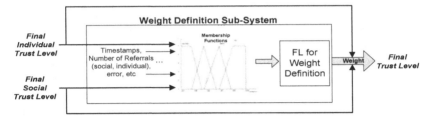

Fig. 2. The architecture of the sub-system for the final trust value extraction.

Table 1. FL rule base for final trust calculation.

SR	IR	Er	w_s
Low	Any value	Any value	Low
Any value	Low	Any value	High
High	Any value	Low	High
High	Any value	Medium	Medium
Low	Any value	Medium	Low
Any value	High	High	Low
Medium or High	Medium	High	Medium

5   Experimental Evaluation

We evaluate our system with a comparative assessment with another trust calculation model based on [14]. We adopt the *Root Means Square Error* (RMSE), defined as $\text{RMSE} = \sqrt{\frac{\sum_{i=1}^{n}(\hat{y}_i - y_i)^2}{n}}$, where y_i and $\hat{y}_i$ are the actual and estimated value, respectively. We insert 100 referrals for 20 entities into our system and consider that 50 IAs participate in a pervasive computing application. Referrals for speed and quality of interaction are randomly generated in $[-1, 1]$. We run the system and take the final trust value $\hat{y}_i$ for each of the 20 entities. Then, we consider deception values for every referral. Deception values are updates in true values, negative and positive. Negative deception is realized by adding -0.1, -0.2, -0.3, -0.4, and -0.5 to normal referrals. Positive deception is calculated by adding 0.1, 0.2, 0.3, 0.4, and 0.5 to normal referrals. When we apply a deception value, we retrieve the final trust (y_i) from the system and calculate the error.

Figure 3 and Fig. 4 show our results for negative and positive deception. In these plots, we use $d_{max} \in \{50, 100\}$ (days) and see how the parameter affects RMSE value. When $d_{max} = 100$ results are similar to [14]. However, when $d_{max} = 50$ our results outperform results in [14]. For example, for deception of -0.1 our system gives RMSE $= 2.6\%$ while in [14] the result is over 3% for the EFL model and over 4% for the EWL model (approximately). For deception of 0.1 the results are 2.93% and over 3% (EFL model) and -4% (EWL model) respectively. For deception values of -0.5 and 0.5, the results are 9.71%, 9.83% for our system and close to 15% (EFL model) and -19% (EWL model) for the system presented in [14].

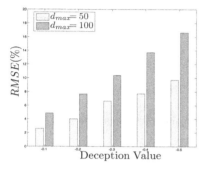 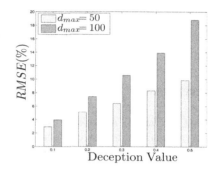

Fig. 3. RMSE for negative deception values.   **Fig. 4.** RMSE for positive deception values.

Finally, Table 2 presents our results for parameter Δ_T. Δ_T shows how d_{max} affects RMSE value. Δ_T is given by $\Delta_T = \frac{T_F - T_S}{T_S} \cdot 100\%$, where TF and TS are the trust value calculated with $d_{max} = 50$ and $d_{max} = 100$ days respectively. We see that a high d_{max} lead to a high RMSE. This means that the fluctuation of referrals age negatively affects the trust value and RMSE. When d_{max} is low, the IA takes into account only 'fresh' referrals, thus, it is less affected by possible deceptions.

Table 2. Δ_T results for negative and positive deception values.

Deception value	Δ_T	Deception value	Δ_T
-0.5	71.27%	0.1	34.47%
-0.4	78.31%	0.2	45.10%
-0.3	56.95%	0.3	65.57%
-0.2	91.98%	0.4	67.59%
-0.1	86.92%	0.5	91.35%

6   Conclusions

This paper studies trust estimation for entities in pervasive computing applications. In such cases, IAs need an efficient mechanism for calculation of other IAs trust. We propose a FL system comprising three subsystems. The two subsystems determine the trust level of an entity based on referrals or on IA's individual experiences. The third subsystem results weights for each trust category (social, individual). We present the architecture of each sub-system and mathematical formulations for trust calculation. We compare our system with models in literature and provide results. Experiments show that the system outperforms others for specific values of the parameters. We allege that IAs should pay attention on recent referrals in order to have an efficient mechanism for calculating trust levels of other entities.

Acknowledgment. This research received funding from the European's Union Horizon 2020 research and innovation programme under the grant agreement ARESIBO (Augmented Reality Enriched Situation awareness for Border security) No. 833805.

References

1. Aref, A., Tran, T.: A trust establishment model in multi-agent systems. In: AAAI Workshop: Incentive and Trust in E-communities (2015)
2. Bharadwaj, K., Al-Shamri, M.Y.H.: Fuzzy computational models for trust and reputation systems. Electron. Commer. Res. Appl. **8**(1), 37–47 (2009)
3. Czabanski, R., Jezewski, M., Leski, J.: Introduction to fuzzy systems. In: Prokopowicz, P., Czerniak, J., Mikołajewski, D., Apiecionek, Ł., Ślezak, D. (eds.) Theory and Applications of Ordered Fuzzy Numbers. SFSC, vol. 356, pp. 23–43. Springer, Cham (2017). https://doi.org/10.1007/978-3-319-59614-3_2
4. Daronnat, S., et al.: Human-agent collaborations: trust in negotiating control. In: Proceedings of the Workshop Everyday Automation Experience in Conjunction with CHI (2019)
5. Devitt, S.: Trustworthiness of autonomous systems. In: Foundations of Trusted Autonomy, pp. 161–184 (2018)
6. Esfandiari, B., Chandrasekharan, S.: On how agents make friends: mechanisms for trust acquisition. In: The 4th Workshop on Deception Fraud and Trust in Agent Societies (2001)
7. Griffiths, N.: A fuzzy approach to reasoning with trust, distrust and insufficient trust. In: Klusch, M., Rovatsos, M., Payne, T.R. (eds.) CIA 2006. LNCS (LNAI), vol. 4149, pp. 360–374. Springer, Heidelberg (2006). https://doi.org/10.1007/11839354_26
8. Hnativ, A., Ludwig, S.A.: Evaluation of trust in an eCommerce multi-agent system using fuzzy reasoning. In: Proceedings of the FUZ-IEEE, Korea, pp. 757–763 (2009)
9. Huynh, D., Jennings, N.R., Shadbolt, N.R.: Developing an integrated trust and reputation model for open multi-agent systems. In: Proceedings of the 7th International Workshop on Trust in Agent Societies, New York, USA, pp. 65–74 (2004)
10. Jøsang, A.: Trust and reputation systems. In: Aldini, A., Gorrieri, R. (eds.) FOSAD 2006-2007. LNCS, vol. 4677, pp. 209–245. Springer, Heidelberg (2007). https://doi.org/10.1007/978-3-540-74810-6_8
11. Josang, A., Ismail, R.: The beta reputation system. In: Proceedings of the 15th Bled Electronic Commerce Conference, Bled, Slovenia (2002)
12. Kolomvatsos, K., Hadjiefthymiades, S.: How can we trust agents in multi-agent environments? Techniques and challenges. In: Krol, D. (ed.) Intelligence Integration in Distributed Knowledge Management (2008)
13. Lesani, M., Montazeri, N.: Fuzzy trust aggregation and personalized trust inference in virtual social networks. Comput. Intell. **25**(2), 51–83 (2009)
14. Ludwig, S.A., Pulimi, V., Hnativ, A.: Fuzzy approach for the evaluation of trust and reputation systems. In: Proceedings of FUZZ-IEEE, Korea (2009)

15. Marmol, F.G., Marin-Blazquez, J.G., Perez, G.M.: Linguistic fuzzy logic enhancement of a trust mechanism for distributed networks. In: The 10th CIT, pp. 838–845 (2010)
16. McKnight, D.H., Chervany, N.L.: The meanings of trust. Technical Report, University of Minnessota, Management Information Systems Research Center, 1996, Accessed 01 April 2000
17. Nefti, S., Meziane, F., Kasiran, K.: A Fuzzy trust model for e-commerce. In: Proceedings of the 7th IEEE International Conference on E-Commerce Technology (2005)
18. Ramchourn, S.D., Huynh, D., Jennings, N.R.: Trust in multi-agent systems. Knowl. Eng. Rev. **19**(1), 1–25 (2004)
19. Rasmusson, L., Jansson, S.: Simulated social control for secure internet commerce. In: Meadows, C. (ed.) Proceedings of the 1996 New Security Paradigms Workshop, pp. 18–26 (1996)
20. Sathiyamoorthy, E., Iyengar, N., Ramachandran, V.: Mobile agent based trust management framework using fuzzy logic in B2C e-business environment. IJCTE **2**(2), 308–312 (2010)
21. Wang, Y., Vassileva, J.: Bayesian network-based trust model. In: Proceedings of the 6th International Workshop on Trust, Privacy, Deception and Fraud in Agent Systems (2003)
22. Wang, Y., Hori, Y., Sakurai, K.: On securing open networks through trust and reputation – architecture, challenges and solutions. In: 1st Joint Workshop on Information Security (2006)
23. Zytniewski, M., Klement, M.: Trust in software agent societies. J. Appl. Knowl. Manag. **3**(1), 93–101 (2015)

Author Index